ROBESPIERRE

THE FORCE OF CIRCUMSTANCE

JOHN LAURENCE CARR

ROBESPIERRE

THE FORCE OF CIRCUMSTANCE

CONSTABLE LONDON

First published in Great Britain 1972
by Constable and Company Limited
10 Orange Street London WC2H 7EG
Copyright © 1972 by John Laurence Carr

ISBN 0 09 457850 8

Set in Monotype Garamond
Printed in Great Britain by
Cox & Wyman Ltd,
London, Fakenham and Reading

CONTENTS

CONTENTS

ILLUSTRATIONS

FOR CATHERINE,
STACY AND PHILIP

FOREWORD

'Ce qu'il nous faut, c'est un Robespierre'

BARBEY D'AUREVILLY

'Why Robespierre?' asks J. M. Thompson.[1] Because like a colossus he straddled the age in which he lived, in and out of parliament but always more and more in the public eye, until at last his own crisis coincided with one of France's great turning-points, namely the collapse of the Jacobin republic. When he died, the Revolution died too in all but name.

So he is important. Confirmation abounds on all sides and in nineteenth- and twentieth-century writers alike. One day Victor Hugo was to refer to him as the 'algebra of the Revolution—the immense power of the straight line' and if we substitute 'geometry' for 'algebra' it is easier to understand what he meant. Similarly, Anatole France confessed to having discovered in the politician from Arras the dominant statesman from the period 1789–94. Similarly too, Romain Rolland referred to him as the most con-siderable figure of that age and the poet Péguy concluded that he could find no one to set above Robespierre in the whole *Ancien Régime*. More extravagant still was George Sand, who called him the greatest man, not only of the Revolution, but of recorded history.[2] A huge personality, therefore, like the *Énorme Figure* of André Frénaud's ingeniously arranged poem and one whom students of history and serious-minded readers cannot afford to overlook. Here indeed was a person whose tormented soul vibrated to the vicissitudes that beset a France in transition, harbinger of modern Europe.

Important, yes; but opinion has not stopped there, for, with our insatiable mania for moral judgements, we have tended to ask another question: 'Was he good or bad?' At one time the answer was invariably that he was a blood-thirsty villain and dictator of the worst type; but we have had to revise our opinions about this traditional picture, since it became clear, from the press of the time, that the legend had been forged in advance of the Terror, in the years 1789–91—long before the Thermidoreans seized upon it and embroidered it to serve their own ends.

Truth prevails slowly, alas. Even the efforts at rehabilitation expended by devoted modern Robespierrists like Mathiez have not won over Right-wing opinion. Republican France has barely a memorial to the colossus of '93 and in the capital, which, in 1971, was celebrating the stalwarts of the second Commune, you will find a Rue Danton, even a Rue Hérault de Séchelles, but no Rue Robespierre! Moreover, at the time of the bi-centenary of the tribune's birth (1958), it was clear from the proceedings of the Paris Conseil Municipal that the politician, who had dominated the life of that city for more than a year, was still capable of arousing the most determined opposition. In fact, he is still anathematized by many Frenchmen who have failed to understand not only their own democratic history but this singularly unsmiling northerner as well. The debate continues today, often in virulent terms, which are to be regretted, since the only way to view moral problems is in their context or since, as Montesquieu pointed out so often in his day, relativism is the only guarantee of fair-mindedness. Justice cannot be achieved without a sense of history and a sense of proportion. That is why our sub-title refers to the force of circumstance, without which history would have been unfolded in an entirely different way. Given other conditions, Maximilien (de) Robespierre might have stayed at home, a small-time lawyer in Arras, and might never have been heard of outside that town. In different circumstances, he could well have lived to the age of ninety, with a large family to enliven his declining years. Destiny decreed otherwise.

So our aim in this book is not so much eulogy or castigation (though we must occasionally pass judgements on most matters) but rather location. If we approach our objective in that manner, we may perhaps understand the man in his evolving *ambiance*. Some will find this easier than others. Were we, for instance, Mao or Castro, we might come closer to our subject. We might be able to feel for him amidst a growing predicament of power, as most of his problems would have been met by us too in our own political progress.

At which point another question naturally follows. Blessed with such privileged insight, how could we be sure that our career would not end, like his, on the scaffold? The answer is that we could not guarantee anything of the sort. Revolution breeds violence and dying in one's bed becomes a rare luxury. Revolutions are also notoriously difficult to understand, either in advance or with hindsight. For one thing, the rebel leader cannot afford to sit back and let things take their course. A cold revolution is sometimes worse than a hot one, and certainly equally unpredictable. Once the flames begin to subside, the leader is likely to be displaced by some new incendiary and does not usually survive to complete his task. Such is the central problem of revolt. As a playwright knows very well, it is difficult to find the right ending to the play. If the curtain is rung down too soon, the audience will find another writer better suited to their taste for prolonged excitement. If, on the other hand, the play lasts too long, the author will be accused of boring his public and will suffer just the same.

So every tribune of the people has two thorny questions before him. More or less agitation and violence? When is it opportune to close? Of course, it is the politician's job to take awkward decisions, after he has weighed the arguments for and against. Here, however, another *caveat* rears its head: the politician is human, and this too is important. In our study we shall consequently endeavour to savour the strange *ragoût* that was Maximilien—that compound of blazing integrity, sober intent and a magnetic self-sacrifice which occasionally borders on the masochistic. But we shall always see him silhouetted against the backcloth of his times; strong moral principles against an age struggling to emerge from its amoral cocoon; unique honesty against war-time corruption; a golden future, instead of a dingy present.

Robespierre offered man a vision of what France could become in the next century, for he adumbrated a new deal, in which obliquity, self-seeking and vice would not be rewarded. His heavenly city was a place for the hitherto oppressed and underprivileged—for Jews, Protestants, actors and coloured people, for instance—and as such is woven into the glorious tapestry of humanitarian progress.[3] It was even more a city where welfare in general enjoyed pride of place. We think in this connexion of his many remarks in favour of large families, of the elderly and infirm; and we reflect that our politician was the precursor of penal abolitionists. Perhaps, therefore, under his care France perceived a new way of life and by his austerity was temporarily steered from Epicurean cynicism towards an ideal neo-Platonism.

In taking this course, Robespierre was revealing that he was rarely original in his ideas. As in most things, the influence was that of Rousseau; and, in itself, this heightens Robespierre's significance for us, who are in so many respects the heirs of the great Genevan; who worship the General Will in its various guises; who despatch our offspring to progressive schools or are involved as parents in classroom-activity experiments—novelties which remind us of Robespierre's promotion of a pseudo-Rousseauist scheme for primary education. So when Robespierre said of Jean-Jacques 'I wish to follow in your hallowed foot-steps',[4] he was guilty of no exaggeration. For good or ill, we have done the same thing ourselves.

It is true, in fact, that Rousseau's great disciple of 1793–94 blazed a trail for modern social reformers: Robespierre would surely have approved of modifications to the French legal code in favour of bastards[5] which were effected in the spring of 1971. He would also have understood President Pompidou's disquiet about the death penalty[6] and in so many other ways would have shared the feelings of statesmen of our own times. His problems were our problems—classic dilemmas of our own century; pacifism versus war, protest versus complacency, economic liberalism versus prices-and-income controls. His failures are our failures. We too have repeatedly failed to solve the problem of law and order, as opposed to freedom and anarchy; of destruction, as opposed to constructive reform. We too must honestly admit that we have not been able to reconcile the rival claims of liberty, equality and fraternity; but conscious of our shortcomings, we are still trying. Thus the life and times we are now to examine are not historically remote from our own situation. This is obvious when we read that Robespierre opposed the employment of a shorthand writer during the trial of the Hébertists in 1794,[7] or that aerial recon-naissance helped to win the battle of Fleurus. Multiply these instances, and the story assumes a modern appearance and vividly demonstrates the relevance of Robespierre.

Logically our examination proceeds from background to fore-ground—from the period to the man who dominated it. The Revolution, from which sprang modern political man and such technical innovations as national conscription and the decimal system, is important in its own right: for us it has a double significance, since it produced this unusual man of parts. Consequently, following a review of pre-Revolutionary circumstances, we propose in Part I to set Robespierre against his times. Continuing the same theme, but with a change of emphasis, Part II will deal with his character and culture; and we shall hope to discover the man afresh through his general activities. The third part is concerned more specifically with his professional performance as a politician, faced with the tremendous affairs of State; and in the fourth part of this study, we shall attempt to estimate the effects of events and circumstances upon personality and career. In the last chapter, we consider the reasons why this apparently unattractive man should have enjoyed such acclaim in his own day and excited so much attention in ours.

Most quotations involving ideas have been translated, but literary examples of Robespierre's poetry and prose are printed in the original French, so that the writer's style may make its true impact and our own critical opinions be fully supported.

Finally, I should like to acknowledge indebtedness to learned institutions in Paris, Glasgow, Leeds and Southampton, principally for their invaluable help with bibliography; to Constable, for unfailing courtesy, kindness and forbearance; and to all friends and colleagues whose conversation has stimulated my ideas or crystallized them for the task in hand.

J. L. C.

INTRODUCTION

BEFORE THE DELUGE

'Après nous, le Déluge!'

LOUIS XV

In 1751, D'Alembert prophesied in his preface to the famous *Encyclopédie* that the mid-century was apparently going to be a decisive event in the history of man's ideas, because of the ideological changes which seemed to be in course of preparation; and about the same time the Marquis d'Argenson was busy writing in his memoirs about a political revolution which he judged to be imminent. Thus a mere seven years before Robespierre's birth in 1758, men of wisdom and judgement were already foreseeing stirring events and regarding their own times as pregnant with possibility.

First, legal concepts had been shaken by the appearance in 1748 of Montesquieu's *Esprit des lois*, which ushered in the age of sociology, of comparative jurisprudence and of the rule of law, ultimately to replace the arbitrary grace-and-favour system of the *Ancien Régime*. This work, produced by a southern aristocrat of liberal inclination, was to transform western thinking on legality and make Frenchmen seek a constitutional arrangement. Secondly, with the studies of human instincts and senses undertaken by Condillac—the only real philosopher of the century, in the accepted sense of that term, contrasting with that of the French word of the period which relates to reformers and propagandists— the more personal and individual aspects of modern psychology were given birth. At the same time, Rousseau's investigation of the origins of inequality and his enthusiasm for sensibility, apparently at the expense of reason, meant that values of a different sort were stressed and other time-bombs were set, ready for the inevitable explosion.

The mid-century was noteworthy on another account. In 1736 Voltaire had written a poem extolling fairly sumptuous living. The senses were given for man's enjoyment; progress was a fact and a

I

good thing; therefore civilization was also a great boon and should be enjoyed to the full—so ran the *Mondain's* argument. By 1750, however, seeing the reign of royal mistresses in extravagant flight at Versailles, serious-minded thinkers and moralists were beginning to turn the tide of public opinion against luxury, one of them being Rousseau, who, in the *Discours surs les sciences et les arts*, cast doubts upon the value of eighteenth-century good-living and intellectual sophistication. So around the year 1750 another revolutionary war-cry was heard: primitivist austerity, based on a rigid ethical code. As if to echo this cry, some *Philosophes* were soon preaching the charms of a rustic, agricultural economy, instead of an industrialist, mercantilist capitalism. If they had their way, basic values would be located in the land, in the soil and in peasants. These Physiocrats, who founded agronomist societies and launched appropriate reviews, were liberal in politics.

In religion, the mid-century was already well on the way to replacing Christianity by deism, a basic religion which, rejecting all dogma and ceremonial, regarded God as a universal force hardly distinguishable from nature. Once the flood-gates were opened, it was not surprising that some advanced thinkers continued beyond mere deism into materialism and atheism, as pagan theories culled mainly from the much-admired Epicurus came out into the open. And, whereas Christians had always been encouraged to consider soul and body as separate and distinct, the opinion now widely held was that these were aspects of the same thing; and thus the doctrine of hylozoism gained considerable favour in France, promoted by men of repute like the chief Encyclopaedist, Diderot.

Crisis became the order of the day. In the political sector this was very evident. Eighteenth-century France had no parties as such until the years immediately preceding the Revolution of 1789; but political opinions were expressed in religious distinctions, and especially that between Jansenism and Jesuitism. To be a Jansenist generally meant that one was in opposition to the Court of Versailles, which was staunchly Jesuit, and that one was therefore something of a reformer. So Paris became filled with Jansenist liberals, chiefly from the merchant classes, disaffected as their financial commitments and investments grew larger and their say in government remained derisory. These bourgeois citizens were to come very much to the fore in the second half of the eighteenth century—the culmination of a progress begun in the seventeenth —and, painted in virtuous, theatrical, domestic settings by Greuze, they were similarly idolized in Diderot's *drames*. One day they were to rule France, but not before terrible things had been enacted. Meanwhile disunity grew apace; and, for reasons just given, in this fascinating twilight of the old order, religious disputes tended always to underlie political disputes. The best example of this is provided by the *billets de confession*—certificates demanded by the Catholic Church before sacred rites were made available to some members. Since these certificates were a proof that Frenchmen had accepted the Bull Unigenitus condemning Jansenism, insistence upon the *billets de confession* served to inflame passions, especially amongst the middle classes who had Jansenist sympathies, and amid the legal bodies named *parlements*, traditionally associated with that religious faction and by no means the equivalent of British parliaments. When, in *La Pucelle*, Voltaire called Unigenitus the origin of French parties and disputes, he was simply stating that this apparently trivial disagreement was generating strife, destined very soon to make its existence felt in more important ways.

Politically speaking, then, the mid-century period was potentially catastrophic. Already in 1748 the disastrous Peace of Aix-la-Chapelle had changed the monarch's relative popularity into distinct unpopularity. Already French society was showing signs of a return to the *Frondes* of 1648–53, when civil war was waged by refractory aristocrats and princes of the royal blood, by the *parlements* and ultimately the common people. The same classes were flexing muscles again for the labour which awaited them in the political field.

Why then, we may ask, did the whirlwind harvest, foreseen so clearly by the Marquis d'Argenson, take another forty years to ripen? Some answer that, although many rebellious elements were already in existence in 1751, theories had to be formulated and turned into compelling arguments; that, precisely in 1751, the first volume of the bible of the revolutionaries, the great *Encyclopédie*, was launched; and that it was this massive work which crystallized political disaffection into party strife leading to rebellion. Indeed, as event followed event and deterioriation continued, the likelihood of a revolution became even clearer.

Two years before Robespierre's birth came the Seven Years War, which was to last until 1763 and end disastrously for France (especially in the colonial sphere). Then, in 1771, attempting to resolve the eternal wrangles between the Government and the Bar, Chancellor Maupeou had exiled the regular *parlement* (meaning principally that of Paris which was all-important) and set up an *ad hoc* body. This change was of significance to the budding lawyer, expecially as, a mere three years later, Maupeou himself was dismissed by the new king and the former *parlements* came back with all their pristine arrogance and awkwardness. By 1789 they were thirteen in number.

Besides allowing back the old *parlements*, well-known trouble-makers that they were, Louis XVI in his fumbling inexperience and natural incompetence made many mistakes which were to contribute to his downfall. He recalled to power Maurepas, the exiled minister of Louis XV, whose frivolity and impudence had rightly earned him disgrace in 1757. His one supplier of liberal economics, the Encyclopaedist and Physiocrat Turgot, was dismissed on forged evidence in 1776, largely because he offended the privileged classes with his projected reforms. Finally Louis allowed France to participate in the American War of Independence, at a time when she could not pay her way in the world. Worse still for him, brilliant American ideas, embodied in the 1775 Declaration of Rights, flooded into France, to highlight reactionary moves—like the 1781 *règlement militaire* which decreed that henceforth only nobles could become army officers.

As a last straw came the Necklace Affair which, though Marie-Antoinette was clearly guiltless, discredited the monarchy and formed the preface to a revolution which began four years later. Thus during the time when Maximilien was practising law in Arras—that is, in the years 1781–89—epidemic revolts of all kinds were incubating or breaking out amongst the *parlements* and certain elements of the aristocracy. Paris, already alienated from Versailles, was furious since a new local customs wall had been set up in 1785 to restrict economic intercourse between the capital city and the provinces. In 1788, when Robespierre addressed a pamphlet to the Artesian Nation,[1] the Revolution was imminent.

But there is another cause, which few historians have noted.

Approximately a quarter of the *Conventionnels* elected late in 1792 were born within two years of Robespierre's birthday in 1758— the same generation of public-school boys in fact. For many decades now they had been notorious. From Voltaire to Diderot and Condorcet, a large number of eighteenth-century reformers had been educated in Jesuit colleges, where, with worldly tutors, they had developed into freethinkers, whose ideas were formed partly by the pagan authors they had read. At the same time they had been told about the importance of restraint and tact, particularly in making disclosures to the common people. Though privately they were deists or worse, in public they encouraged, the masses to accept divine Providence as a moral policeman. Then came a significant event. The expulsion of the Jesuits from education in 1762 and the consequent training of boys like Maximilien by lay teachers or secular clerics, meant that they were not brought up in the traditional Jesuit manner of colleges like Louis-le-Grand. So a quarter of the future Lower House was not drilled in restraint, as their forebears had been. To make matters worse, these forebears, members of the Philosophic Party, were nearly all dead by 1789 and, in the Revolution proper, only minor characters like old Abbé Raynal survived to recall the real principles of mid-century *Philosophes* and sound a note of warning—and we shall see what happened to him!

The scene was set and the principal actors had no scruples about inciting their compatriots of any social class to seize their birthright.

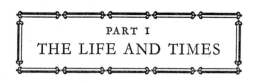

PART I
THE LIFE AND TIMES

'La Révolution, pour Robespierre, de plus en plus, est un état de son âme'

CLAUZEL

Chapter 1

THE CANDLE IS LIT

'Robespierre a grandi déjà avec la Révolution . . .'
RATINAUD

The modest Rue des Rapporteurs (originally *Rats-Porteurs*) in Arras was narrow and dull. No gardens bordered the pavements, which in any case were terribly narrow. Frequently the grey houses were shuttered up and on Sundays black-frocked *bourgeois* hid behind their shutters or peeped through lace curtains to see what their neighbours were up to. Normally a rather depressing street, as banal as the cobbles forming the roadway.

One day in early May 1789, however, something happened. Suddenly people were at their doors or standing in full view at unscreened windows. Others who had been loafing about in the Place de la Comédie were now looking expectantly towards the Rue des Rapporteurs. For outside the Robespierre residence there stood a porter's truck, gradually acquiring a modest burden of baggage. A few simple cases and a time-worn trunk left the corner house and were safely stowed in the tiny barrow.

Then out of the house came a woman dressed in black, followed by a small, thin, neatly but shabbily dressed man, who looked nervous and self-important at one and the same time. Charlotte Robespierre was seeing off her beloved brother, Maximilien; the convenient arrangement which she had so long enjoyed since Joseph Fouché had jilted her was at an end. She had the Versailles meeting of the Etats-Généraux to thank for that. But what to her was a minor tragedy and a major dislocation was for her elder brother an opportunity and a challenge. The challenge brought all his nervous tension vibrating to the surface: on the other hand, the opportunity made him feel that at last he was someone who mattered.

Maximilien-Marie-Isodore de Robespierre was born on May 6, 1758, the son of Maximilien-Barthélemy-François de Robespierre. Two unusual derivations of the name Robespierre have caught the public imagination at various times. In 1757 a college servant from the same part of France stabbed Louis XV with a pen-knife, the very one in fact with which he sharpened the quills at a Jesuit college. Louis did not die, but of course the miscreant, Damiens, had to be punished according to the full rigours of the *Ancien Régime*: he was pulled apart by teams of horses. Any persons possessing his name were naturally determined to change it; and it is at this point that rumour maintains that Robert and Pierre Damiens combined their Christian names to produce an unsullied replacement. The second theory is that there was Irish blood in the Robespierres, and that consequently their patronymic had been corrupted from some form like 'Robert Spiers'. This second explanation has at least the supporting evidence that one of Maximilien's early portraits could easily pass for that of an Irish youth.

Other historians claim that the family had been French since the fifteenth century, being sprung from one Gilles de Romespierres [*sic*]; and that 300 years of native family tree are sufficient to guarantee that we need not look outside France for origins. On the face of it, this would appear the more reasonable solution: no one quite knows who started the Irish theory, but it occurs in Lewes, Hamel, Michelet, Lamartine and Belloc, in each case with somewhat tenuous support. The other story is equally romantic and equally suspect, for it must be more than a coincidence that Maximilien had a schoolfellow called Damiens, a detail which may well account for the association of his name with that of the unlamented desperado.

Maximilien's French grandfather, the first Maximilien, had also been a lawyer; and this was to have its influence on the choice of career of the young tiro. An even more important influence, of course, was exerted by his own father, who had studied law at Douai and was subsequently attached to the Conseil d'Arras at the age of twenty-four. Two years later his wayward ways had led to a hasty marriage with Jacqueline, a daughter of Carraut the brewer, from which union had sprung Maximilien a mere four months later. The father had fulfilled his obligations more or less well during the birth of two daughters and another son, but, on the occasion of his wife's death in childbirth with a fifth child, who did not survive, things began to go very wrong for the impoverished widower. He did not even attend his wife's funeral and some months later walked out on his responsibilities altogether, leaving them to the eldest son, who lacked the toughness he was now called upon to display.

Brought up very much by his mother, Maximilien had developed a few interests more often associated with the opposite sex—for instance we are told that he learned to make lace. Consequently at the age of seven Maximilien was shattered by the family tragedy—a tragedy sharpened by the ineptitude and moral flabbiness of an absconding father. Soon after this deplorable event, the little girls passed into the care of aunts on the father's side and the boys were taken in by their maternal grandfather. The year was 1767 and Maximilien was nine years of age.

The significance of this early privation becomes more compelling if we take account of Mrs Iremonger's intriguing ideas. According to this writer, prime ministers (fifteen of the twenty-four studied) were spurred to ambition by handicaps, bereavement or bastardy and developed into neurotic, religious recluses, disliking sport and junketing, suffering from periodic depressions and other psychosomatic symptoms. Undoubtedly, Maximilien fits snugly into this diagnosis. Indeed, it is possible to go even further with the author of *The Fiery Chariot*, agreeing that an unfortunate consequence of early privations is that they make the man in question unlike the people he is to represent in parliament.

Happily the gloom was relieved to some extent by the solace of a substitute-father, who had the good grace to do his duty by the young Robespierres. Grandfather Carraut sent his grandsons to the Collège d'Arras, where they were taught by Oratorian priests.

The Oratorians owe their origin to Bérulle, who was bent upon reform. His reform represented, in a rather superficial and insignificant way, the triumph of the salons, of polite society, of preciosity and refinement. Some of this had undoubtedly rubbed off on Robespierre, as we shall see when we study his poems and consider his relationship with the ladies. But there were much more serious aspects of the Berullian revolt. In religious matters, the Oratorians—and in this respect Malebranche was typical—were unusually theocentric. Man was made to adore God; God was not there to oblige or serve man. So the essential cult of this Supreme Being, this God-centred religion, was the basis of a kind of deism later to be expressed anew in the Robespierrist State religion.

Equally deistic is the Oratorian insistence upon erudite and rational study of the Holy Scriptures. It is therefore logical that this order should have produced an exegetist like Richard Simon, whose *Histoire critique du Vieux Testament* has a title that speaks for itself. So theology began to be eroded and modified, thanks to philology, chronology and other scientific studies. Admittedly, in that year, 1678, Simon had been expelled from the Oratoire, but his ideas lived on to confirm the trend. So it is not surprising that Oratorian *alumni* followed him into heterodoxy.

The Oratorians were similar to the Jansenists in their views on grace and predestination. This *rapprochement* with a sect agitating against Jesuit Versailles and favoured by Parisian bourgeois and lawyers, is a further link between Oratorians, Robespierre and revolt. Being in opposition, as it were, Oratorians shunned the Court and all its decadent pleasures, preferring a more austere way of life, devoid of luxury. In this respect also, the young man from Arras must have been in his element with the reformers who taught him. Gallican tendencies accentuated this bias, for, whereas the Ultramontane Jesuits were obedient to Rome and universal in their activities, these secular priests inclined towards a national church, and in this were semi-Protestant. So it is not surprising that Maximilien was more than heterodox.

On the positive side too, the renowned eloquence of the followers of Bérulle came in useful. Distinguished humanists, who were much at home in Latin and Greek, these tutors had a lasting influence on young Robespierre, whose speeches reflect this classical bias and undoubted expertise in language, which afforded him lasting satisfaction.

Even though it is reported that at this school he lacked friends and kept himself to himself, writing to Daunou in January 1791, Robespierre recalls his happy days with his Oratorian tutors.[1] So much aptitude in the art of speaking had already been displayed by the enterprising orphan, that he was the natural choice for public exercises held at the end of the school year. A master called Gaillard had selected Henri IV as the subject for oratory and asked Robespierre to open the proceedings. Great was the pupil's success on this occasion, to the delight and pride of his teacher. Fired by enthusiasm for his subject, Maximilien had praised the good king's concern for the common people in such eloquent terms that even this stolid northern audience had been reduced to tears. Realizing in a flash what power he possessed, Maximilien was soon ready to repeat in Paris this singular performance.

In Paris, he did not feel out of place. Like Montesquieu before him, young Maximilien was trained by the Oratorians, but in this case twice. This was because, after attending their school in Arras, he proceeded to the old Jesuit College of Louis-le-Grand which, in contradiction of what Mathiez asserts,[2] was no longer in Jesuit hands, but had been handed over to the Oratorians when the Society of Jesus had been banned from education. To this Latin-Quarter establishment, the young tiro was admitted by scholarship. When first he travelled to the capital which was to provide the setting for the momentous years to come, Maximilien was eleven years of age. The year was 1769. Basically the curriculum was what he had expected. With religious instruction, the classics still held pride of place, so the paganism of Greeks and Romans provided an alternative to Christianity on many subjects of importance—for instance, Cicero's condoning thoughts on suicide, which Christians traditionally reproved. How many other pagan ideas outshone Christian ideas? Undoubtedly, here was fuel for intellectual revolt and, as we have said, a string of rebels from Voltaire to Sade proves the case. The tutors were not very different either: for instance, the Abbé Bérardier was to enter the National Assembly as an M.P. for the Third Estate—a revolutionary, in fact, like so many of his former pupils.

The generation, thus equipped by the best college in France in the late 'sixties, was to come to flourishing manhood in the 'nineties and therefore to control the great Revolution. Of the many methods of self-expression available to these mature young men, the press was one of the most popular. Consider as examples Sulleau, who founded the *Actes des Apôtres*, or Stanislas Fréron, who was to edit the *Orateur du Peuple*. More important still was the famous *Vieux Cordelier* of Camille Desmoulins, who, having sent the crowd on its way to attack the Bastille in 1789, was to live to regret that he had ever put pen to paper.

Others entered politics more directly: Lebrun became War Minister after August 10, 1792. There was also Maximilien Robespierre. When his mentor, Canon de la Roche, died in 1772, he turned his back on religion, especially since the Principal of long standing, the Abbé du Mesnil, had been succeeded by a more permissive cleric, the Abbé d'Enthienloy, who allowed the great Encyclopaedist, D'Alembert, to discuss hitherto forbidden subjects with his charges. In any case, young France was ripe for subversion, since, in 1775, the American colonists on whom it kept a friendly eye were involved in fighting their British overlords; and since an especially exciting rebel, Benjamin Franklin, was soon in France seeking support from fellow Masons and other well-wishers for the American cause.

Meanwhile, in July 1775, Robespierre had met his king. Seeing that His Majesty was to be crowned in Rheims and would be passing through Paris, it was decided that he should pause awhile at the college bearing the name of his illustrious ancestor, Louis XIV; moreover, since Robespierre was the best boarding-pupil, it was agreed that he should read the loyal address. Naturally the youth of seventeen was both honoured and dismayed at the prospect of this ordeal, which would surely not have been his if he had really been descended from the would-be regicide, Damiens! Anyhow, attired in his ill-fitting borrowed suit and clutching a damp manuscript, the trembling classical scholar waited and waited. At last the coach arrived, but, because of the inclement weather, Louis XVI and Marie-Antoinette decided to stay within it; and so it was that the future republican leader read aloud to his future victims a Latin oration in carefully contrived measures. It did not last very long. Maximilien barely had time to raise his dripping head again before the coach was rattling away towards Versailles. Louis the Bored had had enough. So incidentally had his young entertainer.

After hours of nervous tension, it was over. It ended in a sort of fiasco, because His Majesty could not be expected to consider the feelings of this young *collégien*. How humiliating it was! The grooming of the martyr had begun already in that rain-soaked Paris street and the young man never quite forgot the shame he felt during those terrible moments of despair. However, he did not immediately give up and, in 1784, when he wrote his first Discourse, he expressed the confidence that his opuscule would not be offered in vain and the hope that the monarch might find in these brief pages something useful to humanity.[3]

If the encounter with his king was destined to end in frustration, Robespierre's meeting with, or perhaps merely the sight of, another important personage was to affect him in precisely the opposite way. Of all the lyrical passages penned by this college classicist on the threshold of romanticism, the most florid and most sincere concerns Jean-Jacques Rousseau. He probably did not, as Thompson affirms, meet the great man in a Paris garret;[4] but rather travelled to Ermenonville, about twelve miles from the capital. Entering that peaceful park with its grottoes and temples happily located to catch the eye, and skirting the neat manor-house where the great man had spent some of the most contented hours of his latter days, young Maximilien had made his way towards the lake surrounding an island, later to be the temporary resting-place for his hero's mortal remains. Old as he was now, the Citizen of Geneva was still able to 'herborize', and he was taking his morning constitutional along familiar paths lined with wild flowers that had long been his refuge and joy. From some distance probably, the young man studied the stooping, emaciated figure and the care-worn face of the noblest *Philosophe* of all, and for the rest of his life was inspired by what he saw: 'I saw you in your last days, and for me this memory is a source of pride and joy; I gazed upon your majestic features and I saw there evidence of the dark despair to which man's injustice had condemned you.'[5] Often subject to blank despair himself, he was already beginning to identify himself with the great thinker who became his life-long idol and who had experienced endless suffering, during a career dogged by illness and poverty.

In such sympathies, Maximilien was already displaying the characteristics of the northern scholarship-boy, as delineated for us so admirably by Richard Hoggart. Which means that he was glum, sensitive, unsure of his social status, thrifty, gauche and relatively unaccustomed to travel—a clumsy pedant with a veneer of social graces.

At the Collège Louis-le-Grand Robespierre learned jurisprudence, graduated *bachelier-en-droit* in July 1780 and was awarded the *licence* of the University of Paris one year later. These qualifications permitted him to be enrolled on the register of lawyers attached to the *Parlement* of Paris, where he had already worked part-time with the procurator, Nolleau, by the side of a future enemy, Brissot, who was also learning the practice and incidentally how to be a Girondist politician. It should be added that Maximilien was *not*, as some erroneously state,[6] a schoolmate of Danton—a boarder of the Lazarists of Troyes (where he attended Oratorian classes) and later a graduate of Rheims. In 1781, after twelve useful years at college, Maximilien received a prize with a testimonial and returned to his home town of Arras. He had asked the Cardinal de Rohan if his scholarship could be passed on to his younger brother, Augustin, a request which was granted.

In Arras the young *licencié* expected to have ample choice of work, because there were five ordinary and four royal jurisdictions in that region. Thanks to the help of Maître Liborel, at the age of twenty-three he was appointed to the Arras Bar by the Conseil and, to start him off on the right foot, was offered a prepared case to present in court. Unfortunately he lost it, but such things are taken phlegmatically by sensible pleaders and he was none the worse for this initial setback. Next day he was successful in a different case.

Shortly after this, Maître Delarsé, a judge of the Episcopal Court of Arras, conveniently died, and Robespierre was appointed in his place after much lobbying by the candidate and his devoted sister, Charlotte. Thus by March 1782 young Robespierre had become a judge with a tidy income to match his new post. His job, ironically enough, amounted largely to defending the Catholic religion against Protestantism. Though poverty was a daily companion and he was desperately in need of civil briefs to pay the bills, he was making his mark.

One of Robespierre's most important legal battles centred round Benjamin Franklin's great invention, the lightning-conductor. A fellow lawyer of the town of Saint-Omer, Vissery de Boisvallé, having placed such a device on the chimney of his house, was immediately assailed by his neighbours who, in superstitious fear of the new object, demanded its prompt removal. The consequence was the decision that it should be taken down within twenty-four hours by the owner or, failing that, by the bailiff of the town. Vissery appealed againt this judgement; the locals threatened physical violence if it were not executed quickly. Meanwhile the Conseil d'Arras was to deal with the appeal. A certain Maître Buissard having prepared an elaborate defence of lightning-conductors, Robespierre was given the task of reading this *mémoire* before the tribunal—a task which he relished, since it chimed in with his up-to-date scientific views.[7] It also enabled him to display a predilection for scientifically-orientated nations to the north, favoured on 'philosophic' grounds—that is, because, unhindered by tradition and authority, they were committed to the secular pursuit of truth by empirical methods. He did so because he shared the eighteenth-century opinion that the Renaissance was a continuing phenomenon, which had commenced in the south with art and letters and had spread to countries like Holland and, via Great Britain, to America—the point at issue here. It is especially important to note this approval of Holland and Britain at the time of the Vissery trial,[8] because later on, under the stress of warfare, this natural inclination towards enlightened nations had to be stifled for patriotic, political reasons.

America, however, never presented such problems to the French of the Revolution. Not only did Maximilien delight in paying tribute to the great American scientist-politician, Franklin,[9] but he was fortunate enough to be able to draw attention to the installation by Louis XVI of the transatlantic device at his Château de la Muette. The famous *Mercure de France* praised an eloquent defender of novel ideas and poor Buissart, who had done most of the spade-work, was ignored! A singular triumph at twenty-five: now the young judge could consider himself famous. He had won not only a case, but national acclaim, such as would ensure that in future he would enjoy exceptional consideration as Arras's most accomplished legal orator.

One result of this was that he was busier than ever before. For instance, between February 27, 1782 and March 17, 1789, he spoke 118 times before the Conseil d'Arras and twenty-seven times before the Echevinage. It is also true that, at the age of twenty-seven, the man destined to lead had already been made Director of the literary and scientific Academy at Arras—one of thirty throughout France. This helped to reinforce the conviction that Robespierre would undertake with exemplary conscientiousness any case with which he was charged, and soon after the *paratonnerre*, he was involved in the Deteuf affair, which was important in that this young judge of an episcopal court was to defend an individual against a Benedictine abbey.

In 1783 a rope-maker, Deteuf, was accused of stealing from Dom Brongniard, the superior of this abbey, a certain sum of money. Deteuf appealed against the judgement of the abbey's federal court, and the appeal went before the Conseil d'Arras and into the capable hands of Robespierre, who took full advantage of the discovery that Dom Brongniard was guilty of misappropriation of abbey funds and privately dissolute into the bargain. An indefatigable moralist was now launched on the national stage. The case was won and Deteuf declared innocent; but not before the young lawyer defending him had fulminated against the abbey, which had shown such criminal complacency towards its superior,[10] and not before Robespierre had been in trouble for daring to make public certain aspects of the case which was still under litigation at the time. So there were snags and, in spite of a sensationally successful début, he does not appear to have been very settled in the legal profession, where established members stole all the ripest plums. Although such discontents help to explain his decision to quit the law, the coming meeting of the States-General unfolded new and tremendous possibilities too. Already he had shown predilection for cases in which, like Voltaire before him, he defended victims of the tyranny, oppression and vices of the *Ancien Régime*; already, during his career as budding *plaideur*, politics had been influencing his decisions and colouring his utterances. This was especially the case in the Dupond affair of April 1788, when the young advocate raised his voice against arbitrary imprisonment.[11] The Revolution was close at hand; Robespierre was caught up in advance in some of its ideals. His colleagues showed their disapproval by not inviting him to attend a conference upon legal reform. Considering himself pre-eminently qualified to discuss such a promising subject, Maximilien complained bitterly about such treatment; and his legal mentor, Maître Liborel, replied in similar terms, but the wound did not heal. In any case, what use was an episcopal judge who went off his food for two days when he had to pass the death sentence? Such a man would be much better off in politics.

There was plenty of work for any future politician trained at the Bar, for, in 1788, Lamoignon had issued edicts denying the *parlements*' right to oppose the financial measures the Government was now forced to take in an unavailing attempt to balance the budget. So, one year before the holocaust, all thinking lawyers were up in arms, many of them sincerely convinced that they alone represented the best interests of the little man of the Third Estate, and indeed his only hope of standing up to the hegemony of Versailles. Robespierre consequently joined in the lawyers' protest at the Establishment's so-called 'reform' of the legal system and against denial of the *parlements'* hallowed and age-old right to register, or decline to register, royal edicts. Thus a new kind of Fronde, in some respects resembling those which bedevilled Louis XIV's minority, was now prepared. As on the former occasion, most lawyers were in it for what they could extract for themselves and their own *cadre*; but quite a few saw themselves as defending nobler ideas—for instance, law versus favour; France versus Versailles.

This was the agitation which snowballed into a demand that the States-General should be called for the first time since 1614—a demand which achieved success in August 1788, when the Government agreed to convene this vaguely representative body for May 1789. This was Robespierre's cue. By an appeal addressed to his fellow-Artesians, the young idealist had already launched himself into the fray and, since in many places it read like an address to constituents, there is not the slightest doubt that this aspiring young orator considered himself the best choice as M.P. for Arras.

It was no sinecure that he was seeking. For one thing, France was in a severe financial crisis. In 1783 the Finance Minister, Calonne, had tried in vain to sustain confidence by spending money and undertaking national works; but he was forced by public disquiet to return to some economies and reforms initiated by Turgot. When his proposals were turned down by the Assembly of Notables, in April 1787 he resigned. He was superseded by Brienne, who found himself in conflict with the Paris *Parlement* about the registration of edicts; so, having announced that the States-General would be convened, the minister resigned in August 1788 and was replaced by the Swiss banker, Necker, who, once he had nullified the judicial reforms proposed by his predecessor, was finally able to insist that the Third Estate should have double representation in the States-General. This bright idea endeared him to the people of France. Impressed by this gesture and fired with ambition, Robespierre paid court to the Swiss wizard. Later, in the gardens of the Petit Trianon, he was introduced to Necker's daughter, Madame de Staël[12]—destined to become one of his sternest critics—who on this occasion overwhelmed him with politeness. But the daughter's goodwill was not enough. Robespierre had bombarded the minister with memoranda of various kinds. Predictably, his spirits were raised when he received a dinner invitation from the great man. Alas, however, they were destined to take a dislike to each other. Necker did nothing for Maximilien, after all, and the aspiring politician was able one day to denounce the foreigner as a traitor.

Any success the young Artesian was to enjoy was due largely and almost exclusively to his own exertions. They had been significant already. For example, that appeal to the Artesians was resounding to his benefit. Many remembered his picture of the lamentable state of agriculture, commerce and industry. Many more had been moved to emotion and principally to anger by such passages as this: 'Most of those living in our towns and country-side are weighed down by poverty, in that extreme state of degradation where man, entirely taken up with problems of subsistence, is unable to reflect on the causes of his afflictions and to acknowledge the rights nature has bestowed on him ...'[13] Compassion was there already; but the call to citizens to do something about their woes was there too. The author of this *Appel* was already a marked revolutionary.

In March 1789, he had played a prominent part in the preliminary meeting of the Artois section of the Third Estate. Twelve men were chosen to draw up the *cahier de doléances* and he was one of the twelve. As though this were not enough responsibility, he was engaged by the local cobblers' guild to draw up a special protest on their behalf. Finally, he was selected as one of the forty-nine entrusted with the job of producing a composite document for the entire bailiwick. At last the great day dawned when the Third Estate chose its deputies to send to Versailles. Elections took place on the basis of 'universal' suffrage, which means that some fiscal qualifications were imposed, none the less. In all areas the three estates had submitted *cahiers de doléances*, in which were set down complaints and criticisms coming from the electorate. Generally speaking, these notebooks requested the retention of the monarchy but demanded a constitution to safe-guard essential freedoms. They were neither republican nor egalitarian.

Robespierre was one of the eight deputies chosen. All that good work both in the wings and on the courtroom stage had brought him the part he had so long coveted. At long last, he was now really in politics, and his legal training would stand him in good stead, for it is no coincidence that so many representatives of the Third Estate were from his profession. After all, the revolutionary situation had been provoked largely by ideas stemming from Montesquieu and Rousseau; and who better to interpret such ideas than men professionally trained to orate and determined to ensure that the arbitrary should be replaced by a new concept of legitimacy?

Chapter 2

THE CANDLE BURNS

'L'Assemblée constituante a tenu dans sa main la destinée
de la France et de l'univers'

ROBESPIERRE

Those destined to martyrdom must begin as they intend to continue—with austerity and toil. At home in Arras, Robespierre had been an early starter—a habit which was to continue in Versailles and Paris. Rising between six and seven, he had worked on till eight, at which time his taste for decorum and neatness was satisfied by the arrival of a barber to shave him and powder his hair. Breakfast had been of the simplest, consisting usually of a cup of milk or of a little bread and his favourite drink, coffee. Having spent most of the early part of the working day in court, in the late afternoon, following a light lunch accompanied by diluted wine, he would indulge in the luxury of a short stroll. The evenings he would generally spend reading briefs for the next day or working out some new defence, though sometimes he enjoyed some short relaxation with friends. But in company he was awkward and ill-at-ease and, whilst others played cards, Maximilien had the annoying habit of sitting alone in some corner pondering higher things, as though he were alone in the room. Work never left him, even when he was supposed to be at leisure. Effort and meticulous care were already his deities. For instance, he was always anxious to keep his quarters tidy and, had he been born a woman, would undoubtedly have spent most of his time cleaning the house from top to bottom and then starting again.

Fresh from Arras, the budding politician established himself in the Hôtellerie du Renard in Versailles with three peasant colleagues from his native region. He also frequented the Café Amaury, where tradition has it that a special chair was kept for him each evening. Alas, the café has now disappeared to be replaced by a smart modern furniture store. But the proprietors have not forgotten the illustrious M.P.s who once graced this same plot of French soil. Outside the Huchers Minvielle, as the shop is now called, a neat notice is displayed above the window facing the Avenue de Paris: 'Here in 1789 stood the Café Amaury, where representatives of the Third Estate to the States-General held their meetings; where often Mirabeau and Robespierre held forth and whence originated the Jacobin Club.'

His association with the Jacobins instead of the more plebeian Cordeliers was, in provincial circles, a further guarantee of political respectability; yet the choice was not as automatic as some of his supporters imagined. At least half his natural inclinations were directed to the poor and oppressed already, as we have seen in his appeal to the people of Artois. There was the dilemma; he had not been sent to Versailles in order to represent the working classes. On the contrary, in an age witnessing the beginnings of the Industrial Revolution and which since the Regency had been acquiring the habit of investment, he was in the States-General to speak up for the new capitalists who, though commoners, had a large financial stake in France's survival, but so far no voice in her councils. Coming as he did from a professional, middle-class household, and being himself a lawyer, Robespierre was ideally placed to represent the bourgeoisie from which he had sprung. His election programme was that of a reformer, but of a reformer with conservative reservations, particularly in respect of the sacred right to own property. Moreover, he was still loyal to Necker and the Crown and this too enhanced his reputation as a steady, middle-of-the-road fellow.[1] Consequently, the bourgeoisie esteemed his patent rectitude and 'his vague and rhetorical platitudes hung like illuminated texts in their tidy parlours', as Thompson has it.[2] Deprived of a focal point for their religious sentiments, these people found in Robespierre an idol on which to focus their adoring attention, the answer to a middle-class prayer.

Middle classes made up most of the huge submerged third of the parliamentary iceberg; and, in order to take advantage of double representation, the Third Estate demanded that, instead of voting by 'order' (i.e. by block votes for each social class), they should express individual choice. Receiving no satisfaction on this point, the Commons proclaimed themselves a National Assembly and, finding their meeting-place barred against them, met in the royal tennis court, where they swore an oath that they would not disband until a constitution had been agreed. Unwilling, tragically as it turned out, ever to make firm concessions in the direction of social equality, Louis ordered the three estates to meet separately, but Bailly and Mirabeau sat tight, so Louis finally allowed a joint body to be formed—the Constituent Assembly, as it came to be known. How would the Court and the monarch react to this first act of defiance?

Concentrations of troops near Versailles worried the Parisians, already incited to violence by the Duc d'Orléans (an ambitious minor scion of the royal house) and now driven to action by the dismissal of the popular Necker. Arms depots were despoiled and, on July 14 1789, the Bastille was attacked and razed to the ground. Louis recalled Necker and on July 17 came to the Town Hall to receive the Revolutionary cockade. Robespierre was one of the reception committee of deputies.[3] Whilst Paris was seething and perspiring in the heat, an attack of fear visited provincial France, with tales of brigands and awful threats to ordinary folk. By October, Paris effervesced still more and, whilst the new constitution was being discussed, by exploiting unemployment and food shortages, agitators persuaded Parisian women to march on Versailles on October 5. The following day, the royal family was forcefully brought back to the Tuileries, where the mob could keep it under surveillance.

On October 6, 1789, when the Assembly moved to the capital, Maximilien was obliged to find lodgings there too. Leaving his three Artesian colleagues to fend for themselves, he booked accommodation with a young fellow called Villiers in the Rue de Saintonge, in the Marais area. Not long ago, when Walter paid a visit to this establishment,[4] which had at that time been empty for some six years and was due for demolition, he found two large windows opening out on to the street and providing, as they did for Robespierre, a view of the tips of two famous arches, the Porte Saint-Martin and the Porte Saint-Denis, both dating back to the reign of Louis XIV. The room occupied by the deputy from Arras was rectangular and in its time had been clearly comfortable, being still spacious and airy, whilst outside, a narrow corridor led to a tiny kitchen. Near by there was a second room looking on to the courtyard with a small summer-house at the far end. This Walter presumed to be the abode of Villiers, a small-time playwright who incidentally helped to awaken Robespierre's early love of the theatre. Villiers also wrote memoirs, in which he tells us how he spent some seven months in the presence of greatness. This leads Walter to calculate that the first three months of Robespierre's stay in the Marais were spent alone.[5] It is possible that Villiers helped him in 1790, though perhaps he did not reside with him, but merely came to perform his duties each morning.

The help which the loquacious memorialist rendered to the future leader of France was mainly secretarial. There was much to do, for already Maximilien was face to face with the eternal ogre—the problem of gross overwork, which was to plague him for the rest of his life. How often he wished he were in the position of the *Homme champêtre* of his own poem!—

> Who, remote from artificial man and from the courtier,
> Cultivates a modest plot and, returning home from toil,
> May consume in peace within his humble cabin
> The bread, which by the day's labour
> His noble, ungrudging efforts have secured for him.
> With satisfaction he sees his wife and children
> Preparing with dear, diligent hands
> The simple meal and the garments
> He is in need of now.
> ... He alone can be happy and he alone is always so![6]

But it was not to be, since duty loomed large in his sights and there were so many abuses to shoot at.

Though in later years he was to turn savagely upon the atheistic and materialistic Encyclopaedic Movement with whom his beloved Jean-Jacques had quarrelled in 1758, in Constituante days Robespierre's notoriety rested upon enthusiasm for their precious shibboleths, justice and reason, without which he was convinced that popular aspirations would never be canalized or popular demands satisfied. Furthermore, justice and reason would not, he argued, be achieved without a fight against their enemies, the vested interests of the privileged. In other words: he was thoroughly conscious of the class struggle and of the need to achieve social justice. Speeches of progressives like Maximilien were already bearing some fruit, for by August 4, 1789, partial renunciation of feudal privilege by aristocrats and landowners had been effected in the Assembly, though admittedly when the first flush of euphoria had faded, some regretted this idyllic orgy of self-renunciation.

In the early days he had been ignored so much that, in writing up debates, the *rapporteur* was at a loss how to spell this unusual name.[7] However, Maximilien learned to catch the eye of those who mattered, to the extent that other M.P.s began to mock the provincial lawyer, old before his time and devoid of humour, whom they nicknamed the 'Candle of Arras'. This of course made him more rebellious and choleric than ever. Nevertheless, ridicule was to some extent balanced by sincere admiration in certain quarters. For instance, it was in 1790 that he first heard from a young blood called Saint-Just who, writing as *électeur* for the Aisne department, sent the renowned Revolutionary a tribute, in which he professed to know the Artesian wizard just as he knew the Almighty—namely, by his miracles; and in which he also alluded to him as the deputy not only of France but of mankind![8] The extravagant epistolary introduction of the younger to the older man was pregnant with portent.

There followed a period of consolidation, during which the aspiring politician continued to keep his name before the public. Even his attitude to his own profession had led him into ambivalence in December 1790, when he spoke in favour of citizens defending themselves in court, instead of employing advocates;[9] at the same time he recalled that the Bar had been traditionally useful in defending freedom against absolutism and in vindicating justice, humanity and oppressed innocence; and he certainly could not forget that practice under the old system had first awakened in him a sharp taste for liberty. Fighting in court for the weak and underprivileged had taught him an art which already stood him in good stead when searing invective was called for.

For instance, in June 1791 there was that all-important happening. Accompanied by his family, Louis, upon whom rested one pole of the new constitution and opinion had generally relied, escaped from the Tuileries Palace to make his way towards Germany and the *émigré* army, which would presumably have been prepared to overthrow the Constitution and restore the *Ancien Régime*. The fact that the *berline* was stopped at a small village called Varennes merely increased the embarrassment of those who wished the Constitution to work. Maximilien was still one of these. His first reaction to Varennes was different from the violent Left-wing explosion of hatred and indignation. Generously, the young politician pointed out that freedom, equality and virtue could be still ensured under a monarchy as well as under a republic and not all republics were renowned for the preservation of these things;[10] but this attitude was short-lived, as more and more the sovereignty of the people appealed to his imagination and pushed out the monarchy. In July he was already calling Louis a traitor.[11]

Both the Jacobin and Cordelier clubs would have no nonsense and decided to press for Louis's deposition, though so far a republic was not openly considered. On July 16 Danton read a petition to the crowds on the Champ de Mars and met with opposition when the phrase 'by constitutional means' came out. The Assembly finally voted for the king's suspension until he had fully approved the Constitution of 1791. Considering that this made the petition read by Danton illegal, the Jacobins quashed it, whereas the Cordeliers, Danton's Left-wing friends, decided to get up a new petition demanding that the monarch be put on trial. It was this petition, signed on the Champ de Mars on July 17 by some 6,000 citizens, which resulted in fifty of them being shot by National Guards under La Fayette. Though not a Cordelier, Robespierre was associated with the Left because he realized that the Assembly's pretence that the king had been kidnapped by men like Fersen and Quentin Crawford was nonsensical. He therefore urged that the king and queen should be questioned about their degree of guilt in this shameful breach of faith. Furthermore, since violence had been the Assembly's answer to working-class protest, the struggle would henceforth be on a different basis. Not only was His Majesty a rogue, but indirectly the Assembly and the Mayor of Paris were accessories to a crime against the people. For the clique in power time was running out, so Maximilien decided to side more and more with the poor wretches who had been gunned down in the 'White Terror' by bourgeois guardsmen. Otherwise one might as well say farewell to the gains of the early Revolution. The appeal could not be made to parliament, which now denied him a hearing, so it was published.[12] Addressed not specifically to Paris, but to the nation, it embodied a stern warning against allowing the Revolution to lose its way and against imagining that principles could necessarily be saved without bloodshed; for, just as violence had been used against the legitimate objections of ordinary folk, violence might have to be used to save liberty, equality and virtue. The real struggle was in fact just ahead.

Since he was so resolutely incapable of joining his conservative colleagues in whitewashing the royal reputation, Maximilien became a marked man from July 17, when La Fayette and his 'Fayettists' did their utmost to save the king. As he passed through the Rue (Saint-) Honoré on his way home to the Marais, the tribune was jostled by an over-enthusiastic crowd and at the same time exposed to danger from government troops in the very congested area. It was to save him from this ambiguous plight that the carpenter, Maurice Duplay, offered him his hearth and home—a generous gesture towards a man who was later to be accused of acting like a Tartuffe in the carpenter's home and whose final ruin dragged down the Duplays too.

For three years Robespierre was to reside at 366 Rue (Saint-) Honoré, which today, after structural modifications and a short spell as a night-club bar ('Chez Robespierre'), bears the number 398. The building was constructed around a yard with a tiny garden on the left as one entered. On the left too and attached to the ground-floor apartments, there was a lean-to which served as a workshop for Duplay's men. The yard backed on to the convent garden belonging to Conceptionist nuns. The entrance gate was flanked by a jeweller's and a working-class cook-shop. The ground floor boasted a living-room and dining-room, whilst, facing the convent, were a study and kitchen. An external stair led to the first floor, which could be reached from the dining-room too. On the south side this floor facing the street had a small room which, for odd periods, was occupied by Couthon or Robespierre's brother or sister, as required. To the west, towards the Place de la Révolution, were located the rooms of Jacques-Maurice, Simon, Robespierre himself and Monsieur Duplay, whilst Madame's bedroom was on the north side, where her three daughters also slept. Robespierre's room was sparsely furnished, as befitted a puritan by nature and conviction. There was a wooden bedstead, with damask curtains which Madame had run up out of one of her cast-off dresses; a small desk, some poor chairs with cane seats and a bookcase in a cupboard. It would have been unseemly for the future saviour of France to be accommodated more luxuriously; for the wilderness lay ahead with its sackcloth and ashes.

On November 28, 1791, Maximilien returned to Paris after a short trip to Arras.[13] At this point he finally broke with the middle-class electors who had sent him to Versailles two years before and frankly became a Left-wing militant. So, whilst he declined the title when in 1792 Brissot alluded to him as the *agitateur du peuple*, he significantly added that 'the people are just, good and magnanimous'.[14] He was wrong, of course. They were not as he imagined them to be and they were certainly not much like he was. Above all, middle-class Arras was different from the Faubourg Saint-Antoine, as he would one day realize to his cost.

Chapter 3

THE JACOBIN

'Ceux qui ne sont pas Jacobins ne sont pas vraiment
vertueux'

A CONVENTIONNEL

Few are the politicians who, on the threshold of a promising career, dare to vote themselves out of office and desert the welcome glare of publicity.[1] Yet that is precisely what Robespierre did in 1791. New men were needed and the old faces should not be seen again for some time, he argued.[2] Secretly also he thought the Assembly too conservative to represent the forces that were seething, surging, anxious to break out from below—the very power that the Establishment wished to suppress. La Fayette and his friends had no sympathy whatsoever with the workers, whom they feared more than the *émigrés*. Their revolution was over and they wanted nothing more than to stabilize the present situation, i.e. the constitutional monarchy. This would not do at all for the deputy for Arras, who had reacted angrily to the use of the royal veto, authorized in the Constitution. Though he admitted that, in times of crisis, freedom might have to be waived or restricted for the duration of the emergency, he never faltered in demanding the expression of popular will and the establishment of equality, neither of which had yet been realized. It was better to remain in the wings whilst the Assembly continued to abide by a document in which no one had nowadays much confidence and under a king who had been despised and mistrusted since Varennes.

Curiously enough, Maximilien had the support of the Right for his proposal that present M.P.s should stand down. The wily Conservatives considered that this would ruin the Moderantists and provoke a political crisis to the advantage of the royalists. Of course, on almost every other topic the latter found Robespierre distasteful and with good reason. He had been one of the few who spoke out against the inequality of fortunes; and, though at no time a communist, he was well aware of social tensions caused by excessive differences between the 'haves' and the 'have-nots'. He had also proved an eloquent partisan of (almost) universal

30

suffrage.[3] This too added to the suspicion with which he was usually viewed by the Right and brought him still closer to the Left. However, in the end, he prevailed with a Constituante who lacked the guts to spurn his lead in self-effacement and consequently reluctantly agreed not to form part of the Legislative Assembly. The new House was therefore packed with greenhorns —a situation which led to difficulties for the nation, but, on the personal level, Maximilien's decision turned out to be very shrewd indeed. Relying more and more on the Parisians, he could at the same time be sure of a good platform at the Jacobins, where he held forth on many controversial issues and, especially on one of great importance.[4]

War appealed to both constitutional 'poles': to the king, whose courtiers obviously thought that a French defeat would mean an end to the Revolution and to the restrictions placed upon them by the new régime; to the Girondins in power, for reasons already given. In fighting militarism, the Incorruptible was right, for the war was to change a fairly peaceful lawyers' revolt into a soldiers' holocaust. Alas, the idealistic Girondins were not clever statesmen. If they had been, they would not have committed their country to a foolish adventure, against which Robespierre had warned them desperately in detailed speeches, and which would result in either failure of the popular revolt or the creation of a military dictatorship. They refused to face the fact that (as Robespierre repeatedly said) the enemy to fear was within the camp. They also turned a deaf ear to his claims that France was totally unprepared for war on the scale that would necessarily ensue. At the Jacobins Maximilien poured out arguments against war-fever.[5] All in vain; on April 20, 1792, with the Assembly's approval, Louis declared war on the King of Hungary and Bohemia. The fatal die was cast. It was small comfort that, within a few days, Maximilien's worst fears were justified, in that war brought humiliation and hardship. The first phase began with a French assault upon Tournai, followed by a retreat towards Lille and Valenciennes, so that by May 18, 1792, the generals were refusing to attack again until their forces were adequate and properly supplied.

Whilst Robespierre was being proved right in one respect, the Assembly and the king were being justified in another. War certainly changes things and military defeat is political dynamite. What the king and the politicians did not know, however, was

that a very few months later the Legislative Assembly would be
at an end and France would become a republic. Once it became
clear that the Assembly was not meeting the exigencies of a
national emergency, it was only a question of time before the
hated Constitution was thrown out along with the king who
'sanctioned' it. The defeat of French forces persuaded the Assembly to issue certain decrees which the king refused to accept,
and this led to the first penetration of the Tuileries Palace by a
Parisian mob, on June 20, 1792.

This relatively peaceful demonstration was to be the dress
rehearsal for a much more bloody engagement on August 10,
1792, once more at the Tuileries. Robespierre was right. At home,
the situation had been changed with war-induced brutality and
speed. Temporarily an insurrectional Commune ruled Paris.
'Communist' Paris ruled France; the National Legislative
Assembly was a pale shadow of its former self. The ill-fated
Constitution still held good, but no one cared about it any more.
Two days before the proclamation of the Republic, the Legislative
Assembly had its last meeting, and six weeks after the violent
attack upon the royal palace and the massacre of the Swiss guards,
the National Convention came into being.

In February 1792, Robespierre had been appointed Public
Prosecutor for Paris, but he had later resigned this post, because
he wished to promote justice on the wider scale, the national
scene. Now came the awaited opportunity to find the job he really
desired. Return to politics was marked by definitive identification
with the common people—not the bourgeois Artesians, but the
people of Paris—a wise decision, as it turned out, for in this latter
part of 1792, it was becoming political suicide to disagree with the
capital, as 1793 was to prove conclusively. The acknowledged
king of the Jacobins was soon to be the uncrowned king of Paris
—a situation full of dangerous paradox, since henceforth, on the
one hand, *laissez-faire*, and, on the other, controls; on the one,
property ownership and on the other, socialist nationalization,
were constantly to pull him in different directions until at last
they dismembered him. In late 1792, he did not see this clearly
ahead; for after all no man had better right to enter the Convention. Steps were duly taken and, even though some of his critics
could say later that he proclaimed his principles in the Republican

parliament after he had let others die for them, his friends excused him, because they knew how opposed to violence he was by nature.

Characteristically, the enemy of capital punishment and of war[6] had taken no direct part in the stirring events of August 10. Nor had he been a member of either the federal or sectional committees that had organized the mini-revolution, but, as August 10 approached, he had said in his newspaper that he hoped that the king and the Assembly would shortly be replaced by another body[7] and, at the end of a momentous day, he had turned up at the Jacobins to demand the creation of a democratic parliament of this sort.[8] When, in its indignation, the Legislative had quashed the Commune and ordered elections, Maximilien had written for Tallien to read to the Lower House on August 30 a petition in which there occurs this sinister and pointedly prophetic sentence: 'We have had the troublesome priests arrested and in a few days' time the soil of freedom will be purged of their presence.'[9] So, if he did not personally butcher the priests in their prisons, he knew of the impending carnage and even endorsed it; but of course many judgements were utterly warped at this time by the danger from foreign invaders threatening the very existence of France. Luckily, at the very end of this period, by one expedient or another, the Prussian advance was arrested at Valmy on September 22. At last a much-needed victory could be celebrated. Being relatively near the front line, the terrified Parisians could breathe again in this nightmare conflict undertaken by forces ill-equipped and unprepared for the task.

At home, the new government was taking office.

The National Convention, which lasted from September 1792 until October 1795, falls into three distinct periods: first, the Girondin Convention; secondly, the Montagnard Convention; thirdly, the Thermidorean Convention, following the fall and death of Robespierre. In the first of these, the Girondins, who had been Left-wing in the previous Assembly, now found that they were regarded as much more moderate and even conservative in their outlook. On the whole they tried to represent provincial and national opinion, whereas the Commune episode had brought into greater prominence already the Jacobin-Montagnard element, which above all enjoyed the favour of Parisians. Between the two lay a centre party, known as *Le Marais* or *La Plaine*.

The Convention began by voting that the monarchy should be abolished and a republic established. Immediately thereafter the real conflict between Left-wing Jacobins and Right-wing Girondins broke out. France had been very much a divided nation since Varennes and the consequent Massacre du Champ de Mars. So political choice had been inevitable, but political reality was not the same as good intentions and fine theories. In the Convention Robespierre now represented the urban workers, as we have seen; but he did so with relative restraint, since he could not subscribe to the rabid socialism of extremist *enragés* and was still apprehensive of the anarchy released the previous August. Political colours were purely relative, however, and the Girondins accused him of a form of communism—had he not been a member of the insurrectional Paris Commune? Dangerous talk, meriting a sharp reply: the Incorruptible hit back in September by accusing the Girondins of having a soft spot for the enemy commander, the Duke of Brunswick.[10] Whatever may have lain behind this accusation (as we shall speculate later), there is no doubt that the tide of war had turned in favour of the new Republic at Valmy in September 1792. Subsequently, a French victory at Jemappes was achieved, and soon all Belgium became French.

At home, warfare of a different kind continued unabated and especially virulent on the subject of the fate of Louis XVI, the Girondins resisting Left-wing demands for the execution of a traitor to France, such as those which in November and December came from the mouth of Robespierre, who, fortified by Saint-Just's ruthless logic, claimed that Louis must die so that France could live.[11]

The Girondins continued to be inept in war. By the end of 1792 a further military crisis had ensued and a levy of some 300,000 men was raised to fill gaps in the lines. Meanwhile all Europe had taken note of French expansion, especially into Belgium, a situation which worried Great Britain most of all. To justify these apprehensions, in February 1793 France declared war upon Britain and Holland; and, as if to punish impertinence, fate decreed that at Neerwinden (March 1793) France should be overwhelmed and routed. The defeated general, Dumouriez, the favourite of the Girondin faction, aggravated the mortal danger by defecting in

Robespierre at the time of the Assemblée Constituante (1791).
The so-called 'Irish' portrait by Vaquelin, engraved by Guyard
(see p. 10)

The opening of the States General 5 May 1789. Robespierre is immediately in front of the seated figure turning to speak to a colleague. The engraving is by Prudhomme from a painting by Couder

April.[12] To Maximilien this appeared conclusive proof that the Girondins were either treacherous or inefficient—neither of which could be condoned in war-time. Moreover his thesis was seized by others with the greater eagerness since it was already widely known that La Vendée was in revolt against the central authority and in the south federalists had begun to demand autonomy for their regions. This complex war on three fronts provoked the gravest military crisis of the Revolution and was to be Robespierre's supreme opportunity. He was the one man who had a chance of uniting Jacobins and *sans-culottes*. Already he had made a bid to be considered the architect of a new French system of government.

It is a commonplace of history that those seeking power first make striking suggestions and sooner or later may find themselves called upon to act upon them. Practical proposals had been put before parliament in March 1793.[13] In this manner Maximilien suggested the type of Committee of Public Safety which was set up three weeks later and the kind of Tribunal which was to complement it and do its bidding. Criticizing the régime whose ineptitude had made it possible for battles to be lost, he urged more centralization, so that the State could regulate all movements of the Revolution. In addition, he stressed internal dangers. Efficiency would only be regained when treachery became truly hazardous to the traitor. To achieve this, the gap between legislators and the executive would unfortunately have to be temporarily narrowed and the latter would have to consist of known patriots full of energy and worthy of a nation's trust. Such was his lofty conception of the hard-working Committee which he would one day head. In addition to these internal improvements, Maximilien urged the French to set up a ministry of information and propaganda to divide and debilitate the allies fighting the Republic.

Thus he blueprinted the machinery of the terror, which was not conceived without safeguards to protect the innocent, and for this touch of humanity Robespierre was most responsible. Secondly, we must understand that the harshness of most of the remaining laws and provisions were a kind of anticipatory protection for the Revolutionary government and for Robespierre himself in the role he envisaged. Caution and vigilance were to insure the executive against home-made perils: the Convention was rife with plots and counterplots. Maximilien was clearly one of the principal targets of the Gironde Party, who did not hesitate, for instance, to foster damaging rumours concerning the alleged family connexion with the would-be regicide, Damiens. His own party, the Montagne, riposted by proposing that all deputies who had not voted for the immediate execution of the king should be put out of the Convention.

At this crucial juncture the Girondins made fatal mistakes.[14] They impeached the Montagnard Marat for inciting the common citizenry to pillage and murder and they did not foresee that the Tribunal would acquit this popular hero, who would be carried shoulder-high in triumph from his place of trial. Maximilien capitalized on the wave of indignation against the Right in a pair of vaguely socialist speeches delivered on April 21 and 24, 1793.[15] Furthermore, since he now desired to dominate the upper Committee instituted in April, on May 10 he proclaimed his constitutional doctrine.[16] His ideas may be summarized briefly as follows; submission of government to the rule of law; protection of citizens against excessive use of authority; limitation of power of officials to be accompanied by restriction upon the number and tenure of public charges. Another mistake made by the Girondins was the setting up of the Commission of Twelve to investigate an alleged Leftist plot hatched by the Commune against the Convention. As though these were not enough blunders for one season, they further proceeded to have the deputy clerk, Hébert, arrested along with other municipal officials. Isnard, the Girondin President of the Convention, was even foolish enough to imitate the Duke of Brunswick in threatening the city of Paris with destruction. In Brunswick's case this red rag had brought the bulls on to the streets to sack the Tuileries: in Isnard's, it prompted Robespierre to invoke popular insurrection.

On the following day, May 27, the Girondins shouted him down in the Convention, when he protested about arrests ordered by the hated Commission;[17] but Maximilien had good friends in the 'boulevard de la liberté', as he liked to call the capital.[18] Four days later the Commander of the National Guard seized key positions in the city and closed the gates. Several leading Girondins were arrested and a Jacobin motion was carried abolishing the Commission. Meanwhile Robespierre's humane hesitation led to a delay in the expulsion of the deputies of the Gironde party, and as a result a dangerous political situation dragged on into June. On the second of that month Paris forced the issue: the Tuileries were surrounded by popular soldiery, with cannon and a vast crowd of Parisian supporters. Force prevailed: the Girondins had to consent to the Jacobin motion concerning the seizure of their leaders. Twenty-three were placed under house arrest; twelve escaped to the provinces and eight more followed a short time later. Robespierre's party had won, thanks largely to Marat and Henriot—the determined men of action. The lesson was thus made abundantly clear: procrastination would not do against resolute enemies at home or abroad. Poor Maximilien: as on so many occasions, confined to his bed with yet another bout of that mysterious malady which laid him low—sick with contemplation of future responsibilities in a régime he had tailored to suit himself as well as republican France!

Chapter 4

ANNUS MIRABILIS

'Robespierre aspire à rester maître moins par ambition que par crainte'

MALLET DU PAN March 1794

During the hegemony of the Montagne, parliament was, as we saw, served by two subsidiaries, the Committee of Public Safety and that of General Security, concerned more specifically with police matters, though later in the crucial year, even these functions passed partly into the hands of the dominant Committee, consisting now of twelve men—surely a Parisian answer to the Commission des Douze!—with Robespierre as a minister without portfolio, though prime minister would have been nearer the truth. His closest associates were the crippled lawyer Couthon and the proud young fanatic, Saint-Just. Carnot was in charge of military matters, assisted by the Prieur from the Côte d'Or constituency, and Lindet, who tackled the problems of logistics and supply. Naval affairs were handled by Jeanbon de Saint-André. Two *enragés*, Billaud-Varenne, a former actor and teacher, and Collot d'Herbois, a playwright, were holding a watching brief for popular factions. Young Saint-Just and another Prieur (from the Marne) were often sent on missions to see that the Committee's decisions were carried out. Barère proved a very versatile member, and Hérault de Séchelles was concerned with constitutional matters. It was late in July 1793 that Maximilien joined the major Committee, instituted the previous April, and thus placed himself in the line of fire.[1] He hoped to accomplish his task before he was gunned down. His final year had begun. He had some initial advantage in that the Convention was purged of the Girondins who were soon to be outlawed too. On the other hand, the Centre contained elements hostile to him.

When he entered the Committee, Maximilien persuaded the other members to accept new procedures, to reorganize the clerical staff and to hold weekly meetings with the other Committee. The press, which, from intimate knowledge, the leader regarded as dangerous, was to be temporarily deprived of its freedom. Only when true democracy had been established would it be possible to allow journalists to have their say again! In all such decisions, the will and interests of the majority of citizens of France were both the pretext and the inspiration. In other words: the government was to remain revolutionary until peace had been restored and all enemies put to flight.

Involved in almost every department, Robespierre performed his labours with exemplary enthusiasm and fortitude. Some members of the team could not be trusted beyond the end of the corridor, but faithful Saint-Just and Couthon were keeping a watchful eye on them. When Maximilien sensed plots on all sides, he was not entirely wrong. It was therefore fortunate for him that the carpenter and his equally devoted family acted as watchdogs as well as landlords, companions and fans. Not that they saw much of him most days. During the months when he was a member of the Committee of Public Safety, Maximilien was obliged to leave the Duplay residence in good time, because he put in an hour's work before the Convention met.

The Committee met in the wing of the Tuileries connected with the Louvre and now named the Pavillon de Flore, but in Revolutionary times called the Pavillon de l'Egalité. It had set up its headquarters in apartments formerly used by Marie-Antoinette, located on the ground floor and in the *entresol* overlooking the Tuileries gardens. Robespierre went up to his work by the Escalier de la Reine, on the first landing of which he was afforded a good view of the gardens. On the right was a door leading to the rooms along the terrace, separated from those overlooking the courtyard on the other side of the building. The Committee sat in the large drawing-room, later used as an office by Napoleon I and his royal successors in the nineteenth century. Hitherto located (as we said) mainly in the queen's apartments on the ground floor, from 1794 with its extension of bureaucracy, much of the Committee's activities had to be transferred to the first floor of the palace. At the end of the Reign of Terror, offices were housed in the king's suite. It is also likely that each member of the potent oligarchy had his own *pied-à-terre* in the Tuileries. The committee-room proper was hung with magnificent Gobelins tapestries to match the sumptuous royal furniture of a former epoch. Guards were on duty inside the former palace and cannons protected its entrances. Robespierre and his hard-working colleagues were taking no chances!

So to the Convention, which was at first housed in a royal riding-school. Of course, a riding-school is not the best place to hold parliament. For one thing, the floors were never really strong enough to support all that weight. Time and again buttresses were added; the joiners were never out of the place. Access to the parliament chamber was effected via a vestibule from which led two offices. Many other bureaux were improvised in neighbouring buildings hastily added to the riding-school itself.

After the vestibule had been crossed, M.P.'s found themselves in a corridor which ran round the whole circumference of the *Manège* and led into the main chamber at several access points. This large hall was about six times as long as it was wide, which was a nuisance. Deputies adapted to circumstances, however, arranging themselves on six rows of ascending benches in the form of an ellipse, leaving the *piste* in the middle free. Half-way along the garden side of the hall was the President's elevated rostrum, furnished with a table covered by a green cloth. There were also secretaries grouped about a round table. Opposite, on the convent side where runs the present Rue de Rivoli, was the Bar of the house. In selecting one's seat—right or left of the Speaker's tribune—there was established a custom which has provided modern political distinctions. The Montagne occupied high benches on the left and in the middle was the *Plaine* or *Marais*. At the ends of the hall were public galleries, though privileged guests were housed in boxes.

Later, when parliament was transferred to better quarters in the Tuileries Palace itself, access was gained by way of a vestibule, which led into the *Salle des Machines*—the effects' department of the old Tuileries royal theatre. This large room, cleared of its equipment, was divided by a new floor to make the Salle de la Liberté and the Salle des Séances. The latter, 130 feet long and 45 feet wide, became the new home of parliament, the amphitheatre occupying the whole left-hand side as one entered. Ten rows of seats in tiers formed something rather less uniform than an ellipse. Placed there for safety's sake by a vigilant architect, four large pillars restricted the activities of the deputies and spoiled the view a little. Opposite this amphitheatre there was a wooden construction housing the Presidential offices. The President himself was perched on top of all this and reached his dais via two ramps, one at each side of the office block. The other two walls supported public galleries, which were more like theatre boxes, and at the ends of the room there were arcades with stagings, so that a total of 1,400 spectators could be accommodated.

The general sessions of the Committee of Public Safety began early, and from seven onwards some of the keener members were at their desks preparing for the beginning of the daily session. About ten in the forenoon, the real meeting began. Formality was not a characteristic of these working sessions, there being neither chairman nor set agenda. After decisions had been taken, resolutions were drawn up on the basis of unanimous opinions.

When some members of the Committee of Public Safety had to slip away to attend the Convention from which they drew their authority, the rest laboured on. Their motto was that there is no time like the present and that time was seldom on the side of revolutionaries anyhow. The only pretext for postponing discussion or decision-making arose in the absence of a key figure—Maximilien's pilot-fish, Saint-Just, for instance, who was at the Front. About five or six in the early evening members left the Tuileries to snatch a hasty meal in a neighbouring restaurant, but two hours' break was the maximum. About eight they were back at their desks or in committee, their deliberations lasting so long into the night that there were two carriages on hand to take them home. Robespierre rarely needed this facility, for his lodgings were situated so near to his places of work.

On afternoons when not required at the Convention, it was his custom to stroll in the Marbeuf Gardens, the still rustic Champs-Elysées or on the more distant heights of Montmorency, communing with nature or the shades of Jean-Jacques, whilst his faithful dog, Brount, which he had brought back from Arras, afforded him more tangible companionship. In the Champs-Elysées he loved to play with the Savoyard children, whose fathers ran messages around Paris; and these tiny southerners would dance for the great man.

Because of the proximity of his lodgings and the peculiar hours he had to observe, Robespierre dined about five o'clock. His meal was invariably spartan. It was soon over and then, from six till eight, nine or ten, he was at his third place of business, the

Jacobin Club, where the audience was generally more sympathetic than the *Conventionnels*. This club met off the Rue (Saint-) Honoré, at first in the refectory of the convent, then in the library and finally in the church. Though architecturally undistinguished, this building was striking since it contained a high altar decorated with the Annunciation and, in a side chapel, a fine Coysevox tomb. All around the place were tiers of seats. Speakers faced the Chair across the narrower middle of the nave. Several offices were to be found in other rooms of these conventual buildings, for more than a thousand provincial branches kept up correspondence with Paris.

Meetings took place on alternate evenings. That left some spare time and, in the early days, Maximilien devoted these free evenings either to theatre visits, which he appears to have enjoyed very much, or to musical evenings at the Duplays', where Lebas sang Italian songs, Buonarroti played selections on the piano and Robespierre himself either declaimed poetry or read aloud to the assembled company. This consisted of Madame Duplay's brother and a friendly blacksmith from Choisy; Vaugeois, a carpenter; a distiller from next door; the painter David and Cietty, an Italian artist; a printer Nicolas, who lived a few houses up the road; another neighbour, the *ci-devant* Comtesse de Chalabre, infatuated with the young politician; a doctor Tranche-la-Hausse; a cordwainer by the name of Calandini and a grocer, Lohier. At Duplay's place he also found the opportunity to play the Rousseauist hero and to liken himself to Saint-Preux at Wolmar's house or to Emile either in the workshop or with Sophie's father—all of which afforded consolations to a romantic soul. Such consolations were sorely needed, for the young tribune was increasingly obliged to spend his spare time preparing speeches for the morrow. Even when out for the evening, he was unable to forget the Convention and, when dining at Méot's restaurant, Maximilien remained silent and thoughtful. Truly, it was a terribly busy life, calculated to undermine the nervous stamina of one twice as robust as he was. To add to the strain, Maximilien was never a fast worker; which makes it all the more remarkable that this highly-strung individual found the energy to cram so much into each day that Mathiez refers to him as the *contrôleur-universel* of the new republic.[2]

There was always something to keep him from his sleep—for

instance, the Constitution of 1793, that most democratic of documents drawn up by Hérault de Séchelles, closely supervised and prompted by Robespierre. Nothing before or since can match the liberality of this constitution, which gives expression to principles announced two months before. Whilst the notion of the separation of powers remained in cold-storage until the nineteenth century, this document closely associated with Robespierre's régime envisaged direct consultation of the people by way of referenda— a preview of Gaullist France; universal suffrage—the natural corollary of belief that salvation could only come from below; a lower House elected for one year only, and an executive of twenty-four men. The propaganda-value of this new charter was enormous and desperately needed at the time, because in the provinces Girondins who had escaped their enemies had managed to excite federalist feeling, stirring up those discontented people who disliked centralized unity and longed for devolution of power and authority. The situation became very dangerous for the Montagne. One young lady from Caen, Charlotte Corday, expressed her Girondist sentiments by murdering the agitator, Marat, and imminent personal danger was brought home to Jacobin leaders. Soon sixty out of eighty-four departments had gone over to the federalist cause and to trouble in royalist Vendée were added widespread disturbances on this new issue.

However, Republican France responded to the challenge. Glorious is the military history of the Montagne period from mid-1793 to mid-1794. The army had been thoroughly reorganized on more democratic lines, so that the common soldier had now something to fight for and opportunities of promotion unknown before. In August 1793, the *levée en masse* of a million men had evoked the response to peril which brings out the best in patriotic citizens. Consequently victories came one after the other: Hondschoote, Maubeuge, Wattignies, Landau, followed by successes in Savoy and Roussillon. Finally, in December 1793, the Vendean revolt was crushed and the civil war was checked.

Things would not be the same now. In Anouilh's play, *Pauvre Bitos*, Mirabeau is made to anticipate the attitude of the Indulgent-Moderantist faction, once they could make themselves heard again. The opinion began to be proclaimed that pleasure-seekers have always caused less misery and bloodshed than the austere idealists. This hedonist doctrine was dangerous at the moment of victory. Moderantists began to oppose the reformers, who remained convinced that the Revolution should continue until more had been achieved. Spurred on by a variety of motives, these counter-revolutionaries were a real menace to the leader and his small band of trusted colleagues and were therefore, in his view, true enemies of the people, for they were consciously or unconsciously serving the cause of nobles, clergy and financiers—those egotists, many of whom had started the Revolution but now wished to stop it because the people were taking control. Robespierre's only hope lay in cowing them into cooperation or surrender. From the timid leader's point of view, pre-emptive, official terror was the only effective answer to unofficial, anarchistic terror, the guillotine the only real deterrent. Protesting since Marat's murder that all France's leading politicians would be assassinated,[3] he obviously thought that the best antidote to fear was superior fear; the most powerful argument against the assassin's knife was the *couperet* in the Place de la Révolution. Such thoughts betray obsession with political murder and suspicions about some sort of plot, eternally hatching against avowed democrats who refused to be trimmers and compromisers. Indeed, the case of Marat was potentially so like his own that it was natural that he should foresee similar events happening to every Committee member. Something drastic was required and, in the summer of 1793, was proposed by the Committee of Public Safety, accepted by the Convention and welcomed by the *sans-culottes*. The Law of Suspects of September 17 was the outcome of this agitation.[4] Though Robespierre did not script it, he did not oppose it—except to ask that it be applied mercifully.

On the other side of the balance-sheet must be placed the execution of the Hébertists and Dantonists in mid-March and early April 1794.[5] The Hébert group had made themselves a nuisance and a menace on the extreme Left by demanding popular control of military appointments, a purge of the civil service and a stricter use of identity cards as a check on suspect persons. This appeared as an attempt to outbid the Committee of Public Safety precisely at a time when Robespierre was straining after greater unity. The Hébert faction was also in the front rank of the dechristianizers. This too militated against unity, since it antagonized the unofficial Catholic lobby. The situation was delicate and had to be dealt with carefully. Though he may have had little choice as we shall see, in February 1794 Maximilien allowed the eager Saint-Just to steal some of Hébert's thunder by sketching out measures relating to the redistribution of property belonging to arrested suspects among the deserving poor. But Hébert came back fighting strongly and on March 4 at the Cordeliers he attacked Maximilien, who was currently ill.

The only effective answer to a presumed *coup d'état* would be the *coup de grâce*. Robespierre had no alternative. On March 24, eighteen conspirators went to the guillotine. As it turned out, this was not a good decision, inevitable though it had been; for the Parisians never forgave the leader for this onslaught on their scribbling sacred monster. In any case, cutting out the tumour did not cure the political cancer, closely associated as it was with economic *malaise*. Another symptom complicated the illness. The Right of the Jacobins, led by the newly re-married Danton, had become lukewarm about the Revolution. Danton himself, as we shall see later, was suspected of 'feathering his love-nest' with bribes. Other men in conspicuous office were involved in the Indies Company scandal, which seemed to illustrate the widespread corruption that reigned amongst those who wished the Revolution played down so that they could drool over illicit perquisites.

A week after the Hébertists had met their end, tactics to be employed against the Dantonists had been worked out in the Committee of Public Safety, whose proceedings went unrecorded. Indeed, secrecy was vital, since the new *fournée* was to include not only the powerful Danton (whom Maximilien suspected of dealings with Orléans and Dumouriez, not to mention Brunswick);[6] but also Desmoulins (who had criticized recent policies in his newspaper), the dubious Hérault de Séchelles (whose constitutional draft did not excuse everything) and Fabre d'Eglantine (inventor of the republican calendar, but up to his neck in the Indies Scandal).[7] This wholesale purge of front-line Revolutionaries was necessary if the pure fire of the great cause was not to peter out in self-seeking and ignominy. Robespierre appended his signature and fed the Jacobins with more and more evidence against the accused. At the trial all but one were condemned and, on April 6, fourteen prominent statesmen were executed. Robespierre's retributive justice had done its work and his peril and power were proportionately increased.

In a sense his power has been 'centred'. Marat to the Left and Danton to the Right had represented the extremes of Robespierrism. In a short space of time Marat had been done to death and Danton despatched to the guillotine. From now on, the all-powerful tribune would walk the narrow rope running down the centre of Revolutionary politics. But heaven help him if he leaned too much to Right or Left, as he performed this death-defying funambulism.

Chapter 5

GOVERNMENT BY GUILLOTINE

'Robespierre ne peut gouverner ni vivre longtemps de
cette manière

FROSSARD, April 14 1794

From April until July 1794, France was ruled with a blade of steel.'
This was the high tide of Terror; the reign of an all-powerful
oligarchy. As leader of the great Committee, Robespierre set the
tone of austere virtue guaranteed by fear. At last, he surmised,
the golden age of republican ecstasy was at hand, and indeed
would be here tomorrow, if only the tares of self-interest could be
killed off. Rousseau had done his work well, and his most enthusiastic disciple had learned his lesson well too. Now he was to
institute what amounted to a new State religion, the Cult of the
Supreme Being. Proclaimed before the Convention, this cult was
merely an affirmation of the deistic minimum—that is, belief in the
godhead and perhaps the immortality of the soul, for the good of
the people. That they needed such a moral policeman was now
painfully obvious. Hébertism had seriously eroded public
morality, especially in Paris, and guillotining the man himself
would not necessarily stop the spread of the pernicious contagion
of the *Père Duchesne*, which was now revealing itself in
dechristianization on a wide scale.

By now the disciple of the Genevan *promeneur solitaire* had
acquired a small carriage to take him around Paris, but, with
typical modesty, had insisted that it should bear a number, like a
hire-cab! In fact, this new means of transport had been supplied
not for ostentation, but entirely for reasons of security. For it was
now the dangerous season in the political calendar—that warm,
disturbing interval between spring and high summer when
violence lurks in the bright shadows. Opportunities were not
lacking. On June 8, Paris was crowded with sightseers from the
provinces and with Parisians in holiday mood. It was a lovely day
and the streets were suitably garlanded. The painter David had
done his work well, for the various didactic models in stucco
and canvas were ready for the great occasion. Members of the

Convention advanced in procession, each bearing a bouquet of flowers, corn and fruit—a pantheist tribute to Mother Nature, bountiful and good. Leading the group was Robespierre, President of the Convention, set apart and wearing clothes that singled him out still more; for, whilst the other deputies wore a ceremonial uniform, he had chosen yellow breeches and a sky-blue coat. In front of the Tuileries he set fire to David's contrivance representing atheism, which, in the course of conflagration, disclosed a statue of wisdom pointing to the heavens. He then made the second speech of the day.[1] From the Tuileries it was a fairly long processional walk to the Champ de Mars, where an even more elaborate mumbo-jumbo had been arranged. David had contrived an artificial mound, so that deputies could ascend, whilst a choir intoned a song duly composed for the occasion by Méhul.

Once more Maximilien stood apart from his colleagues and alone at the head of the procession; once more there were nudgings and murmurs about the Supreme Being's true identity! The object of this criticism was well aware of the danger. Robespierre was afraid—with good reason, since, a few days before the Fête, a man called Admiral had attempted to assassinate Collot d'Herbois, because he could not locate Maximilien himself;[2] and, within twenty-four hours, a girl called Renault had tried to emulate Marat's killer, Charlotte Corday, by concealing in her shopping basket two sharp knives when she came to Duplay's to offer the tribune a gift of his favourite fruit. To make matters worse, on the following day, Lecointre had threatened to assassinate the Incorruptible in the Convention. No wonder, then, that the chief target felt that something more should be done to protect him and his colleagues from all these fanatics. The Committee of Public Safety decided to act and, against a background of protest from many members of Parliament that the new decree deprived them of parliamentary immunity, the Convention was persuaded to instigate ruthless repression.

Intensifying the campaign initiated by the Suspects' Law, the Prairial Law of June 1794 allowed the number of cases before the Tribunal to be doubled. Executions rose from 346 in May to 689 in June and 936 in July. Such remarkable productivity proved the efficiency of oligarchic business methods. Surely it could not be long before all the weeds had been successfully mown down! But the new law made an implacable enemy of the Committee of General Security, which should surely have been consulted on a matter so closely linked with the policing of the State. Suspicions and a whispering campaign against Robespierre thus spread to the second seat of delegated authority and made the leader still more resolute.

Ruthlessness is frequently the *sine qua non* of military success— undeniably a factor in the situation changing in favour of the young Republic. In May 1794, Moreau was victorious at Tourcoing, and the next month Jourdan prevailed at Fleurus, where observation balloons were employed for the first time. Then Antwerp, Liège and Brussels fell to the Revolutionary armies, whilst the Sardinians were driven from Nice by Dumerbron; in the Pyrenees the Spaniards were routed by Dugommier and Moncey invaded the Basque country. Of these resounding triumphs, Fleurus (June 26, 1794) was perhaps the most decisive and the most fatal for the pacifist turned war-lord. Like the Terror itself, controls appeared to be no longer necessary; a government which had kept Frenchmen in a state of economic restriction for some time now became redundant and execrable; requisitioning was no longer considered justified and it was hoped that rationing would quickly be abandoned. Idleness and cynicism, selfishness and personal violence rose to the surface once more. Reaction was already under way, with criminals and eccentrics to the fore. The crusade against privilege, vice and prejudice was over. Opposition grew almost hourly, led by Fouché, Barras and Tallien, who sought to profit by a change of régime and who naturally solicited the assistance of a disaffected Committee of General Security.

But this opposition needed some matter with which to polarize discontent and they found it in the curious affair of Catherine Théot, the so-called 'Mother of God', an eccentric visionary who suffered from religious mania and claimed the gift of prophecy.[3] It was unfortunate for Maximilien that Dom Gerle, one of Madame's associates, had a *certificat de civisme* signed by the Incorruptible himself and that the Théot woman should have chosen the great leader as her idol and referred to him in a letter (perhaps forged), found in the old lady's mattress, as the Messiah and Saviour. The situation became more dangerous for the Incorruptible when he rescued the old seer and her friends from the guillotine, for this was taken as proof of complicity in an alleged process of deification of the revolutionary tribune or his eccentric priestess. In particular, his enemies found that *Théot* was remarkably close to the Greek word for the deity, and that the whole thing smacked of Robespierre's new religiosity demonstrated in the Cult of the Supreme Being. In this matter, the spearhead of opposition was the redoubtable Vadier.

The real assault on Robespierre, Couthon and Saint-Just was to come when the leader had been absent from the Convention for some time with ill-health. Back again, on July 26 he made a long speech in self-defence.[4] He complained of the attacks which were already being made upon him and once more committed the fatal error of referring to his enemies in vague generalizations, so that many who were not implicated joined up with the opposition to save their own necks. Vadier's hostility to Maximilien now paled into insignificance compared with the vitriolic, purposeful, desperate initiative taken by Charlotte's former boy-friend from Arras days.

Having just laid to rest the body of his beloved infant daughter, Fouché could not sleep anyway. So he spent the fateful night of July 26–27 in scurrying hither and thither, reminding some of his associates in the Convention that they were probably due to be proscribed when this veiled accusation took more precise form, perhaps on the morrow.

The Ninth of Thermidor dawned with the plotters more numerous and more determined than ever.[5] When the meeting began, the issue of which faction would be guillotined next day remained open. Saint-Just tried to speak eloquently in defence of his friend and his faction; Robespierre endeavoured to reach the rostrum, but was impeded. At the same time, brandishing a dagger turned against himself, Tallien claimed that he would rather die than submit to tyranny, and the Convention shouted down Saint-Just and refused Robespierre a hearing when he begged to be allowed to reply. The Centre or Plain abandoned him; several deputies demanded his arrest and, when the proposal was put to the vote, it was carried. Accused of betraying his own class, the former bourgeois deputy turned demagogue was deserted by old and new friends alike. The man destined for martyrdom was on the threshold of fulfilment of his tragic and glorious destiny.

· · · · ·

The arrest of Robespierre. Detail from a painting by Moave, after a drawing by Barbier (see p. 50)

Robespierre the dandy. (Painter unknown)
(see p. 58)

Once the arrest of the two Robespierre brothers, Couthon, Maximilien's former school friend, Lebas, and his most ardent disciple, Saint-Just, had been unanimously decreed by the Convention, the prisoners were taken out by gendarmes amid general shouts of approval. The hour was five-thirty and the parliamentary session was then suspended to allow time for refreshment. Meanwhile friends of the 'Triumvirs' had not been idle. Since midday the Mayor of Paris, Fleuriot, and the Commander of the National Guard, Henriot, had been at the Town Hall, where, having summoned municipal officials, they were waiting to see whether insurrection would be necessary to save their heroes. However, doubts were dispelled by an usher from the Convention who demanded that Fleuriot should present himself at the Bar of the House. This he declined to do, whilst ugly little Henriot, blustering as usual, sent the fellow back with the message that Robespierre was not to lose his nerve.

The news of Robespierre's arrest started things in motion at the headquarters of the Paris Commune. An alarm was sounded, the city gates were closed and both the Council and Sections were immediately convened. At the same time the National Guard was to proceed with its cannon to the Tuileries, where the Convention was due to resume its sitting at seven. The Jacobins went into permanent session, demonstrating that they recognized the gravity of the crisis. With wild approval, members saluted the envoys of the Council attempting to stiffen their resistance. Thus two important streams of opposition to the Convention were confluent in this hour of trial for democracy. The excitable Henriot felt that the time had come for more personal intervention, and brandishing a pistol he rushed into the Paris streets urging citizens to take up arms. Happening to pass along Henriot's route and hearing these boisterous exhortations, Merlin de Thionville ordered gendarmes to apprehend the impromptu speaker for incitement to rebellion. Seized in the Rue (Saint-) Honoré, Henriot was handed over to the police at the Comité de Sûreté Générale. There matters stood, in a situation resembling stalemate, with a slight advantage to the forces of the Commune during the parliamentary adjournment.

Following arrest, the proscribed politicians had been taken to their respective prisons—Robespierre to the Luxembourg, his brother to Saint-Lazare, Saint-Just to the former Scots College in the Rue Cardinal Lemoine of our own day, Couthon to the Bourbe prison and Lebas to the Conciergerie. In each case, jailers refused to obey the Convention and therefore to detain their illustrious prisoner. Thus Maximilien was gladly entrusted to a detachment of armed men sent out for this purpose from the Town Hall. Further evidence of the temporary supremacy of the Commune-cum-Robespierre faction was furnished by the boldness of Coffinhal, Vice-President of the Revolutionary Tribunal—like Henriot, a man of independent action. His eyes ablaze with legal authority, Coffinhal rushed forth to deliver Henriot from the hands of the police and free him for further exploits likely to help the Robespierrist cause. So once more we discover Henriot arrived at the Place du Carrousel, between the Tuileries and the Louvre, where he ordered his artillery to threaten members of parliament, who by this time had returned to their seats after the comfort-break and were already discussing this present menace to their security and their very existence as a legal body. Members sitting on two government commissions arrived in panic to inform the House that Coffinhal was making a nuisance of himself and that Henriot had directed his cannon on to the palace where parliament was in session. So the deputies resolved to do their duty or die at their post.

This was the climax, the crisis of this Greek drama. Naturally, then, *hubris* had to be punished and the fatal flaw in the Commune's case was to be made clear. Angered at the reduction in their wages proposed in the new Maximum decrees, Parisian workers were not going to support a faction responsible for the prices and incomes policy. So Henriot's heroics produced little effect: the National Guard's artillery refused to fire and the balance of power tipped in favour of the Convention. To make matters worse, since escape from detention Robespierre had done very little to save himself. Dispirited and apathetic, maybe he did not really care to survive the horrors of this terrible day. Not so his enemies, desperate men, determined not to forfeit this all-important battle—men like Fréron, Bourdon de l'Oise, Léonard Bourdon and Legendre who, having a lot to lose, stiffened the determination of remaining members of the Committee. If Parisian workers in the National Guard would not fight for a government they had come to dislike, neither would their friends in the Parisian Sections rally to support the Town-Hall clique. Admittedly, at the instigation of the Commune, they had met about nine in the evening, but their minds were troubled, and when representatives of the Convention came to claim their support, they complied with little hesitation. Meanwhile Barras had been nominated to replace the outlawed Henriot as commander of the National Guard, which was thus taken over by parliament. Two columns of armed men marched against the refractory Paris Commune a little before midnight.

Although, in a confrontation between rebel municipality and legal parliament, many discovered conflicting loyalties, back at the Hôtel de Ville all was not yet lost. Assembled on the wide Place de la Grève were 3,000 armed men with artillery of sorts, waiting to be directed by the dismissed Henriot. They were also waiting for the support of the Paris Sections, but by half-past midnight none was forthcoming. Then came the *deus ex machina*, the climatic act of Fate. At midnight a sharp shower demoralized the bored supporters of the Commune and of Robespierre, who began to slip away, especially when a proclamation was read out officially banning the Commune movement. So, when at last he turned up brandishing his sabre, Henriot discovered that his legions had melted from sight.

What happened next at the Hôtel de Ville remains a matter for conjecture. A gendarme named Méda (or Merda) claimed later to have shot Robespierre through the jaw. If so, he was a poor shot! A better explanation is that, using Lebas's other pistol, the leader tried to commit suicide,[6] but that his aim was not good. This theory is rendered more credible by the fact that the wounded tribune was still playing with the white leather holster when later seen by a group of intruders. (This holster he subsequently employed to staunch the flow of blood from his mouth.) The reason why this appears to be the more credible solution in the case of a neurotic is that, on that day, his apathy had made it certain that he would not lift a finger to save himself; and those who lend credence to the trigger-happy gendarme should ponder the second official report made by Courtois: 'Robespierre who, in the forenoon, was manipulating a penknife with which he dare not stab himself since he still hoped to carry the day, aims at himself a shot which does nothing more than punish him in that organ whence originates eloquence . . .', to which is appended this note: 'Leonard Bourdon introduced to parliament a gendarme, saying: "This excellent gendarme you see before you has not left my side. He has killed two of the conspirators. The gendarme may have thought he had killed Robespierre and told Bourdon so, but the testimony of Bochard, the Town-Hall janitor, shows that it was Robespierre himself who fired the shot which wounded him." [7] If Anouilh had known or believed that, he would have lacked a crucial development in his 1956 play, *Pauvre Bitos*! The editors of the tenth volume of Robespierre's complete works certainly opt for the suicide theory, citing a contemporary account, which tell how the younger Robespierre brother threw himself from a window and landed on a passing citizen; how Lebas, lying on a wood-pile, was found with multiple stab wounds, as was the invalid Couthon, who was discovered under a table; above all, how Maximilien de Robespierre shot himself through the mouth and was shot at the very same moment by the famous gendarme—a nice compromise solution to the dilemma, perhaps. [8]

The Archangel of Death, Saint-Just, remained impassible. Coffinhal resorted to desperate action. Flinging Henriot out of a window on to a pile of manure below, he fought his way out and temporarily evaded his enemies. Then troops of the Convention entered the Hôtel de Ville and Robespierre was taken to their headquarters at the Tuileries, where he was deposited on a table in the Comité de Sûreté Générale—turning the knife in the wound with a vengeance, for the first had been his empire and the second the centre of opposition to his rule. There he remained, insulted by bystanders, until he was carried across Paris in a litter to the Conciergerie, only to make the same horrifying journey in reverse in the late afternoon of the following day, 10 Thermidor, when they put him in the tumbril so often filled with his own victims and trundled him along the Rue (Saint-) Honoré to the Place de la Révolution (Concorde). He travelled between Henriot and Couthon, both suffering from wounds, contusions or abrasions and presenting a very sorry sight indeed. Taunting crowds filled the Place too. Saint-Just died with proud, stoical, defiant calm; Robespierre was vaguely insensitive to the events until the executioner, Samson, removed the band around his shattered jaw, which fell open to the accompaniment of a terrible cry from the victim. The blade fell and the virtuous Terror was at an end. A martyr's road had been traversed. At last, it was accomplished.

PART II

THE MAN

'Robespierre fut-il un monstre ou un martyr vertueux ?'

CLAUZEL

Chapter 6

A LEADER AND HIS FOLLOWING

'Ce Robespierre avait des vertus et des vices en même
proportion'

BARÈRE

What kind of person was this revolutionary leader? Small in
stature (about five feet, three inches), stocky but slim, he was of a
nervous disposition which showed itself in his brusque manner of
walking and changing direction. It revealed itself also in nail-
biting, twitching of the hands, shoulders and neck and in a gesture
likened to the descent of the guillotine-blade. But, since he was
above all an orator, it was his face which had particular significance. It was not the face of a man's man, or a good mixer. The
eyes were the detail one noticed first. Usually shy and shifty, but
on other occasions domineering and angry; deep-set, blue, fawn
or green, according to the situation; sometimes fiery, sometimes
dull and clouded—the optics, therefore, of a mercurial person;
more than that, of a disagreeable, sick man, with his spirit
stretched to near-breaking point; myopic eyes, with a paranoid
glint in them.

His voice gave similar indications—a shattering, hostile, strident
voice with an Artesian accent; the voice of a combative person,
demanding to be heard; the voice of a small man with an oversize
task before him. His hair was chestnut in colour and in curls,
though he frequently covered it with a wig, or had it powdered.
His skin has been variously described as sallow, yellow or of a
bilious hue, the whole effect being offset by greenish veins. His
complexion was pitted with the small-pox, whilst its pallor foretold the romantic recluse. Maximilien's nose was flat. This gave
his wide face a feline appearance. On this detail at least one writer
has exercised his imagination, adding the comment that, after
having been in his early days a domestic cat, Robespierre became
a wild, and finally a tiger cat.[1]

All agree that he was never at all like the Cheshire Cat, for smiles
rarely invaded that dour countenance. Old before his time, the
tribune from the country took everything so seriously. Admittedly

in his works we come across a trip to near-by Carvin, reported in a light-hearted manner;[2] but a glance at any considerable eighteenth-century prose anthology will prove that in exploiting this semi-facetious *genre*, the man from Arras was merely obeying convention and following custom. Nearly all similar travelogues were couched in prose interspersed with light verse, in the manner of Chapelle and Bachaumont of a century earlier. Forgetting this rare example, it remains a fact that Maximilien was no comic. How could any-one with the slightest sense of the ridiculous stand on the site of the former Bastille prison catching water from the breasts of a statue of Mother Nature? Lack of humour made any situation much worse, as for instance when he clamoured 'I demand a measure' in the States-General and was angrily humiliated by the reply from some parliamentary wag: 'Give him a measure of oats!'—as though he were a donkey![3] Unlike many wiser men, Robespierre could not laugh at such slights. Unlike smoother parliamentary manipulators, he failed to respond in kind; failed to confound by malicious repartee. Not for him the coruscating wit of a Mirabeau or a Danton. Indeed, Danton's wit in particular he could not abide. Cut somewhat on the cross, austere, unsociable, he loathed hand-shakes; puritanical, stoical, sulky, often boring, Maximilien was not at first sight a lovable character. He was not lovable, in the first place, because he was a proud and vain person—so much so, in fact, that often vanity outstripped prudence and good sense.

It has often been asked: why did this representative of the people, this enemy of the *Ancien Régime* dress in a manner archaic and almost aristocratic? The answer lies in an exacerbated ego. For instance, in early days the family purse was so empty that he was obliged to borrow clothes for important occasions; and, when he left Arras, his wardrobe was painfully bare. He also borrowed the coach-fare. At school he was obliged to economize in order to buy books and in 1778 applied to the Prefect of Studies for a suit in which to present his respects to the Bishop of Arras.[4] So it continued. In 1790, in order to honour the death of one of his heroes, Benjamin Franklin, this northern-schoolboy-made-good begged a black suit from a man unfortunately four inches taller than he was—with ludicrous consequences.[5] Having finally made his mark, he could no longer afford to be poorly dressed. Inferior raiment would have recalled an insecure, ridiculous past and sapped his confidence. For him dress had become the outward, physical counterpart of intellectual classicism acquired at school— a form of snobbery, but one that, in his own view, separated the man of 'virtue', or true quality, from the louts. In a dictator or a monarch this would have been understandable; in a democrat it seemed incongruous. For instance, on the Fête de l'Être Suprême it would have been very much wiser if he had not dressed in a more showy way than his colleagues of the two Committees; if he had not carried two bouquets of flowers, instead of one; if he had not walked ahead of his fellows; if someone else had set light to that statue of atheism. ... Such stupid behaviour supplied wonderful ammunition to his enemies, who were numerous because democracy crawls with levellers who pass as egalitarians and are part of the arrangement. Fully aware of this, the wise democratic leader assumes a modesty he may not really possess, declining to wear decorations when taking salutes beside be-medalled military experts, for instance. If he stands out, he does so for simplicity and austerity, not for ostentation, and everyone says how ordinary he is. The height of absurdity is reached when we consider that basically Maximilien *was* austere and simple, indeed more so than any of his associates or enemies. His sartorial idiosyncrasies were not assumed or indulged to denote a love of luxury or fine living, but merely as compensation for privation in early life, as we said. The matter was therefore individual but, as we shall see later, it was precisely when the personal dictated decisions that Robespierre lost credibility and support.

The effect was cumulative, since he could never keep the personal out of politics. At the end of the Constituante he had put aside his lawyer's threadbare black gown and, in sharp contrast to Marat who indulged in studied filth and unkemptness, was proud to become the dandy of the Left wing. Then the indignant fop, who already stood out from the democratic rabble by using *vous* in place of the more fraternal *tu*, had the temerity to do what Louis XVI had not dared to do, namely cast aside the Revolutionary bonnet because it would abase him and remind him of humiliation. His comment is revealing: 'To believe that the common people are responsive to such external symbolism is to belittle them.'[6] He himself was quite partial to external symbols—for example, the cockade, yet, like the brightly-hued waistcoat and jacket, the nankin breeches, the silk hose, the buckled shoes, the neat cravat, the wig or powdered hair was prized above all symbolic bonnets by a Revolutionary who dared to hark back to the sartorial elysium of successful men of the *Ancien Régime*. Not for Robespierre the plebeian headgear popularized by his friends, the army mutineers of Nancy, lately become galley-slaves.[7] Not even for him a symbol of his other friends, the Rosicrucians![8] All these personal considerations were secondary to a much more deeply-rooted personal consideration, namely escape from humiliation. This attitude was dangerous. For who could forget the offence taken by Parisian patriots, excessively alert to symbolism, and rising in violent indignation at the very outset of the Revolution against the Régiment de Flandre, who, dining in the opera-house at Versailles, had allegedly insulted the tricolour cockade? That incident had been a godsend to trouble-makers and such an incident could be useful again. The man who displays such illogicalities and personal idiosyncrasies at the expense of public approval is asking for trouble. Pride comes before the fall.

To dangerous vanity Maximilien added a peevish lack of red-blooded masculinity and a tendency to be caddish. He was unable to fit into a human situation, because his ideals were inhuman or superhuman. Thus he declined Desmoulins's invitation to a banquet with the comment: 'your light champagne brews are poison to freedom.'[9] Joviality, the good life, virility itself he shunned and feared. The fear irritated him and made him angry and, though Charlotte (his sister) attributed to him an equable disposition, there are recorded examples of his bad temper. For instance, 'Save the country without my help!', he shouted to the Committee, when they refused to sack Fouquier-Tinville.[10] Very occasionally he could tell lies too. For instance, he denied his share in provoking violence in the September Massacres, when Parisian cut-throats emulated the Marquis de Sade in experiencing a sort of orgasm by murdering the innocent; and he claimed that Pache had been threatened at the Hôtel de Ville, when in fact he had not.[11] Perhaps, with Clauzel, we may judge him guilty of nepotism in respect of his brother, Augustin;[12] or we may underwrite the opinions of Dussault who found him 'Short and vain, cowardly and ferocious, bold when supported, timid in the face of peril ... a clever hypocrite ... knowing no other god than his own pride'; or agree

with the disaffected Pétion who dubbed him 'touchy and suspicious ... overbearing in his opinions, listening only to himself
and never forgiving others'.[13]

Of course, some of his most unpleasant traits had their value in
time of stress—for example, fanaticism. It is a well-known fact
that excess of theory produces intolerance. Consider the difference
between the academic educational theorist and the teacher faced
with the practical problem. The likelihood is that the first will be
less tolerant, because he or she is inclined to dogmatism. So it was
with politics. Maximilien was sure he was right in following most
of Rousseau's ideas. His assuredness in this theoretical sphere was
monumental. In a revolutionary context, this had much to offer.
Here was splendid fuel for a firebrand, but, like many good
fuels, it had the disadvantage of being volatile and explosive.
To change the metaphor: Robespierre's certitude, self-righteous-
ness and confidence were potential boomerangs. He was clearly a
man of absolutes, a person to dominate or be dominated, with no
medial factor to soften the extremes of his policies. In 1793–94
it could hardly have been otherwise, for in revolution pity
destroys its possessor. Consequently, revolutionaries are wise to
strike pre-emptively, especially revolutionaries suffering from
natural shyness; and Maximilien did. But he was shy in a special
way; he resembled a statesman of our own age, Neville
Chamberlain, in that, as we have seen, shyness did not partner
humility, but pride. Like the Man of Munich, the Man from Arras
was proudly shy.

Was he also a coward? The question is a thorny one. Let it be put
on record first of all that there were times when he showed considerable fortitude. For instance, after the Massacre du Champ de
Mars (July 17, 1791), he did not follow the example of many of
his liberal colleagues seeking by flight to escape the fury of
counter-revolutionaries.[14] Instead, he stood his ground, leaving
Danton, Fréron and Legendre to melt out of sight in cowardice
and fright; and, whereas his friend, Camille Desmoulins, penned a
final dramatic number of his newspaper, embodying a journalistic
testament and sounding the knell of departing liberty, the more
obvious human target stayed in Paris and at that very moment
took up residence within yards of his worst enemies in a conspicuous area, at first defended only by the Duplays, their three

daughters and a lad of thirteen. This demanded courage and was to his credit. So was his behaviour in his final appearances in the Convention, for his colleague, Prieur de la Côte d'Or, says: 'he bore himself very courageously in his last debates'.[15]

Robespierre's revolutionary reputation rests also, alas, on absence when derring-do was afoot. For example, when the dangerous revolt of August 10, 1792 was being prepared, Panis organized a tactical conference in Duplay's house. It was held not in Robespierre's room, but in that of another deputy, Anthoine. The reason for this is understandable. Representing values that had to endure if the Revolution was to prevail, Maximilien did not wish to be compromised by ephemeral plotters, who had not even the sense to close their windows. Indeed, the landlady had to beg them to keep their voices down, because she had no intention of having her important lodger butchered. To which remark Anthoine replied that, since the precious lodger was hiding away in his own room, there was little danger for him![16] Clearly, behind such bitterness lay the suggestion that the tribune was saving his own skin, whilst others risked theirs in the great August 10 *putsch*, when, according to Vergniaud, the Incorruptible was skulking in a cellar. The following January, when Louis XVI was due to pass by on his way to be decapitated, the Incorruptible ordered Duplay to close the outer yard-door so that his distinguished and sensitive lodger could hear and see nothing. On another occasion, Robespierre is reported to have indulged in deception of a more positively cowardly kind. Apparently, as he left the Committee of Public Safety, he was obliged to pass close to a number of unfriendly plebeian faces, at which point he resourcefully turned on his heel and shouted back to bewildered colleagues that he refused to 'decimate' the Convention.[17] There were those who found him guilty also of allowing his colleagues to take the rap for the Prairial Law, whilst he absented himself from the Convention; and on numerous occasions it was reported that Maximilien allowed Saint-Just to fire the rhetorical salvos. Then there is Maximilien's reticence, when he could have spoken up more openly in defence of Marat, impeached by the Assembly.[18] Though charitably it may be conceded that he had sometimes had a score to settle with the *Ami du peuple*, it is possible to find little to admire in the way Maximilien behaved on this occasion, for Marat had defended him and had often praised him; finally,

Marat's principles were closest to his own, the differences between the two being temperamental rather than ideological.

Maximilien himself seems to have had no doubts about his own moral courage. In 1788 he had declared:

'I have an honest heart and a resolute soul; I was ever incapable of yielding beneath the yolk of baseness and corruption . . . If I may be taxed with anything, it is with my inability to conceal my way of thinking, with never having said yes when my conscience cried out no .., never having paid court to an Establishment from which I have always considered myself independent, however many attempts may have been made to persuade me that it costs nothing to put one's self forward by making a few obsequious gestures in the ante-chamber of some important person.[19]'

—which sounds like priggishness. No wonder Robespierre was to die young; for such a man was too 'saintly' to live long. Above all, what conceit this auto-encomium reveals! Pride is dangerous, in that it attracts dangerous support. Vanity in high places is nourished both by base sycophants and honest admirers to such an extent that the very optics of life can be utterly distorted. The papers he left behind in his lodgings prove that this actually happened. Lyrical and distasteful is one of the letters he received: 'The esteem in which I held you . . . made me situate you in the heavens next to Andromeda in the scheme for an astral memorial.' Here is another example: 'I wish to feast my eyes and my heart upon your features'[20]—who but a swollen-headed fool would leave such extravaganzas for posterity to read and laugh at? Yet there are many others in like vein that could be quoted.

Of course, there were more genuine and more restrained tributes. An ex-capucin, Chabot, explained that he had baptized a child with the forename of Robespierre.[21] A rich haberdasher wrote requesting that the great man should act as god-father to his child, whom he desired to bring up under the auspices of one who set such fine standards and whose name would be eternally venerated.[22] Private panegyrics were supplemented by others. In 1791 a pastel-study of the young politician exhibited in the *Salon* of that year bore the subscription *L'Incorruptible* and a celebrated title was launched; but it widened the gulf between him and the average politician of Right, Left or Centre, to whom it could never have been applied and who hated him for his immaculate repute. They did not declare their hatred openly yet. At the end of the Constituante period, the French still knew him as '*le héros de la Constitution*'[23] and popular societies like the Jacobins placed his bust in a place of honour at their meetings. The Bishop of Bourges wrote to the Incorruptible to the effect that he would be happy if he could 'deserve the glorious surname of *Little Robespierre!*'[24], and a former colleague from the Arras Academy, Beffroy de Reigny, provided this assessment: 'An exalted mind, coupled with an honest heart..' much ability as well, whatever may say those who have never seen him. That, in a word, is Robespierre.'[25] There can be no doubt that such encomia prove that the tribune had many admirers who considered him the heaven-sent man-of-the-hour. Sublime irony: a *future* man-of-the-hour called Bonaparte was to spend a short time behind bars for *his* alleged admiration of Robespierre, as we shall see!

On the whole, women admired the Incorruptible even more than the men. For example, a rich English gentlewoman by the name of Shepen offered him a present for the cause[26]—a gift which incidentally Maximilien declined. Ladies found his austere habits to their liking. Some, like Madame Théot, carried their affection a step further, turning him into a kind of deity; and, before dismissing this as sheer nonsense, we should remember the adulation reserved in our times for entertainers. In those days, such devotion tended to be directed towards religious or political leaders. The man who could speak well in public—in the pulpit or in the hustings—was certain of a zealous feminine following and had the makings of a fan-club. Two pious crones from the Saint-Roch parish were so moved by his speech of December 30, 1792 that they demanded a repeat;[27] a lady with the intriguing name of Olympe de Gouges offered to commit joint suicide by plunging with him into the Seine, suitably ballasted with heavy weights to ensure non-survival.

Another proposed marriage, on the grounds that she would love to perpetuate his name; a young Nantaise widow wrote to say that she had loved him since the start of the Revolution, but had not been free to act upon her infatuation until now, when, before the Supreme Being, she declared her love.[28] There can consequently be no doubt about the man's fascination for females of many types.

Ladies found themselves worrying constantly about the man's safety, especially since that terribly exciting deed accomplished with a household breadknife by that attractive Corday girl. It was all so domestic and *real*. So, when the beloved leader narrowly escaped Mademoiselle Renault's lethal shopping-basket, one woman wrote: 'I thank the Supreme Being, who has watched over thy days' (forgetting that he disliked *tutoiement!*),[29] whilst others flatteringly speculated that this desperate young person had perhaps made the attempt out of unrequited love for the great man. At the Jacobins, ring-side seats were constantly filled with admiring ladies, hanging on the famous orator's every word and expressing romantic emotion when, at the close of one particularly eloquent period, old Madame de Chalabre stepped forward to wipe the beads of perspiration from the beloved brow.[30]

Timid though he was, Maximilien was sought after socially. Madame Buissart, Madame Marchand and Madame Roland[31] (who also offered asylum after the Champ de Mars incident in 1791) opened their salons to the educated lawyer. Frequentation of such a host of affectionate socialites revived in the object himself old-world gallantry associated with that *de* in his patronymic and with a good education that had not spurned the blossoms of poetic philandering, culled from the gardens of Horace, Ovid or Anacreon. Now, as a background for prominent rebels, classicism allied with nascent romanticism were common enough. The difference between Maximilien and the rest lay chiefly in the proportions of these two ingredients and was therefore largely temperamental. We have noted this fact when we contrasted him with Marat. How much more important was it in the rivalry between Maximilien and Georges Danton? For, whereas the 'bull of Arcis-sur-Aube' burned with earthy passion for the female, the 'Candle of Arras' glowed with more idealized concepts. Both came from the provinces; yet, whilst Danton loved with the lusty enthusiasm of the farm labourer, Robespierre, being more delicately contrived, retained the dying conceits of the pastoral.

A demonstration of this truth is to be discerned in Maximilen's relationship with the painter, Madame Labille-Guyard, who stayed on to depict Revolutionaries after painting courtiers of yester-year. Naturally she was out to catch the expressions, moods and appearance of personalities who might one day be as famous as kings had been. We have met her already, for, spotting Robespierre's aptitude for this role and sharing his republicanism, it was she who offered to make him immortal in her canvases and in fact supplied the title *l'Incorruptible* which passed into legend. The detail is not of importance: Robespierre's reaction *is* important, however. Penning a reply to her professional invitation, in *Ancien-Régime* style—a style which paradoxically looked forward to some aspects of the Restoration—the former *alumnus* of Louis-le-Grand produced some elegant turns of phrase:

'On m'a dit que les Grâces voulaient faire mon portrait. Je serais trop indigne d'une telle faveur si je n'en avais vivement senti tout le prix. Cependant, puisqu'un surcroît d'embarras et d'affaires ou puisque un dieu jaloux ne m'a pas permis de leur témoigner jusqu'ici tout mon empressement, il faut que mes excuses précèdent les hommages que je leur dois. Je les prie donc de vouloir bien agréer les unes et de m'indiquer les jours et heures où je pourrais leur présenter les autres.'[32]

Curiously analogous with his costume and worthy of the highest traditions of Céladon and *Astrée*, of Versailles and Marly in the good old days, this 'poetic' missive reveals a foppish anachronism; but one who could produce such gallant prose obviously had some real poetry in his desk-drawer; and amongst the *Poésies amoureuses* we find two addressed to Henriette; some verses for Mademoiselle Demoncheaux on the occasion of her marriage; one for Flore and another for a timid beauty by the name of Sylvie. The most sincerely lyrical is a *Madrigal* dedicated to a lady who masquerades under the romantic and Shakespearean name of *Ophélie*. His regard for the modest, fair maiden appears to shine through youthful lyricism:

Crois-moi, jeune et belle Ophélie,
Quoi qu'en dise le monde et malgré ton miroir,
Contente d'être belle et de n'en rien savoir,
Garde toujours ta modestie;
Sur le pouvoir de tes appas
Demeure toujours alarmée
Tu n'en seras que mieux aimée,
Si tu crains de ne l'être pas.[33]

Traditional sentiments, perhaps, and certainly similar to those expressed by budding poets to their ladies since the days of the great salons and before that; and yet through the purely conventional one catches a rarer note. A gossamer piece, it suggests that, before harsher realities took a grip upon his soul, Maximilien was well-equipped to please the ladies and was not indifferent to their responses.

Of course, the following he knew best was about him in the Duplay household, who took full advantage of proximity. Completely captivated, the homely Madame Duplay monopolized the young celebrity to such an extent that sister Charlotte became jealous and quarrelsome. Then there were the four Duplay daughters who provided a supporting quartet of adulation, though admittedly one of them, Sophie, was obliged to admire the tribune from the fastnesses of the Auvergne. The remaining three were, however, on the spot to thrill to this elegant young man. None of them appears to have been in the beauty-queen category, but then it is unlikely that the shy Maximilien would have responded to overwhelming comeliness.

The most presentable daughter, Elizabeth, married Robespierre's faithful political ally, Joseph Lebas, in August 1793. Mademoiselle Victoire was totally lacking in personality, as she is hardly mentioned; on the other hand, the plain Eléanore came to be known as 'Madame Robespierre', though they certainly never got as far as that in their relationship. This is surely the Duplay daughter who loved him most; yet Robespierre showed little interest in her hints about marriage, which means that, to some extent, Eléanore herself invented or embroidered a rumour to enhance her status with fellow-students of the artist, J.-B. Regnault, whose studio in the Rue (Saint-) Honoré allowed her to watch the tumbrils pass below. It is said that sometimes she denounced people, but more often saved them. Perhaps out of spite, perhaps speaking the truth, one of her fellow-students summed the matter up in a way calculated to discourage romantic speculation, when she explained: 'Eléanore thought she was loved, whereas she simply scared him.'[34] So the mystery remains and we are left wondering precisely what relationship existed between Robespierre and his landlady's daughter.

We have said that he neglected to respond to Eléanore; yet, on the intellectual level, he preferred her, because she had the soul of a man. At the same time, he was disposed to help the nubile Elizabeth, who declared that she and her sisters loved more than a brother this prestigious lodger who took their side against their parents. He apparently gave good advice—after all, he was used to sisters at home—and patiently listened to their troubles. He fell naturally into this habit, since sentimentality and tenderness were part of a hangover from the provinces and from the century which bred him; and, seeing that 'betrothal' to the rather masculine Eléanore appears to have led to nothing more intimate and rewarding than holding hands—which was an engagement-gesture in northern France at that time—regard for the feminine Elizabeth is all the more intriguing. Was it true that his protectiveness was evoked the more readily when she was spoken for by another, on whose behalf Maximilien had managed to overcome parental opposition? Indeed, his attitude to Elizabeth may well have transcended the fraternal, which explains a number of things. For instance, without obvious self-sacrifice, at one point Maximilien suggested that his brother Augustin should marry the plain daughter, but the hotter-blooded fellow declined the noble gesture.[35] One reason why Maximilien never married Eléanore may have been that he was in love with the future Madame Lebas, whom he sacrificed to the other *Conventionnel*, either because for him France held priority over wives, or simply because he was too shy or strangely wrought to commit himself.

Secondly, and more important still, affection for Elizabeth explains his attitude to Danton and Desmoulins as newly-weds. For it is clear that Robespierre grew to hate the former, who had made immoral suggestions to *Babet*, and Camille, who had used this innocent girl to convey unsolicited obscene illustrations to the Incorruptible in his lodgings. Maximilien was the last to see a dirty joke and the fact that Elizabeth had intercepted and opened the package (and could perhaps have been disillusioned concerning her influential 'brother') was enough to provoke Robespierre's implacable enmity. Thus it is possible that the political campaign he waged against certain people was prompted by personal motives—motives reflecting the damage done to an idealized relationship with a comely girl attached to him in an innocent way.

At all costs, it would appear, Robespierre kept his hands clean, striving to preserve the image of a decent fellow, a ladies' man but never a husband. Indeed, when Pétion jokingly remarked that his companion needed a wife to make him more sociable, the Incorruptible soberly replied: 'I shall never marry.'[36] After all, it was easier to be a ladies' man at a distance than in the intimacy of the bedroom. Marriage itself seemed to annoy Robespierre, who reacted so badly to Danton's quip about the supreme virtue consisting in what he did nightly with his young wife.[37] In the case of Desmoulins, he made it clear on occasion that work came before pleasure, especially marital pleasure. On February 14, 1791 he wrote: 'I would point out to Monsieur Camille Desmoulins that neither the lovely eyes not yet the appealing qualities of the charming Lucile are sufficient reasons for omitting to give notice of my work about the National Guard which I sent him! ...'[38] Perceiving in these words some John-Knoxian bile, we are not surprised that one day he was to send to the scaffold his old friends Danton, Desmoulins and soon Lucile too. That would teach them to enjoy sex! This austere renunciation, this tendency to prize work more than pleasure and duty more than philandering, has misled some of Maximilien's critics into thinking him at the best a mysogynist and at the worst a fetichist. For instance, Ratinaud suggests that he was attracted more by elegant female attire than by sexuality as such.[39]

Was he a mysogynist? 'In his life, there was no room for women', says Renier.[40] There were times when his own sister would have agreed. It is certainly possible to sympathize with this querulous spinster, who appears to have been a nuisance to her brothers (and especially to the younger *Bon-Bon* during his affair with a certain Madame Ricord). On this occasion, Charlotte was sent back to Paris; on another occasion, she was exiled to her native Arras, where she found she had been denounced as an aristocrat in a town controlled by her elder brother's henchman! She was therefore obliged to flee to Lille and demand asylum in the house of one Florent Guiot, an enemy of the Incorruptible, but who nevertheless had the courage to bring her back to Paris with him.[41] There poor, difficult Charlotte was obliged to lodge impecuniously with a Madame Laporte. Later, requesting a pension from the Thermidoreans, she mentioned that she possessed only one poor woollen dress and that failing sight prevented her any longer from making lace for her living. Yet, since Maximilien was by that time dead, she defended his memory with passionate loyalty.

Being nasty towards an importunate sister is, of course, in a category of its own and does not enlighten us on the more general subject of relationship with the opposite sex. Were women, as in many cases, a sheer necessity for the relief of tension? In 1802 that rather dubious authority, the memorialist Villiers, telling tales when his flatmate was no longer there to deny them, said:

'As for chastity, I only knew of one woman of about 26, whom he treated pretty shabbily but who idolized him. Often he would turn her away; he passed on to her a quarter of his professional fees.'[42]

In other words, Maximilien is reported by his fellow-lodger and secretary to have had a *petite amie* or part-time mistress, to whom he handed over a quarter of his income in return for services rendered. Whilst this would scotch the rumour that he was sexually abnormal, it would also suggest that his needs were simply physical during his early months in the capital. Further confirmation of normal potency probably lies behind the information that Robespierre contemplated marriage with Mademoiselle Duplessis, sister-in-law of Desmoulins;[43] and the assumption of normal inclinations underlay two rumours circulating either during his lifetime or soon after.

We recall that Maximilien read to his king and queen an ode he had composed in their honour. Speculating from this performance, Mornand posed some intriguing and shattering questions—'Did he entertain other fancies, more tender and sentimental, after he had knelt at the feet of Marie-Antoinette? Was he in love with the queen, as some have claimed?'[44]—which are clearly far-fetched, as far-fetched as Maréchal's accusation that he had left his job as Public Prosecutor on orders received from above (and presumably from the queen, who was present) during a secret conference at Madame de Lamballe's.[45] His relations with Versailles were never as close as that and the whole thing would have been completely out of character.

A still more engaging and extravagant theory concerns his alleged designs on Marie-Antoinette's unhappy daughter, Madame Royale, presumably with a view to ascending the throne. A

satirical song entitled *Le Tombeau de Robespierre* embodies the
edifying rumour:

> Under the guise of law, he aspired
> By promoting his own dictatorship
> To become the real king
> Of a fictitious Republic.
> This proud plan fell flat
> And, frustrated in his canine appetite,
> Instead of marrying a Capet,
> He espoused the guillotine.[46]

Furthermore, the mercurial Buonarroti reports that, at the time
of the final crisis and in order to have them march against the
Commune, Léonard Bourdon had assured men of the Gravilliers
Section that Robespierre had contracted to marry some royal
person, but this was clearly a desperate calumny.[47]

Considering the evidence, and discounting liars and novelettes,
one love affair remains authentic and decisive, but virtually overlooked. Sister Charlotte tells us he fell in love with a young woman
of Arras, Anaïs Deshorties, with whom he discussed marriage;
and was therefore deeply distressed on his return to his home-
town to find her wedded to someone else.[48] This event, occurring
when he was twenty-nine, may well have broken his tender
fin de saison heart and convinced him that love was not worth it,
after all. Maximilien would not have been the first man to decide
never to take such risks again. It is easy to suppose, therefore,
that the lesion did not heal and that his mind, already embittered
by family misfortunes, incubated a jaundiced cynicism from which
it never truly recovered. This in its turn suggests that some of his
nervous symptoms, which we shall consider later, had their
origin in a love affair gone wrong. Thus Robespierre may not
have been greatly different from another important pupil of the
Collège Louis-le-Grand, recurrently ill after the Dunoyer heart-
break of his youth. Like Voltaire, Maximilien did not shun women
altogether. He simply remained single and suffered inconvenience
and disorder. Romance had shed its filigree covering; women had
ceased to be an indispensable necessity or dream, but the haunting
memory of their perfume and the elegant *frou-frou* of their dresses
remained in the hinterland of emotion to perplex and plague him.

Chapter 7

BETTER THAN WEALTH

'Un hypocondriaque obsédé des hallucinations de la mort'
SOREL

Anxious ladies who worried about his safety worried even more about Maximilien's health, and with good reason.

Some years ago, a new science called psycho-biology enjoyed a brief vogue before disappearing beneath the waves of fashion, never more to be seen. During its short existence, this science claimed that there was a correlation between events in a person's life—joys, sorrows, afflictions—and his medical record. Now, whether valid or not, psycho-biology, temporarily resuscitated for our purpose, happens to provide illuminating explanations. Certain facts became apparent. The first is that Maximilien suffered from psychogenic troubles. One of these was almost the cause of his undoing for, had he not let it be known that he liked oranges,[1] Mademoiselle Renault would not have thought of utilizing a shopping-basket in order to mask her nefarious scheme. The reason why he had an exaggerated taste for this particular fruit is that, subjected to strain engendering constriction of the colonic muscles, poor Robespierre suffered from constipation, which constantly menaced his well-being and brought on other symptoms too—a fullness, a desire to vomit, a general distaste and nagging irritability. In other words, he presented the classic case of the sluggish system which needs, but cannot find, the time for relaxation or exercise.[2] His incessant need to justify himself, his black humours, his depressions, the stomach-trouble which made him avoid official banquets—all these manifold afflictions came upon him more and more as he obliged to work at his desk or speak in the Convention. Rare indeed now were the invigorating strolls with Brount in the forest of Montmorency, communing with the shades of Jean-Jacques—a habit doubly valuable since it refreshed body and soul at the same time.

Ironically, the price of success is often the abandonment of those very habits which would make a man physically fit to accept responsibilities and labours imposed by fate.

72

With so little relaxation, his nerves suffered too. Mind and body were so congested that his soul was covered over with a sickly hue at all times of day and night. He lived in a state of fear, exacerbated by enervating events and political developments. For one thing, the constant threat from Left- and Right-wing extremists, from old enemies and former friends whom he had estranged, gnawed at his composure and gave him little rest. When this condition became acute, he trembled with fear, his eyes appeared more deep-set in their sockets and his whole appearance was haggard and prematurely aged. His voice lost its power, sobs of prostration seized him, his legs became weak with neurasthenia, he suffered from extreme lassitude and exhaustion, he took to his bed, there to be haunted by a form of asthma—another sign of constriction and tension. His sleep was severely curtailed. Sometimes he could not fall asleep at all. However, perhaps there was something to be said for insomnia, for, when he finally achieved sleep, his dreams were so morbid that he awoke in the early hours convinced that he was losing his reason.

Day gave him no relief. Growing absentmindedness during waking hours merely served to reinforce the conviction that madness was his ultimate destiny. So acute was his anxiety-neurosis that he developed fevers bringing alarming variations of temperature and acquired the habit of feeling his forehead to ascertain the severity of this febrile visitation. He was never away from the mirror, looking at his tongue and assessing his pallor. His finger was for ever taking his own pulse and finding that it raced when anxieties mounted.

Enduring all these horrid symptoms, Maximilien found life a living hell, especially, as we have observed already, because his health let him down precisely when he needed all his stamina. Examples are numerous. At the time of the frustrated royal escape to Varennes, Robespierre was described as haggard and overworked—visibly in a dreadful state of nerves. On July 17, 1791, seized with the panic of the marked man, this known opponent of government policy was making his way from the Champ de Mars to his lodgings in the Rue Saintonge. It will be remembered that in the Rue (Saint-) Honoré he was jostled by citizens and potentially hostile soldiery—he did not know which he feared most—and, trembling with fear, was rescued by Duplay, but not before his taut system had been subjected to still more strain.

From that condition he did not recover for a long while, *if at all*. It is possible, in fact, that the lesion was permanent, for a recognizable pattern began to emerge from that time; he tended to hide more than ever, when stirring events were afoot. He was in hiding, of course, when the greatest *journée* of all, August 10, 1792, was being enacted; but in the evening he came out of his funk-hole to speak to the Jacobins in praise of what had been accomplished by the mob. Though he had helped to provoke them, the Massacres of September found him officially uncommitted and a fugitive from bloody reality. There followed the Girondist attacks upon Robespierre himself, spearheaded by Louvet who accused him in the Convention of being the arch-villain of the whole Revolution.[3] When it was alleged that he had supplied the motive force behind August 10, the Commune episode and the prison massacres, Robespierre defended himself skilfully in a reply of some merit, but the effort took much out of him, for, till the end of that year 1792, he was in constant ill-health.

Particularly significant was the psychosomatic bout which kept him from the Convention from November 5 to November 30 of that year. After his election to the Convention, he had set out from Arras for the capital with his sister, Charlotte, who was offered by the Duplays a room formerly occupied by Couthon. But Charlotte was difficult and embarrassingly possessive towards her brother, who finally gave in to her wishes that they should set up house together apart from the amiable carpenter and his family. It will be recalled that Maximilien agreed to move a few yards only, to the Rue (Saint-) Florentin in fact, and that, deprived of the lively comfort of his former host and his family, the new *Conventionnel* fell ill and was easily persuaded to return to the nest by his maternal landlady from across the road. As he staggered back home from his cross-grained sister to his friendly foster-parents, he only wished to get back into his old bed, where he would be relatively safe from a cruel world. Once more Maximilien had found in illness an escape from harsh reality.

Whether his nervous exhaustion was the recurrent outcome of the break between what he wished and what he had to contemplate as reality, is difficult to say. For these illnesses were just as inconvenient on some occasions as convenient on others. On this occasion temporary refuge may have been welcome, since he managed to escape his critics for a while; but the pace of the

Revolution afforded him little respite. A vivid example of this fact was supplied in May 1793 by the struggle against the Girondins, now entering its most virulent phase. Since it was now clearly a question of survival, Robespierre's voice had become shrill and hoarse, and, nearing the point of collapse, he was trembling with fever and exhausted with asthma. This lamentable situation continued through the month of May, past the vital 31st and beyond that to the still more vital and successful June 2. On the 12th of the month, the victorious politician confessed to his friends, the Jacobins: 'exhausted by four years of arduous and fruitless labour, I feel that my physical and mental powers are not up to the demands of a great Revolution'.[4] He did not thrive on conflict. The febrile dyspepsia from which he now permanently suffered was in no way relieved by the assassination of Marat in July 1793, an event highlighted by the Renault Affair in 1794. Spring of that year was very unpleasant. Germinal found him decidedly unwell. That life-or-death struggle, first against the Hébertists, then against the Dantonists, was perhaps the most searching and disturbing of all his troubles, involving as it did close associates of recent months. Contemplating the task, already in December 1793 he was in a state of terror; and, soon after the New Year, he was convinced he had been poisoned, so excruciating were his stomach-pains and so violent his self-induced fever. Nowadays his pillow was blood-stained every morning, so tormented were his slumbers;[5] and when he managed to call upon his tobacconist, Madame Carvin, she noticed that her distinguished customer was wearing a tortured look and was quite worried about him.[6] Just before Danton was finally overthrown, he fell more seriously ill, his nerves finally shattered by the anticipated turmoil and by a most terrible conscience crisis. Poor Robespierre! He simply lacked the stamina required by his unique position; to be overwhelmed had become a recurrent phenomenon. Viewed in this light, the apotheosis of June 8 was less of a triumph than a nervous agony to Robespierre, whose eyes were taut with neuralgic pain and red with insomnia.

It is a frequently proven fact that, when a totalitarian leader travels abroad on business or pleasure, he is never sure that he will have a palace to return to, so hazardous is the power-balance in such a situation. We have said that Maximilien was no traveller; but there are other forms of absence which bring equal perils.

Illness is the most obvious and contributed enormously to the tribune's undoing. For instance, fever recurred in violent guise before the fateful 8–9 Thermidor and, during this long period of absence, his enemies had a wonderful opportunity to plot his undoing. More especially, the Cordelier Club had occasion to rejoice at his illness, for they were now in a position to avenge the guillotining of their former leader, Danton, and his friends of Germinal. Meanwhile, Maximilien tossed and turned in his disordered bed, well aware of these dangers, which added to his hallucinations and nightmares. Like all over-worked politicians, he was exhausted and therefore more vulnerable than ever. He could fight no more, even with his voice, and he knew that the end was near. He hardly cared about the struggle now. After all, in a decadent society which refused moral reform, it was virtuous to be unpopular, just as it was unpopular to be virtuous. He had therefore reached the point where he liked to be disliked!

The seeds of persecution-mania had been there all the time; even his early bucolic lament in favour of the simple peasant life, *L'Homme champêtre*, is laced with fear of murder, of brigands, of crime and of terror. Particularly significant are these three lines in praise of the countryman:

In his dreams he does not perceive a terrifying picture,
Of murder and brigandage.
His waking moments are those of a sober-minded person and he sleeps
    peacefully at night.[7]

How that man feared his own dreams! How he longed for a sound night's sleep!

Already during his early days in Arras, Maximilien had suspected that he was being shunned by polite society,[8] and in this bitterness we may perceive the seed of later troubles. The tendency was quite clearly marked at the time of his election campaign for a seat in the States-General, when he spoke to his fellow-citizens of a conspiracy and said that the country was in danger. Similarly, at the time of Berthier's murder, on July 22, 1789, he was heard to excuse the rabble for butchering the Paris *Intendant*, on the grounds that they had forestalled a plot. Of course, as we have seen, nothing excited Robespierre's nascent paranoia more than

Varennes.[9] His reaction now began to be type-cast. Convinced henceforth of a widespread, all-pervasive royalist plot, he refused ever to be talked out of this suspicion again. The royalists were everywhere. Just before the September Massacres in 1792, we find him vociferously protesting that, since the gates of Paris had been opened, traitors would escape from the city.[10] He was almost hysterical with rage at the plot, of which he was quite sure at that time. Pétion, who reported many of these details, had abundant evidence of his friend's abnormalities—of the obsession with intrigue, treachery and the various pitfalls that beset a man convinced that enemies and enemy agents were constantly sent to persecute and murder him.[11]

The war had now come, and war was a plentiful supplier of evidence. In a sense, the mentally sick man feels more at home in war-time, for now his phantoms acquire real significance. No longer is he talking about imaginary enemies or private enemies. War provides the whole nation with real foes to hate and combat. The war he loathed thus gave Robespierre's fears a credibility they would not otherwise have had. One of his poignant moments of truth and confirmation came when Dumouriez was defeated at Neerwinden in March 1793. Such events had so far provoked in him, not a warm, patriotic determination to fight back, but a cold, searing fear of total defeat, which made him suspect treason behind all military reverses. Of course, such reactions hardly endeared Maximilien to parliamentarians with more traditional emotions. In May 1793 we learn that, increasingly alienated from former associates, he was moving towards that isolation which is the threshold of dementia.[12] Bitterly jealous of Marat's popular appeal and highly suspicious of Danton, he fell ill, but rose from his bed to make this extraordinarily significant assessment of the situation: 'I declare that I shall fight to the death against the agents of this horrible conspiracy . . .'[13]—an obvious touch of paranoia. The war made him more anti-British than ever. Confirmed in his inclination to xenophobia, he accused London of causing France's major troubles.[14] On the Home front, distressed by food shortages, he again attributed them to the enemies of the popular Revolution, who turned out to be those outstanding democrats, Roux and Leclerc of the *enragé* faction! And he continued to regard himself, and refer in public to himself, as the most persecuted of all popular champions. To Maximilien at this time it seemed that the air was eternally oppressive and suffocating in the corridors of power.

Not unexpectedly, religion and paranoia joined forces in his diseased imagination. Speaking on the Cult of the Supreme Being on May 7, 1794, for instance, he claimed that atheism was bound up with a *conspiracy* against the Republic;[15] and, once the Feast of the Supreme Being had triggered off hostile agitation about the Théot affair, Robespierre's savage dementia reached new heights. Turning to the jesting Vilate, who had been overheard saying: 'The Revolutionary Tribunal will amuse itself tomorrow with the Mother of God Affair', he screamed in anger: 'Imaginary conspiracies to conceal real ones!'[16]

Such a person is emotionally, neurotically ill. It gave him satisfaction, for instance, to reflect that he could now identify even more closely with the divine Jean-Jacques, whose shades he might soon join in paradise. For the persecution-mania which was natural to him had been reinforced by reading the *Contract social*, which illogically provided so many injured and oppressed citizens with a reason and opportunity to vent their spleen on the rest of society, the corrupt multitude. It afforded satisfaction to the masochist in him to exclaim: 'It is we who are being assassinated and we who are depicted as ogres.'[17] In these words delivered to the Convention there lies the clue to a state of mind which in some peculiar way chimed in with the birth-pangs of the nineteenth-century, for it was already a romantic trait.

Chapter 8

BROTHER MAXIMILIEN

'En France, la franc-maçonnerie vint d'Angleterre et
renforça certaines sociétés secrètes antérieures'

PRECLIN ET TAPIÉ

In certain types suspicion finds sublimation in secrecy. In this
respect, there was much the century had to offer to Maximilien.
For example, Freemasonry was popular with intellectuals and
middle-class worthies (as well as with royal princes). In particular,
the Encyclopaedists were, almost to a man, devoted to the Craft.
The widely accepted idea that the movement was brought across
the Channel by the Chevalier Ramsay—a Scot from Ayr, who lived
and worked chiefly in France—is open to serious doubt. Medieval
France had its *compagnonnages* which, though principally guild
organizations, were also bristling with esoteric symbolism,
arcane ritual and secret rules of the kind we associate with
Masons. So, in one way or another, a kind of Masonic tradition
existed in France from early times, and the eighteenth century
merely witnessed the recrudescence of an existing interest in such
things. Lodges became political debating clubs, where ideas were
formulated and conspiracies against the Establishment were
hatched. Soon the 200 lodges of 1770 were to be multiplied into
the 600 of 1789, when about 30,000 people could be classed as
regular Freemasons.

It is said that the 'Arras' Lodge, which was in fact probably a
splinter from the near-by Hesdin Lodge, was founded by
Robespierre's father;[1] others say that it was Prince Charles
Edward Stewart, who in 1746 had performed the ceremony, thus
making the foundation a Jacobite one.[2] This would endow the
cell with international, rather than national significance and would
suggest a Catholic background. However, it is more likely that
by that time Jacobite enclaves had ceased to be particularly
Christian and were already filled with deists. Robespierre became
a member of the Hesdin Lodge, for which he composed a Masonic
canticle in his early years. In gratitude for such services rendered,
Masons were to the fore in persuading him to write his *Appel à la*

nation artésienne on the eve of the Revolution.[3] Masonic ties may also explain our young Artesian's attachment to the Club Breton of Versailles, where he met foreign devotees of the Craft like Benjamin Franklin, whose invention of the lightning-conductor he had vicariously vindicated.

There is evidence to suggest another interest, involving an arcane movement, launched in Germany by Weishaupt and known as the *Illuminati*. Among the damning speeches made against Robespierre on 9 Thermidor is one by Vadier, referring to a certain Genevan notary, Chénon (described as head of the *Illuminati*), who had proposed to the French leader a 'supernatural constitution', whatever that means;[4] and, in dealing with the damning Théot case, Vadier found it useful to tear the 'veil', thus disclosing his enemy's contacts with the German group. He further alleged that Madame Théot herself had had dealings with the Bavarian occultists in question. Presented in these terms, credibility grows apace, especially as Morand suspects similar 'occult influences' as accounting for the good publicity Maximilien received in the columns of the *Mercure national*.[5] There are other pieces of evidence. As early as 1791, the British Embassy in Paris reported that (amongst others) Robespierre was bent upon the total annihilation of the monarchy,[6] yet at that time his public utterances speak of the reverse. Did the British, via their spies, know something of Robespierre's *secret* political views and aims? It is certainly possible, and this early republicanism would also suggest Illuminatist infection. In one way or another, therefore, the German sect demands closer scrutiny.

Professing as its aim the delivery of peoples from the tyranny of kings and priests, the *Illuminati* were assuredly in harmony with a Jacobin concept of revolution on an international, as well as a national, scale. It must be stated, however, that their influence upon the French Revolution of 1789 is the subject of disagreement between authorities. Concurring with the French Abbé Barruel, Professor Robison declared that the movement had some influence in bringing about the Revolution, or at least of giving it impetus in its early stages. To justify this, Robison reported that in 1786 Mirabeau and the Duc d'Orléans founded an Illuminatist Lodge in the Paris Jacobin convent; that Mirabeau became its warden and that Sieyès, Pétion, Bailly, Condorcet and La Fayette enrolled as members. The same writer mentioned also that the

Jacobins adopted Masonic head-gear and forms of etiquette in debating; and he spoke of a sinister splinter-group involving amoralists like Sade, Laclos, Rétif de la Bretonne, Cagliostro and Mesmer—near-satanists, in fact, who passed on their ideas to violent anarchists like Anarcharsis Clootz and his *enragé* cronies.

Refuting both Barruel and Robison, Palmer has stated, however, that there was in fact no such international organization and that the French Jacobins were not a secret society at all; and, echoing Palmer's scepticism, Jones tends to discredit the partisans of Illuminatist influence.[7] For instance, this writer claims that the founder of the *Illuminati*, Weishaupt, forecast that, thanks to their efforts, kings and nations would disappear without the use of violence, whereas everyone agrees that the French Revolution knew some very extreme moments of violence. Nevertheless, it could perhaps be pointed out that those other Enlighteners, the French Encyclopaedists, would also have preached non-violent methods.

Secondly, Jones speaks of the Jacobins, whom Robison described as a political offshoot of Freemasonry, and points out that in 1792 [*sic*] 'when the Jacobins were in power' [*sic*],[8] Masonic Lodges were dissolved by government order as Moderantist refuges; he therefore suggests that the top leaders, including Robespierre, had by now turned their backs on Freemasonry. It all depends, perhaps, what is meant by that remark. Admittedly, seeing that the Montagnard government suspended Freemasonry. it is quite out of the question that we should regard Mountain and Masons as synonymous. Still, bearing in mind the military emergency during a large part of the Montagnard Convention, and knowing how much dangerous subversion had been contrived behind locked doors in pre-Revolutionary days, the Jacobins had little choice if they wished to survive—hence the decision of 1793 ungratefully to strike at an organization that had helped them to power. After all, it was not unknown in 1793 for old friends to send other old friends to the scaffold and the action taken in this case was more humane. Above all, it should be remembered that the Girondins had been Jacobins and many were still Masons, prominent members indeed of provincial Lodges, seething with hostility to Paris. A government which ousted the Gironde in 1793 on the issue of federalism was not prepared to stand by whilst enemies plotted its downfall. So, in the Masonic sense of the term, the struggle resolved itself willynilly into 'brother' against 'brother', a common state of affairs, for they had long been accustomed to threaten each other in times of national crisis. Political actions of this nature do not necessarily imply a fundamental change of opinion: one could still be a convinced Freemason, whilst taking inescapable political measures.

'How often in the course of the Revolution did parties threaten each other with "rending this veil"?' asks Mathiez; and Mornand declares: 'That alongside the visible political policy they also had an occult policy; that the veil really existed there is no doubt'.[9] Seen against this 'veil', Maximilien's Masonic connexions appear natural and normal; embroidered by his critics, however, they border on the ridiculous. For example, consider the Sainte-Amarante family—mother, daughter and son—executed with Mademoiselle Renault, the would-be assassin of the great leader. The article *Robespierre* in the *Biographie universelle* reveals the 'true facts' behind 'the murder of the Sainte-Amarante family'! We read on, for what it is worth:

'He had dined in the bosom of this family; everyone had danced attendance on him; but he had not been as abstemious as usual; and upset by vapours from the wine, he had let slip some of the secrets of his policies ... Immediately the whole Sainte-Amarante family, all their friends, all those who had attended the fatal dinner, were arrested ...'

The authors of this tendentious article, Beaulieu and Michaud, claim that all these people to whom Maximilien had unintentionally revealed his secrets were sent to the guillotine before they could talk. No credence should be accorded to this lurid *vignette*. Maximilien drank very little. Furthermore, quoting Beugnot's 1866 *Mémoires*, Madelin tells an entirely different and much less damaging tale, in which 'La Sainte-Amarante' is a prostitute arrested along with her numerous clientèle in a moral clean-up. Yet another version appears in a recent work of Bessand-Massenet.[10] Apparently Madame (whom some detractors described as Robespierre's mistress) kept a gaming-den in the Palais-Egalité, handing over some profits to a partner, Desfieux. Determined to discredit Robespierre and the other Committee, the Committee of General Security were looking for trouble and, since Madame and her beautiful daughter had been saved from the guillotine for some time now by Augustin Robespierre (who did in fact know them quite well), the Committee thought this a good opportunity for a smear-campaign against the Incorruptible himself. The latter did not interfere, but allowed the *fournée*, carefully prepared against his reputation by the second Committee, to proceed to the place of execution. So Madame and her family joined Renault in wearing the red veil of parricides as they travelled along a new route (through the most populous areas of working-class Paris), chosen by Vadier and his friends. Thus, according to this version of the story, the Sainte-Amarante family perished to serve the designs of the lesser Committee, rather than to safeguard any secret doctrine, Masonic or otherwise.

Thus far, we have speculated about Robespierre's probable connexions with Masons and *Illuminati* and we find the evidence partly credible, partly inconclusive. It is when we consider a group to which he definitely belonged, however, that we are on firmer ground. Robespierre was a *Rosatus*, Rosatist or Rosarian—that is, a member of the Arras Rosati Society. The name makes us wonder whether this organization had perhaps Masonic origins, or whether it links up with other movements predating official Freemasonry. One good example springs to mind.

Founded in late-Renaissance Germany, Rosicrucianism gained several French admirers, of whom Naudé is the most important; and, since it erupted strongly 150 years later, the French Revolution may have been promoted partly by its devotees. For instance, it is not generally known that the Phrygian red cap had once been the symbol of the 'Enlightened Ones', or that the common Rosicrucian emblem of a mountain with a burning summit (reminiscent of Sinai and the Holy Ghost) also reappears in the great French upheaval. In fact, the necessary documentation for this revival was opportunely provided for the Illuminatists of 1789, who probably owed much to Teutonic sources, as we shall see.

In a book which appeared just four years before the outbreak of the Revolution and bearing the title *Secret Symbols*, there is an illustration dated 1604 and portraying an alchemist's mountain, the symbol of regeneration to the Rosicrucians. Now the Fête de l'Etre Suprême was intended to mark the regeneration of France, and resemblances do not end there. Both mountains have symbolic trees planted at various levels. Both have a smoking tripod or alchemist's kiln; both have grottoes and caverns on the ascent; both involve animals. In both prints there are bystanders at the base of the mount, making eloquent gestures leading the spectator's eye towards a point of central interest, to which a winding path also guides his attention. Both hills have the same general configuration; both have some sort of balustrade encircling the summit. Both show a supreme device: the Rosicrucians have a crown and orb and a Tree of Life; the Revolutionaries a Tree of Liberty, aptly celebrated in a famous poem by another Brother, called Robert Burns. All in all, it would appear that the similarities are too striking to be coincidental, and we may perhaps conclude that, in designing the 1794 monticule in the Champ de Mars, David, Robespierre and their associates were following a Rosicrucian blue print, happily republished in 1785. This same notion of the emblematic mountain may also have inspired that most enlightening of documents, the *Evangile de la Liberté*,[11] described as having been addressed to the Supreme Being by the *sansculottes* of the French Republic. The *Crédo* contains two allusions to the Mountain—which are nicely ambiguous in that they hallow a party and yet look forward to the earthwork of June 8. Thus 'the sacred Mountain' and 'the holy Mountain' assume a dual significance in this highly deistic document with Rosicrucian undertones.

When in power, it is possible that Robespierre contemplated turning France into a Masonic State. The pressure was there, surely, for the Masonic Lodge for Arras was the Loge des Rose-Croix, and we recall that he himself had belonged to an esoteric circle calling themselves not *Rosicrucians*, nor yet *Illuminati*, but (perhaps by cross-fertilization between the two) the *Rosati*. Now, on the face of it, these rose-fanciers of Arras were not unlike a number of similar groups which had flourished during the past century.

Consider, for example, the Medusa Society, founded by naval officers in the port of Marseilles. In a book containing the *Règlements* are a number of the Chansons de Méduse. The first of these exhorts members to celebrate the goddess in their songs, and a later poem speaks of 'ses plaisans Mystères'. But what are these 'mysteries'? Well, in the first place, there is a special vocabulary for use at meetings. Secondly, the secret initiation: glass in hand, the postulant must praise his sponsor in a speech addressed to the *Grand Prieur*. If accepted, he is then given an appropriate, and often humorous, nickname. In the process of initiation he has been shown certain symbols, which have a recondite meaning. The central ritual is 'petrification'. When a flame springs up from a kind of goblet placed in front of a bust of Medusa, all must remain transfixed and motionless. If they fail to do so, the penalty is more wine and, of course, in time, this in itself makes 'petrification' more difficult, so all ends in riotous laughter. Though founded in the south, the Medusa Society tended to open Lodges wherever naval men were to be found. For instance, one interesting conclave flourished at the end of the seventeenth century in Dunkirk, where the Anacreontic poet, Jacques Vergier, was Prior of the Order.

The army too had its own secret society long before the Revolution of 1789. Having left the forces with the rank of captain, François de Posquières had founded in 1703 an *Ordre de la Boisson et Etroite Observance* (a Masonic title?). This group started its activities at Villeneuve-lès-Avignon, where it was to flourish until 1740. Being partly a drinking-club, it adopted a coat of arms showing two hands, one pouring and one receiving, and bearing the motto: *Donec totum impleat*. Despite this conventional tilt at half-measures, the society delivered home those who had drunk to excess, banned indecent talk or backbiting and encouraged benevolence. These groups thus appear to confirm Le Forestier's perceptive comment that

> 'Even before Freemasonry had crossed the Channel, there had existed in France some more or less secret societies whose meetings were attended by agreeable Epicureans, who kept their pleasures only within the limits prescribed by good taste and good education.'[12]

Just as the Rosicrucians were tied to an annual reunion held always on the same day, so the Arras Rosarians held their main meeting on June 21, at the height of the rose season, in a garden setting at Blanzy by the River Scarpe. The fact that the privet-bower in which they were wont to forgather was adorned with busts of Chapelle, Chaulieu and La Fontaine proves Epicurean attachment and suggests above all the Temple Society of Paris, itself closely linked in tradition with Rosicrucianism, because to this Temple group belonged Chapelle and Chaulieu, as did Vergier, whom we have already met in Medusist circles. Thus we are in process of discovering a network of esotericism involving hedonists, Masons and intellectuals for over a century before the Revolution.

Rosatist initiations run parallel to the ceremonies already examined. First, the postulant was summoned into the private-bower, where a rose was presented to him. He then inhaled the fragrance three times before pinning the flower to his jacket, drinking a glass of wine (made from, or flavoured with, rose petals) and being embraced on both cheeks in token of the welcoming speeches that followed. Very soon, like his forebears of Medusist Lodges, he received a nickname; but in this case for some reason it was a 'transvestite' pseudonym. Thus we hear of 'Sylvia' Charamond (who was a lawyer by profession) and a priest referred to as 'Berthe' Herbert. In Maximilien's fourteen-page *Eloge de la Rose* are discovered some of the ideals of the cult. When we read that 'all their moments are occupied with good works'; that 'they live pleasantly'; that a member's mistress 'can never be unfaithful to him';[13] that participants refer to each other as 'amis' or 'frères' and exist in a kind of 'eternal spring', we re-enter the euphoric domain of the Boissonist and Medusist poetasters. And when we come across the phrase 'victors over death itself',[14] coupled with a reference to the Abbé Chaulieu, we realize once more that our would-be hedonist is harking back to that origin of so many of these libertine assemblies, the Temple Society of yester-year. The allusion to Anacreon, traditionally crowned with a rose wreath and dedicated to pleasure, serves to confirm this attachment and to stress the source of the crypto-Masonic formula employed by Robespierre who, adjuring his peers, says: 'love the rose, love your brethren; these two precepts contain the whole law ... *In his duobus tota lex est.*'[15]

But surely refined hedonism was not all. Published by Reybaud, Maximilien's apocryphal *Mémoires* at least contain some enlightening titbits, amongst which one would select this remark on the subject of 'rose-fancying':

'that was merely the ostensible object of our society; we were in fact concerned with activities other than drinking, laughing and singing.

Our citizen-status, which we appreciated to the full, imposed upon us duties of a quite different character ... We used to meet to discuss the most important questions ..., the writings of the *Philosophes*; especially those of Jean-Jacques Rousseau presented us with a fair number of questions lending themselves to considerable development. Then we sought means of action remaining to citizens and allowing us to escape from a situation that had become intolerable ...'[16]

This statement is very similar to one made by Déprez in the first volume of Robespierre's *Oeuvres*:

'The bacchic meetings could be nothing more than the pretext for more serious work; the Rosati were moreover thinking of things other than drinking, laughing and singing; on certain fixed days they forgathered as colleagues to discuss the most important current problems, the writings of the *Philosophes*—those of Jean-Jacques Rousseau in particular..and also means of action open to citizens wishing to combat abuses that were eternally reappearing and to escape from an intolerable social situation.'[17]

Maximilien's own *Eloge de la Rose* seems to confirm the existence of this serious, but secret, substratum. Taking a clue perhaps from the Freemason Montesquieu, he stresses the value of being a good 'citizen' and a good 'family man' [18]and fights egoism and self-seeking in order to promote concord and friendship. He stresses two other things equally strongly. First, the image of the goddess 'engraved on our hearts' is a flowery reference in not unusual terms to deism or natural religion, another facet of which is revealed in the brotherhood of famous men discussed on the following page. Secondly, the *Eloge* reeks of esotericism. The tone is in fact set at the beginning, when it is made clear that, although everyone can see some significance in a rose, only a 'small number of privileged beings' are capable of *real* appreciation. Throughout, disdain for the vulgar majority goes hand in hand with approval of mysteries suitable to 'the thinking man';[19] with the imposition of silence; with the ban on lifting the sacred veil covering the secrets of the Order, and with ideas much wider in implication than the ignorant rabble will ever comprehend—all of which make up the stock-in-trade of eighteenth-century esotericism. Yet it also has political implications, in that it proclaims the rarity and superiority of those who intend to be the leaders.

Now, we know that the Rosati Society of Arras attracted ambitious future *political* leaders like Fouché, Carnot and Robespierre,[20] so it is doubly justifiable to be suspicious of something *political* behind the façade of flower-fancying—all the more so since the flower in question had long been a symbol of the arcane, as is shown by the use of the expression *sub rosa*, an allusion to the suspending of this bloom above the table at secret assemblies. That is not all: the very word *Rosati* may have special significance, seeing that it is also an anagram of *Artois*. This does more than merely render the title appropriate to the area; it may well suggest the cult of regional autonomy, akin to federalism, which Maximilien was one day to denounce in the name of national unity.

Obediently drinking either rose-petal, or rose-hip country wines, or the more sophisticated grape *vin rosé*, young Maximilien was obliged to make some showing as a versifier, for none would otherwise be admitted. It was traditional to improvise, the verb being interpreted loosely, since in fact authors worked something up in advance so that they could sally forth with the right degree of wit. This habit was still popular in Arras and prompted Robespierre's early incursions into rhyme. Here is such a piece by this eighteenth-century poor-man's-Ronsard, which is as usual about roses, and which his sister Charlotte claimed to have been 'improvised' for his admission to the Rosati in June 1787:

Je vois l'épine avec la rose,
Dans les bouquets que vous m'offrez
Et lorsque vous me célébrez
Vos vers découragent ma prose.
Tout ce qu'on m'a dit de charmant,
Messieurs, a droit de me confondre!
La *Rose* est votre compliment,
L'*Epine* est la loi d'y répondre.

Dans cette fête si jolie,
Règne l'accord le plus parfait
On ne fait pas mieux un couplet,
On n'a pas de fleur mieux choisie,
Moi seul j'accuse mes destins

De ne m'y voir pas à ma place
Car la *Rose* est, dans nos jardins,
Ce que vos vers sont au Parnasse.

A vos bontés, lorsque j'y pense,
Ma foi, je ne vois pas d'excès
Et le tableau de vos succès
Affaiblit ma reconnaissance.
Pour de semblables jardiniers
Le sacrifice est peu de chose;
Quand on est si riche en lauriers,
On peut bien donner une *Rose*.[21]

The fact that these undistinguished lines are described as a song need not concern us here, for, by all accounts, Robespierre's singing was no artistic triumph either! Examined as verse, the three stanzas show on the credit side a clever antiphony and series of contrasts—for instance, we note the balance of *vers* and *prose*, *Rose* and *Epine* in the final couplet of the first stanza, where *compliment* and *répondre* also provide a sort of antithesis, as do *jardins* and *Parnasse* too. But our poet lacks intimate acquaintance with the muse, as is proved by his 1785 eulogy of the third-rate Gresset. More than one line of Robespierre's effort indeed reminds us of Gresset's prosaic verse, although even *he* did not evolve *De ne m'y voir pas à ma place* or *Ma foi, je ne vois pas d'excès*, which are highly infelicitous. One line in particular betrays the true origin of Robespierre's Rosatist inspiration. *Règne l'accord le plus parfait* will be found in more or less the same words in the compendia of the other 'drinking' clubs we have studied.

Another rose-poem offers the reader similar characteristics and similar defects:

O dieux! Que vois-je, mes amis?
Un crime trop notoire
Du nom charmant des Rosatis
Va donc flétrir la gloire!
O malheur affreux!
O scandale honteux!
J'ose le dire à peine,
Pour vous j'en rougis,
Pour moi, j'en gémis,
Ma coupe n'est pas pleine.

Here are antitheses similar to those in the last ballad—for instance, between *rougis* and *gémis*. The word *notoire*, which we shall meet again later, is not a poetic expression, nor is *flétrir la gloire* a very happy combination. Different this time, however, is the anticlimax in the last line. The author has surely built us up for something more important than an empty glass, but he is not original, because this anticlimax is also a commonplace of bibulous verse.

> Eh! vite donc, emplissez-la
> De ce jus salutaire,
> Ou du dieu qui nous le donna
> Redoutez la colère.
> Oui, dans sa fureur,
> Son thirse vengeur
> S'en va briser mon verre
> Bacchus, de là-haut,
> A tous buveurs d'eau
> Lance un regard sévère.

Commonplaces again! We suspected, for example, that we should meet the god Bacchus and we are certain that later his colleague Venus will appear. The expression *jus salutaire* is the kind of euphemism we expected, though admittedly some poets achieve a better line than 'S'en va briser mon verre', which is utterly prosaic and typical of a man who preferred Gresset to Voltaire![22] The stanza that succeeds this one could almost describe the poet himself—at least as he was in later years, when gloom had overwhelmed him:

> Sa main sur leurs fronts nébuleux,
> Et sur leur face blême,
> En caractère odieux
> Grava cet anathème.
> Voyez leur maintien,
> Leur triste entretien,
> Leur démarche timide;
> Tout leur air dit bien,
> Que, comme le mien,
> Leur verre est souvent vide.

It is silly to ask, as some commentators do, how Maximilien

stood up to all this drinking! The fact is simply that, in this kind of hedonist society, such sentiments were expected, even from those with delicate digestions. In any case, the conventions thus duly observed stemmed not only from Bacchic circles but from sheer Gallicism—from writers like La Fontaine, for instance, whose work is the subject of an unacknowledged *pastiche* in the following verse by Robespierre:

> O mes amis, tout buveur d'eau
> Et vous pouvez m'en croire
> Dans tous les temps ne fut qu'un sot,
> J'en atteste l'histoire.

Since La Fontaine had been a seventeenth-century Epicurean, the tribute is no surprise.

The bard continues to regale us with hackneyed and hedonistic comments, quite uncharacteristic, incidentally, of what we generally associate with the sober *prosateur* from Arras, but, it must be admitted, quite characteristic of the group he frequented at the time:

> Ce sage effronté,
> Cynique vanté,
> Me paraît bien stupide.
> Oh! le beau plaisir,
> D'aller se tapir
> Au fond d'un tonneau vide!

To cap this, the next stanza carries the trite quip a stage further. We could have foreseen the sequel:

> Encore s'il eût été plein,
> Quel sort digne d'envie
> Alors dans quel plaisir divin
> Aurait coulé sa vie!
> Il aurait eu droit
> De braver d'un roi
> Tout le faste inutile.

Now this opinion is admittedly consistent with his neo-Platonic opposition to luxury in later years; yet the next three lines betray the fact that this idea too comes from well-tried French sources; and, when he adds:

> Au plus beau palais
> Je préférerais
> Un si charmant asile,

we hear again the plaintive accents of the homesick Du Bellay regretting his little cottage at Liré.

In those days, before matches were invented, it was customary to beg a few hot embers from your neighbour to kindle the fire. In precisely the same way, the Artesian poetaster borrowed his sixth stanza from the classicists of his own day:

> Quand l'escadron audacieux
> Des enfants de la terre
> Jusque dans le séjour des dieux
> Osa porter la guerre,
> Bacchus rassurant
> Jupiter tremblant,
> Décida la victoire;
> Tous les dieux à jeun
> Tremblaient en commun,
> Lui seul avait su boire.

Now, almost anyone with a good education could turn out something like this to order. Furthermore, we may well deplore the repetition of the notion of trembling and the tautologeous use of *Tous* and *en commun*, the second expression looking suspiciously like padding.

Stanza seven contains the grotesque, undignified notion of Jupiter throwing, not thunderbolts, but empty bottles, at the Earth and its inhabitants:

> Il fallait voir dans ce grand jour
> Le puissant dieu des treilles,
> Tranquille, vidant tour à tour
> Et lançant des bouteilles;
> A coups de flacons,
> Renversant les monts
> Sur les fils de la terre:

An elucidation follows, which does not effectively excuse this excursion into mundane extravagance:

> Ces traits, dans la main
> Du buveur divin,
> Remplaçaient le tonnerre.

The more serious side of Rosatist activities, as envisaged particularly by Mornand, who is singularly attracted by the Masonic explanation of almost everything, may perhaps be divined in the next lines:

> Vous, dont il reçut le serment
> Pour de si justes causes,
> C'est à son pouvoir bienfaisant
> Que vous devez vos roses;
> C'est lui qui forma
> Leur tendre incarnat,
> L'aventure est notoire
> J'entendis Momus
> Un jour à Vénus
> Rappeler cette histoire.

Here we may entertain suspicions regarding the *justes causes*, following hard on the heels of the *serment*, exacted of all members of secret societies, many of which did exercise a *pouvoir bienfaisant*; but the evidence is slight and inconclusive.

There follow two stanzas containing the story just promised. It begins thus:

> La rose était pâle jadis,
> Et moins chère à Zéphire,
> A la vive blancheur des lys
> Elle cédait l'empire;
> Mais un jour Bacchus
> Au sein de Vénus,
> Prend la fille de Flore;
> La plongeant soudain
> Dans des flots de vin,
> De pourpre il la colore.

and it continues:

> On prétend qu'au sein de Cypris
> Deux, trois gouttes coulèrent,
> Et que dès-lors parmi les lys
> Deux roses se formèrent;
> Grâce à ses couleurs,
> La rose des fleurs
> Désormais fut la reine;
> Cypris, dans les cieux,
> Du plus froid des dieux
> Devint la souveraine.

This, we feel, is much better poetry than we have met so far, because it rings true and flows more sweetly. Conventional, but at least it is well done. Alas, this vein is soon worked out and we are brought back to harsh reality with the most prosaic verse of all, a mere catalogue of names giving this stanza the appearance of a class register:

> Amis de ce discours usé
> Conclusions qu'il faut boire;
> Avec le bon ami Ruzé
> Qui n'aimerait à boire?
> A l'ami Carnot,
> A l'aimable Cot,
> A l'instant je veux boire;
> A vous, cher Fosseux,
> Au groupe joyeux,
> Je veux encor reboire.

> Si jamais j'oubliais Morcant,
> Que ma langue séchée
> A mon gosier rude et brûlant
> Soit toujours attachée.
> Pour fuir ce malheur,
> Trois fois de grand cœur
> Je veux vider mon verre.
> Pour l'avènement
> D'un frère charmant,
> On ne saurait mieux faire.[23]

Reboire indeed! And that awful Rabelaisian touch about the *gosier*, which just does not ring true from this fake hedonist!

Perhaps this is the real Robespierre—the man who could be eloquent in prose, but not in poetry. In all fairness, though, we should concede that Maximilien's verses are not very much worse than those we discover in Epicurean compendia stretching over a century before his birth. Furthermore, it is to his credit that he did not persist in composing such lines after he left Arras for good; but the literary allusions woven into so many of his stanzas were never wasted, for he could weave them again into his speeches and by so doing stand out amid many uncouth orators—Legendre, Santerre, Pétion and the rest—as a man who could not only write his name but quote the classics by the hour.

Chapter 9

A MAN AND A CULTURAL MULE

'J'ai toujours pensé qu'il avait manqué à notre Révolution . . . des écrivains profonds . . .'

ROBESPIERRE

Some idea of the reading habits and literary tastes of our *Rosatus* can
be discovered by examining the inventory of his library made in
1794. Naturally, as one might suspect, several manuscripts of
speeches, letters and press-articles came to light. Again, it is not
surprising that there was a Bible, duly annotated, for in truth
religion fascinated him and the Bible was to provide him with the
brightest idea of all, as we shall see.

His liking for Voltaire was never very great, but, after the
queen's death, he acquired her copy of the *Henriade*, perhaps as a
souvenir. There were many other unexpected things about his
bookcases. In the collection of one who had been essentially
nationalistic, it was strange to find French, English and Italian
grammars. At first sight it was also amazing to discover that
Robespierre had preserved so few law books—but undoubtedly
he was anxious to forget early days as a struggling student or
barrister. Then again, few proofs of his renowned prowess in the
Latin tongue had been retained—probably for the same reason.
Biggest shock of all: although Mably, Guicciardini, Fleury and
Fénelon were found in his shelves, Rousseau was not. As this
apparently contradicts Madame Lebas's remark that a volume of
Rousseau lay open on his desk as he wrote, we may take it that the
information gleaned from this inventory is perhaps not entirely
reliable, compared with indirect evidence. Speaking of the period
from 1791 onwards, for instance, Renier says: 'There were some
bookshelves made for him by Duplay, full of volumes of Rousseau,
Voltaire, Montesquieu, Racine and Corneille, of papers and
reports.'[1] Consequently one must perhaps assume that he later
disposed of his Rousseau, or that some person removed these
volumes before the inventory was made. How else could he have
been inclined to 'dash upstairs and return with a volume of
Rousseau's *Nouvelle Héloïse* or with a play by Racine or Corneille,

from which he read aloud to an admiring circle, delighted to shed a fashionable tear'—another of Dr Renier's gems of information?

J. M. Thompson explains why certain expected books were missing from Maximilien's bookcase by suggesting that Robespierre carried many ideas in his head and in any case could not afford to possess many volumes.[2] With due respect to Mr Thompson, there is a less flattering explanation of the paucity of this private library. Robespierre was not a highly cultured individual; indeed the fact that he had retained so little of his classical texts argues that his interest in ancient language and literature was shallow or ephemeral, as was that of much of his generation, in love with politics, science and nascent technology. In this sense, then, Maximilien was a true child of an age relatively infecund from the cultural point of view.

It would not be an exaggeration to say that, as a whole, the Revolutionary period was a sort of desert. In asserting this, we are well aware that France was grossly disturbed at the time; yet war need not necessarily affect culture adversely. In Graham Greene's story, *The Third Man*, Harry Lime is discovered examining the moral issues raised by his war-profiteering. Excusing himself, Mr Lime suggests that war often confers cultural benefits and he compares in this respect Renaissance Italy with the peaceful Swiss Republic. Rent by turmoil, Italy gave the world Leonardo and Michelangelo; enjoying centuries of peace, Switzerland produced the cuckoo-clock!

It may be argued that Renaissance Italy and Revolutionary France were different, yet both upheavals involved republicanism, classicism, a struggle for liberty and civic and national pride. The trouble with Robespierre and his friends was that they could not reconcile the conflicting claims of classicism and romanticism. Consider romanticism first. The breeze that blew that long curtain across the Jeu de Paume in David's famous picture was in truth the wind of change. The French Revolution was the orgasm of a fevered ebullience, which had been simmering since the mid-century or even earlier and found its true prophet in the neurotic recluse, Rousseau, Maximilien's idol and model. Tired of rules, restrictions, conservatism, out-moded concepts of society, urban civilization, hedonism, libertinism and salon life, disciples like Robespierre revolted in the name of nature and puritanism against the luxurious opulence of Versailles—that mirrored museum of *grand-siècle* classicism. The new romantic-primitivist cult came to symbolize the violent emotional aspect of mankind and was to supersede moderate liberalism in the political sphere.

But was Rousseau entirely a romantic, or was he not also an apologist for Spartan ways of life? Love of things Spartan would be interpreted by Rousseau's Robespierrist devotees as an example of his clever knack of just anticipating popular taste, for his disapproval of luxury at the mid-century had coincided with a general trend towards greater austerity in national taste. And, as the logical consequence of this trend, on the eve of the Revolution we find Louis-Sébastien Mercier's *Tableau de Paris* expressing disapproval of excessive pomp and display. The versatile Rousseau had also accommodated a bourgeois ideal of virtuous sentimentality, to be found, in bucolic form, at the Versailles *Hameau*, where, unaware, courtiers flirted with death.

This ideal, quietly pervasive in Chardin's domestic cameos, sometimes becomes, at one and the same time, sentimental and melodramatic; and, just as Diderot wanted every picture to tell a story—that is, to point a moral—in canvases like the *Accordée de village, Le Fils ingrat* and *Le Mauvais Fils puni* Greuze had already purveyed a pathetic domestic romanticism. This pathos was a constant companion of the idealistic young tribune from Arras. His other obsessive '-ism' was equally grim and unsmiling. For Robespierre, following both Montesquieu and Rousseau, conspired with David in admiring Romans like the Gracchus brothers, who by agrarian laws had endeavoured to restrain aristocratic society. So, whereas the new austerity could be ascribed partly to nascent homely romanticism, its simplicity was also a reflection of the current interest in neo-classicism. In painting, however, French classicism was far from simple. At the time of the Counter-Reformation it had arrived from Rome, where a French Painting Academy existed. In France it had veered quickly towards a noticeably intricate development called the baroque. So the Revolution inherited an art which was mainly un-French, since it was by no means a return to, or outcome of, Louis XIV's standards of taste and luxury. And, if Poussin may be quoted as an exception, that is because he was truly exceptional. The democratic classicism, or neo-classicism of David owes more to Rome than to France. For instance, the triumph of the *Serment des Horaces* is a result of archeological discoveries at Pompeii and Herculaneum

Robespierre the paranoiac. Engraved by Fiesinger,
after a drawing by Guérin (see p. 77)

Artificial Mountain on the Champ de Mars
for the *Fête de L'Etre Suprême*
(see pp. 83–84 and compare
the illustration facing p. 114)

in the years 1738–60; of the influence of Mengs in 1752; of Clérisseau and Winckelmann whose *History of the Art of Antiquity* had been avidly devoured in 1764; and finally of the appointment of Marigny as Directeur-Général des Bâtiments and of Vien to the Rome Academy. After the *Horaces* canvas, leaders like Robespierre (most of whom were about thirty) devoted themselves almost wholeheartedly to neo-classicism, bastard though it was. And it is not surprising, especially after his education at the best school in France, that Robespierre, when asked which constitution he wanted, replied: 'That of Lycurgus!' Later, when he was at the head of affairs and was assisted by David, Robespierre's Spartan asceticism began to sprout triumphal arches, laurel wreaths and statues to classical virtues. Thus, commissioned by the Jacobins, David lived long enough to contradict the old adage 'official art is bad art', but only because he had that rare genius which transformed the marmoreal pedestrianism of Eléanore's tutor, Régnault, into something of universal appeal. In particular, that early *Serment du Jeu de Paume*, which depicts a fervent Maximilien in the right foreground, proves that a really clever artist can serve two masters and do it very well too.

In the realm of the plastic arts and of sculpture in particular, pyramids, columns, medallions, urns and sarcophagi appeared everywhere, but most of all in stucco and canvas models designed by David for the didactic and idyllic spectacles which Robespierre had thought up. Lesser geniuses supplied the music. Méhul composed the *Chant du Départ* in order to send the 'blues' singing to the front, inspired by naïvely patriotic sentiments such as these:

> La victoire en chantant nous ouvre la barrière,
> La liberté guide nos pas
> Et du Nord au Midi, la trompette guerrière
> A sonné l'heure des combats.
> Tremblez, ennemis de la France,
> Rois ivres de sang et d'orgueil!
> Le peuple souverain s'avance,
> Tyrans, descendez au cercueil!

M.-J. Chénier's lyric, quoted here, provided in the second verse a dreadful lapse into 'conjugation', typical of the *genre*:

> Vous êtes vaillants, nous le sommes.

The second-rate Gossec wrote the deistic *Hymn to the Supreme Being* for Robespierre's most fateful day in June 1794. It was a paean to pantheism couched in terms such as these:

Ton temple est sur les monts, dans les airs, sur les ondes,
Tu n'as point de passé, tu n'as point d'avenir,
Et, sans les occuper, tu remplis tous les mondes
Qui ne peuvent te contenir.

These trifling scraps remind us of Professor Low, famous scientist that he was at the time, busy at the start of the Second World War inventing a cabbage-shredder for use in war-time canteens. They also remind us of Anatole France's character, Gamelin, in *Les Dieux ont soif*, wasting his talents depicting Liberty, The Rights of Man, Constitutional Virtues and Hercules treading on the Hydra of Tyranny—strip-cartoons for *sans-culottes*! And, if we may wonder at the vast necropoles of monuments to Unity, Virtue, Wisdom, Victory and the like, we must bear in mind that the Committee decreed no less than four political and thirty-six moral fêtes a year—enough to sicken most inspired designers.

Expressing the matter succinctly, the Revolution witnessed a contest between the arts and the sciences—a contest already laid before the thinking public in 1749 when Rousseau produced the first of his two famous *Discours*—and the arts lost. This was inevitable in a period when the question 'Is poetry really necessary?' was so easily replaced by the more sinister question 'Is poetry harmful to human progress?'. It was natural that a materialistic and belligerent decade should attempt to make more advances in the technological, than in the cultural sector.

The Incorruptible himself had little time for diversions, but, in his early days before he judged the playhouse sinful, he had regarded the theatre as his favourite cultural luxury. This unfortunately said very little for his taste. True, Shakespeare, in translation by Ducis, proved acceptable to an epoch which could not make up its mind about classicism and romanticism; but, broadly speaking, in the theatre the latter triumphed, sweeping aside the unities of time and place and ushering in wild tirades and physical violence coupled with the horrific. Another budding of *sans-culotte* philistinism produced a crop of melodramas, reminiscent in tone of Laclos and reflecting the depraved tastes of Rétif or Sade and mirroring the gloomy pre-romanticism of a Hubert Robert, in love with ruins and tombs to the point of imagining perfectly sound edifices like the Louvre as they might appear after partial demolition.

This, then, was the chaotic cultural wilderness which Robespierre inherited. For this arid waste he cannot entirely escape blame, but we must not be too harsh. His judgement was distorted by incessant moralizing, which obsessed him, as it had obsessed Rousseau, and caused him to state, in his *Eloge de Gresset*, that he loved virtue more than literature and considered genius less valid than good works.[3] If you thus mix chalk and cheese, you are unlikely to be understood or forgiven by posterity. If, as Rousseau did, you preach virtuous, natural, honest simplicity and senti-mentality; if you anticipate the world of improving Victorian matrons, as Greuze did; if you consider didactic ethics to be more important than pleasure, as in theory Diderot had appeared to do; above all, if like Robespierre and his Jacobin friends you frown puritanically on the debonair delights of civilization, it is not surprising that, despite the dynamic of republicanism and classic-ism, your art and your cultural climate do not resemble those of fifteenth-century Florence. You may even have proved the amoral thesis of Mandeville's *Fable of the Bees*; virtue is essentially sterile; the State flourishes on vice and dissipation; the puritanical hive perishes in its primness.

The barrenness of the Terror in the cultural sector arose, there-fore, partly from the unconscious confusion between Spartan classicism and an even more puritanical romanticism of Rousseauist, and therefore Swiss origin. It is an illusion to suppose that the French are either Greek, Roman or Swiss. In the end, mixed origins proved fatal to culture until the Restoration. Like the mule, that could easily serve as a mascot for this hybrid epoch, the Age of Robespierre, though strong in its stubborn vigour, could display no achievement other than the guillotine, which it did not of course invent. Maximilien's shallow urbanity, consisting chiefly in lip-service to the Ancients, was completely barren too. The 'Editor's' Introduction to his apocryphal *Mémoires* provides the following judgement upon his taste and artistic talent: 'He was expert neither in poetry, painting nor music; he had no taste for urbane accomplishments, for the arts which add beauty and even glory to empires.'[4] That at least, sounds authentic.

It is not surprising that Robespierre had declared early in 1792 that the Revolution had always lacked profound writers. The situation appears to have become worse as the Revolution continued on its sanguinary way, for, by May 1794, the Incorruptible could write: 'Men of letters in general have disgraced themselves during this Revolution and, to the eternal shame of intellect, the people's intelligence alone has borne the brunt of it all!'[5] In fact, culture entered into its bleakest period during Robespierre's hegemony—which is not surprising since France had her back to the wall in all ways. For example, when, after August 8, 1793, the French Academy ceased to exist, the last tenacious guardian of literary standards and linguistic purity was relegated to temporary oblivion. Isolated and cast back on their own resources, writers could do little more than flatter the new leaders in works as ephemeral as politicians themselves. For its own sake, literature had no chance of being read, when all that was asked was that a text should point a civic moral or exhort soldiers to bolder deeds; and it is almost true to say that the best prose of the entire Revolution came from Desmoulins in the Luxembourg prison and from the pages of the *Vieux Cordelier*, in which he criticized the Convention and the Committee of Public Safety. But, as if to offer proof, we are once more back to journalism, to political oratory on the printed page, which, a poor substitute for the real thing, was none the less to become the Incorruptible's secondary means of conversion. For, though he was to be taken to task by Dubois de Crancé for having recourse to an 'external' method of persuasion which allegedly 'was prejudicial to the public interest',[6] Maximilien realized that publication was useful to sway the maximum number of his fellow citizens or to scourge those venal mercenaries who consistently distorted the truth. So it was with a public, as well as a private, motive that he cautiously entered the minefield of Revolutionary journalism.

At what date he first appeared in newsprint we are not sure. Some say that he contributed to the *Union*, which was a two-language paper, written in French and English; others affirm that he helped Marat with his paper. Being an egocentric who preferred independence, he undoubtedly checked any oration of his which was to be published by others, for he had a horror of distortion. In this way Camille Desmoulins, who received many speeches for his

Révolutions de France et de Brabant, had to put up with his old
school friend's careful control of copy, but this was marginal
journalism and smacked of the vicarious. So in May 1792—
perhaps with the financial backing of Duplay—Robespierre
himself founded a paper called *Le Défenseur de la Constitution*.
Between that date and the end of August 1792, twelve numbers
appeared; by which time, in view of the violent events of August
10 and the subsequent abandonment of the 1791 document, he
considered the title no longer appropriate and changed it to
Lettres à ses commettans (*Letters to his Constituents*). Under this new
banner, it continued publication from October 1792 till April
1793, during which period there appeared some twenty-two
numbers, divided into two series, the first stretching from
September till the end of 1792 and the second dealing with the
early months of 1793. The author continued to rely upon the same
format as before—which means that the magazine ran to many
pages and had a strong bias throughout.

In the first number of his *Le Défenseur de la Constitution* we find
a typical example of written propaganda. It was May 1792. Having
suffered sharp defeats in the north, French armies were in retreat
and the generals refused to continue the struggle on the same
terms. A crisis, therefore, and a problem: 'the war is upon us; it
only remains for us to take the necessary precautions to turn it to
the benefit of the Revolution!' Robespierre did not wish it, but
since it was a fact, he and his compatriots had to prosecute it
effectively. Consequently, his article was, first and foremost, a
plea for military efficiency, but there was something more:

'Français, combattez et veillez tout à la fois; veillez dans vos revers;
veillez dans vos succès; craignez votre penchant à l'enthousiasme; et
mettez-vous en garde contre la gloire même de vos généraux.
Sachez découvrir toutes les routes que l'ambition et l'intrigue
peuvent se frayer pour parvenir à leur but; veillez, soit que nos
ennemis intérieurs, d'intelligence avec ceux du dehors, méditent de
nous livrer au glaive des despotes, soit qu'on veuille nous faire
acheter, par la perte des citoyens les plus énergiques, une victoire
funeste qui ne tournerait qu'au profit de l'aristocratie. Songez à
l'ascendant que peuvent usurper, au milieu d'une révolution, ceux
qui disposent des forces de l'Etat; consultez l'expérience des nations
et représentez-vous quelle serait la puissance d'un chef de parti habile
à capter la bienveillance des soldats si, le people étant épuisé, affamé,

fatigué, les plus zélés patriotes égorgés, la roi même désertant encore une fois son poste, au sein des horreurs de la guerre civile, entouré de tous les corps militaires dont on a couvert la surface de l'empire, il se montrait à la France avec l'air d'un libérateur et toute la force des partis réunis contre l'égalité.'[7]

Here we meet the politician in hortatory vein, embodying in his own work the image of a credible statesman. The style of the passage is flowing and very sedulously balanced. Almost every element has its counterpart, so that we almost come to expect that *combattez* will be paired with *veillez, revers* with *succes, craignez* with *mettez-vous en garde, ambition* with *intrigue, interieurs* with *du dehors* and *soit que* with an identical twin introducing an alternative phrase. Indeed, our findings appear to concur with those of Garat, who once remarked: 'I thought I perceived—especially when he was writing for publication—the germs of a talent which might finally grow; which in fact *was* growing and whose development might one day do much good and much harm too. In his style I found an author who was busy studying and imitating those forms of language which possess elegance, dignity and brilliance.'[8] As Victor Hugo was to observe just after the Franco-Prussian War, Robespierre was as careful about his style as he was about dress: 'he never ventured a sentence unless it was decorously attired'.[9] More important is the prophetic reference to a military dictator who, taking advantage of an exhausted people, will appear first as liberator, only in the end to destroy liberty as well as equality. It was courageous of Maximilien to adopt this minority view and perceptive to foresee the role that would soon and inevitably be played by an heir to the Revolution. For, precisely the absence of monarchy, the hatching of a conspiracy and the benevolent support of the army were to supply an ambitious Bonaparte with the triple opportunity he needed at the end of a tedious period of economic distress and moral relapse.

So, like many intelligent journalists, Robespierre had a very personal approach to his paper; and the twelve issues of the *Défenseur* spanning the period May 17 to August 20, 1792 seem to have been designed principally to provide him with a means of self-justification. For example, Number One contains a pointed 'Outline of my principles' and the editor's reply to two leading

Girondins.[10] In 1792 Maximilien had been out of parliament for much too long and was making a bid to return to the House by proving himself a master political theorist—a procedure to be repeated exactly a year later, incidentally, when he wished to lead the Committee of Public Safety. In this article he defends the Constitution of 1791, despite its defects, because it could be a rallying point for reformists. Claiming to be republican, he none the less supports a system of tempered monarchy. In other issues he continues to wage the personal campaign, but adds details of decrees passed by the National Assembly. The fourth number reveals the Incorruptible on his high quixotic mount tilting at 'The Moral Causes of Present Situation' and savouring the didactic possibilities of national fêtes and publicly-bestowed honours.[11] Number Six resembles its successor in printing Robespierre's strictures against the hated La Fayette; and most issues review some aspect or other of the war situation, suggesting ways and means of improving military efficiency.[12] Issue Twelve is especially interesting, since it covers the events of August 10, 1792, as described by one who was absent![13]

When the second publication begins, few contents have changed, for the paper is still a very individual affair. The editor *is* the journal. His feuds with Louvet, the Girondins and Pétion inspire lengthy pieces, whilst topics of special interest, like the vexed question of what to do with Louis XVI, the state of the economy, the food problem, religion, education, the conduct of the war, conspiracies and foreigners, are discussed several times over.

Though he dominates the publication in this way, the head man occasionally provides space for writers like Anthoine, Desmoulins, Dubois de Crancé and Merlin de Thionville—useful second-strings. Naturally the editorial policy is republican and democratic; the clubs get a good airing, especially the Jacobins, who communicate with provincial cells via these columns. As in the *Défenseur*, the lay-out consists first of a moral or political tract and secondly of a 'Hansard' report, often done by a hack called Laveaux.

Summing up, then: the press helped to build up the tribune's prophetic power and reputation as a crystal-gazer or political expert. Revolutionary journalism was largely rhetorical in form and tone, and Maximilien offers a fine example of one who was more at home on the rostrum than in the editor's chair. Once a major political task—the destruction of the Girondins—had been accomplished, the editor lost interest in journalism, which had been an ancillary means. Neither a writer nor a newspaperman by temperament or choice, Robespierre ceased to be both when he felt that political ascendancy was assured; but his powers of oratory were needed more than ever.

Chapter 10

THE REVOLUTIONARY DEMOSTHENES

'La raison et l'éloquence; voilà les armes avec lesquelles il
faut attaquer les préjugés; leur succès n'est point douteux
dans un siècle tel que le nôtre'

ROBESPIERRE, 1784

Naturally hostile because her father, Necker, had been dubbed a
traitor by Robespierre, it was Madame de Staël who drew attention to the supreme historic irony that the man who had relied so
much on his powers of speech was, in his last hours when his jaw
had been shattered by a pistol-shot, deprived of the ability to
defend himself in the manner he had perfected.[1]

Though by nature Robespierre had not been endowed with a
pleasant voice, there is no doubt at all that, when Carra referred to
his 'sublime eloquence' and Mathiez to his 'oratorical genius',[2]
they were not necessarily guilty of exaggeration. Still, whether we
agree with Mathiez that he was 'one of the greatest orators who
ever lived'[3] or, like Madame Roland, find the tribune pedantic and
boring,[4] depends very much on the part of his career chosen
for consideration, for it is true that Robespierre improved
with experience and under pressure, so that the same man who
had never ventured to speak without careful and laborious
preparation learned to extemporize and to profit by the
interruptions of others.[5] In the end, with practice, he became
perhaps a better speaker than Danton, and even more determined to employ reason and eloquence to combat prejudice and
injustice.[6]

The progress he made provides interesting material. Trained in the
legal profession, from the outset the Incorruptible was accustomed
to speaking in public, scoring points in debate and occasionally
winning the case. Yet it took a revolution to overcome his natural
diffidence and timidity. The vehemence of the struggle for
the people, for virtue, for justice, for rationality, nay for sheer
survival of the fittest, helped him to forget his shyness once the
initial blows had been exchanged. He did not make his impact by
wittiness. Although Madame Roland paid tribute to his acidity:

'He often derided; often threw out sarcastic remarks',[7] it is generally agreed that he never achieved genuine laughter with any of his speeches. He was too earnest for that.

His major oratorical début occurred on July 20, 1789—a speech in praise of the demolition of the Bastille; but 'Robert-Pierre', as the records wrongly call him, was still relatively in the background.[8] From May to December 1789 he spoke only twenty-five times, whereas Barnave was heard on forty-two occasions and the famous Mirabeau topped the bill by making no less than 122 'interventions'. Robespierre still needed the sting of sharp adversity and the spur of sensational events to bring him to the front. Alas, the Constituent Assembly failed to liberate him much from his pedantic cocoon and he continued to be tedious until nearly 1792.

As an example of the early style, consider his rigorously geometrical, theoretical, almost Cartesian approach to a national issue.[9] The date is May 31, 1790. He begins with a schoolboy's axiomatic premiss: social laws regulate relations between clergy and society in general. The priest is a kind of magistrate, appointed to provide and maintain worship. From these beginnings, he draws certain principles. All public functions are social functions, having therefore public order and happiness as their objectives. No useless function may exist in society. These observations allow the orator to conclude that all Church livings and establishments lacking specific motivation should be abolished; which means that only bishops and parish priests are worthy of survival. Foreign nominees (cardinals, for instance) must have no rights in France, adds our Gallican nationalist. His second principle is that Church officials should serve society and their salaries should be related therefore to their contribution to public interest and general utility. It is clear that the man of cold principle has applied equally cold logic—the logic of the civil service, perhaps—to the development of an argument which is narrow and monolithic; and, having set down his principles, he leaves the Assembly to proceed further—which it does not immediately do, for Maximilien's impact has been feeble at this time.

On the other hand, a speech delivered towards the end of the Constituent Assembly period,[10] recommending that neither he nor his colleagues of that body should be re-eligible for the Legislative Assembly, is important, not only for its historic influence, but also because it demonstrates oratorical fire, gradually increasing amid adversity and in opposition, and because it strikes a note of real sincerity. First and foremost, he makes a plea for sternness and austerity on the Greek and Roman model. Since classicism is *à la mode*, it is natural and useful to begin in this way. If the Spartan Lycurgus and the Athenian Solon retired into the crowd when they had provided a constitution, then it is right that Revolutionary M.P.s should do the same. After this display of heroic altruism, Robespierre then comes to the more personal and human reason. Clearly, still aware of his immaturity, he is jealous of rivals. Derision poured on the manipulators of the House; upon those exploiting 'parliamentary tactics' suggests envy and proves his continuing inferiority. Yet there is also a subtler motivation. He could at that time afford to strike a blow at his rivals and at his own immediate prospects, since he realized that he already had a following *outside* parliament; and with more spare time, he would one day re-enter the main stream of politics, this time swimming more expertly. And, if the worst came to the worst, he would not go hungry, because in October 1790 he had been elected president of the Versailles tribunal. The speech is significant in another way too, since it shows Maximilien endeavouring to sustain a minority opinion against career-politicians and ultimately managing to carry the day. His discourse had been punctuated, incidentally, by his latest mannerism—thanking the growing number of his supporters with a salute from his inevitable *lorgnette*.

Flushed with the realization of improving oratorical powers, the budding speaker next turned his attention to a less creditable task. Having read and appreciated Raynal's *Histoire des Indes* Maximilien had every reason to revere this ghost from the past, the almost unique survivor of the great Philosophic Movement, without which the democratic Revolution would have been unscripted. At the age of eighty, the Abbé dared to express an opinion about the totalitarian trends of the Constituante. His letter regretted that liberty had been sacrificed and eroded. He criticized the 'false interpretation of our principles' which had been made; he deprecated religious troubles and 'the tyranny of the people'; sadly noticed all around him undisciplined soldiery and a king stripped of real authority. He also dared to complain about the menace of anarchy stemming from excessive egalitarianism—and this before Varennes and the anti-royalist turmoil it aroused!

Clearly, said Raynal, the time had come to stop the Revolution and reinforce the king's authority.

Loving few of the former *Philosophes* except odd-man-out Rousseau, who had furiously quarrelled with his colleagues in 1758, Robespierre took offence and, with Roederer, the Syndic-Général, poured scorn on the ill-conceived missive[11] with such eloquent and vitriolic success that very soon all Revolutionary broadsheets were out for the old man's blood, savage cartoonists had a field-day and, in general, France was made aware that the Abbé was guilty of selling Negroes, procuring women and acting as a police spy. He never effectively raised his voice again. Under the Terror, Raynal was deprived of his fortune, his furniture and silver-ware, and, when he died in 1796 at the age of eighty-four, he left a mere five livres. This shows how successful this vitriolic polemicist already was, even against a former *Philosophe*, who was protesting, as he himself so often did, against the triumph of vice in France.

Then came self-imposed exile. By late 1792 he was back on the benches, ready to demonstrate again his burgeoning expertise. Already in March, he had entertained the Jacobins to this un-acknowledged Rousseauist pastiche: 'All alone with my soul, how could I have shouldered superhuman burdens, if I had not lifted up my soul?'[12] Thus readings in semi-retirement were bearing fruit; Jean-Jacques's style was beginning to run through his quill, vivifying, enlivening, adding vehemence and eloquence for the great occasion that was nigh.

The abortive attempt to flee the country in June 1791 had turned public opinion against Louis XVI; and in November the wall of the Tuileries supplied further confirmation of guilt.[13] To the Convention on December 3, 1792, Robespierre made his position clear: normally he was against the death penalty, but in the case of the traitor Louis he felt that he could not only overlook this principle, but claim that a trial was unnecessary: 'In which republic was the need to punish a tyrant subject to litigation?', he inquired and drove on to the conclusion that 'Louis must die, because the country must live'.[14] Of course, in January 1793, such arguments brought about the king's execution. The harangue had worked very well indeed. That little jousting with old Abbé Raynal was nothing compared with hounding a monarch to his grave. Things were going well for the young tribune of the people, who was already on the look-out for even more numerous fish to net and who, as Durand-Maillane explained, 'strengthened his own power by the systematic destruction of all his rivals'.[15] He did not wait long.

Faced with the problem of eliminating the reactionary Girondins, his sober oratorical powers were to be deployed to the full during Germinal. On April 3, 1793, he went into action,[16] accusing his foes of complicity with foreign enemies and aristocrats and of dealing with traitors like Dumouriez. The continuing list of Girondist crimes was spelt out in a rhetorical anaphora of crushing weight, repeating many times *nous les avons vus, là nous avons entendu, là, nous avons vu* until, reeling under a hail of verbal fire, the Convention was driven to proscribe the Girondins.

A mere three weeks later—before the enemy had been finally hounded out of the House—Maximilien was hot on the trail of another type of big-game, the controversial question of property. The speech is doubly rewarding since we have the scribbled notes from which it was made:

Propriété, ses droits.

> Marchand de chair humaine, navire où il encaisse les nègres, voilà mes propriétés.
> Noble.
> Terres et vassaux, voilà, etc.
> Dynastie de Capet.
> Le droit héréditaire, qu'elle avait d'opprimer, de ruiner, de sucer 20 millions d'hommes.
> Scandale pour les siècles.[17]

From such unpromising material, the Incorruptible evolved this stirring invective:

'Posons donc de bonne foi les principes du droit de propriété, il le faut d'autant plus qu'il n'en est point que les préjugés et les vices des hommes aient cherché envelopper de nuages plus épais.

'Demandez à ce marchand de chair humaine ce que c'est que la propriété; il vous dira en vous montrant cette longue bière qu'il appelle un navire, où il a encaissé et serré des hommes qui paraissaient vivants; Voilà mes propriétés, je les ai achetés tant par tête. Interrogez ce gentilhomme qui a des terres et des vassaux ou qui croit l'univers bouleversé depuis qu'il n'en a plus; il vous donnera de la propriété des idées à peu près semblables.

'Interrogez les augustes membres de la dynastie capétienne, ils vous diront que le plus sacrée des propriétés est, sans contredit, le droit héréditaire dont ils ont joui, de toute antiquité, d'opprimer, d'avilir et de s'assurer légalement et monarchiquement les 25 millions d'hommes qui habitaient le territoire de la France sous leur bon plaisir . . .'[18]

Here with a loaded imagery and emotive force reminiscent of Voltaire recounting in *Candide* the terrible story of the Negro slave ('C'est à ce prix que vous mangez du sucre en Europe') but in a style which is very much that of Rousseau (consider the repetition of *Interrogez*), we find a true product of the age, turning phrases into dynamic prose to sweep along his audience. The orator was now fully, professionally armed. On May 10, 1793, in the Assembly, he once more proved that Rousseau lived on in one who was only twenty when the great Genevan died. 'L'homme est né pour le bonheur et pour la liberté, et partout il est esclave et malheureux'[19] comes almost verbatim from the *Contrat*; yet his own style was evolving too. Forged in the flames of conflict, his technique was ready for all comers.

Read, for example, his report on the current political situation, presented to the Convention on November 17, 1793. Improvement is obvious; his ethic, his likes and dislikes, his political principles, displayed with mature virtuosity; and how proud he is of achievements in which he himself has played a decisive role!

'Pitt s'est grossièrement trompé sur notre Révolution, comme Louis XVI et les aristocrates français, abusés par leur mépris pour le peuple; mépris fondé uniquement sur la conscience de leur propre bassesse. Trop immoral pour croire aux vertus républicaines, trop peu philosophe pour faire un pas vers l'avenir, le ministre de George était au-dessous de son siècle; le siècle s'élançait vers la liberté, et Pitt voulait le faire rétrograder vers la barbarie et vers le despotisme. Aussi l'ensemble des événements a trahi jusqu'ici ses rêves ambitieux: il a vu briser tour-à-tour par la force populaire les divers instruments dont il s'est servi; il a vu disparaître Necker, d'Orléans, La Fayette, Lameth, Dumouriez, Custine, Brissot et tous les pygmées de la

Gironde. Le peuple français s'est dégagé jusqu'ici des fils de ses intrigues, comme Hercule d'une toile d'araignée.

'Voyez comme chaque crise de notre Révolution l'entraîne toujours au-delà du point où il voulait l'arrêter; voyez avec quels pénibles efforts il cherche à faire reculer la raison publique et à entraver la marche de la liberté; voyez ensuite quels crimes prodigués pour la détruire. A la fin de 1791, il croyait préparer insensiblement la chute du roi Capet, en conservant le trône pour le fils de son maître; mais le 10 août a lieu, et la République est fondée. C'est en vain que, pour l'étouffer dans son berceau, la faction girondine et tous les lâches émissaires des tyrans étrangers appellent de toutes parts les serpents de la calomnie, le démon de la guerre civile, l'hydre du fédéralisme, le monstre de l'aristocratie: le 31 mai, le peuple s'éveille et les traîtres ne sont plus. La Convention se montre aussi juste que le peuple, aussi grande que sa mission. Un nouveau pacte social est proclamé, cimenté par le vœu unanime des Français; le génie de la liberté plane d'une aile rapide sur la surface de cet empire, en rapproche toutes les parties prêtes à se dissoudre et les raffermit sur ses vastes fondements.'[20]

Nothing second-rate now! Here, in a discourse which flatters members of the Convention, Maximilien stresses progress towards republican freedom, whilst at the same time the populace is being entertained with aggressive, yet persuasive propaganda, conveyed to them by emotive words like *bassesse, despotisme, immoral*. For the *Conventionnels* there is a dignified use of classical figures, following the accepted custom of associating the Revolution with heroic Greece and Rome. In this connexion, contrasts are not plentiful, but we note that Hercules is faced with nothing more substantial than a cobweb and that royalist immorality is set against Republican virtue. The use of *Philosophic* notions shows that, despite the scourging of Raynal, the speaker is not averse from using Encyclopaedist traditions for his own purposes. Propagandist imagery, reminiscent of political cartoons of the day intended mainly to indoctrinate the working classes, occurs in the hackneyed use of *serpents, démon, hydre, monstre* (all calculated to make a *sans-culotte's* hair stand on end), the first two members of the quartet offering rewarding undertones from Genesis. At first sight, it looks as though Rousseau is responsible for the *pacte social* allusion, but in fact this item is tied more specifically to Robespierre's own attempt to state human rights in 1793. The keynote is freedom through unity. To this end the passage lists some of the enemies of unity: Necker, Orléans, La Fayette, the Lameths, Brissot and generals like Dumouriez and Custine—Maximilien's *bêtes noires*.

In the course of time Robespierre evolved so many techniques that even a hostile critic like Clauzel found his versatility worthy of comment: 'His ideas, his principles, are like soldiers who change places, vary the line of fire and, according to circumstance, take up one weapon or another and modify their tactics.'[21] That is true in large measure, but we must not forget that others found Robespierre boring and prolix, even in maturity. In the final analysis, however, the envelope is less important than its contents. The politician outweighs the stylist.

A Rosicrucian woodcut from Anon, *Secret Symbols*, 1785.
It represents the tomb of Rosencreuz in the
form of a philosopher's mountain, symbolic of regeneration
(see pp. 83–84)

The face of an orator.
Robespierre's death mask
(see Chapter 10)

PART III
THE POLITICIAN

'Législateur courageux, reçois donc la couronne que tes travaux et tes vertus ont méritée. Nous ne faisons que devancer la France et le monde'

A FEMALE FAN

I

Chapter 11

THE TRIBUNE AND HIS PEOPLE

'Le défaut de sa politique fut celui de sa littérature,
l'abstraction'

VICTOR HUGO

No commoner had been called upon to rule France before. So, in
a very real sense, the men of the Revolution were improvisers and
experimenters; and this became the exciting feature of their new
vocation.

On the other hand, it was natural that they should try to make
use of the best ideas in the immediate past—that is, of the eighteenth century. Behind the would-be politician there lay two
supreme authorities, Montesquieu and Rousseau, the one having
dominated political and sociological thought in the first half of the
century and the other having made his impact in the seventeen-
fifties and sixties. As it happened, the Revolutionary lustrum
(1789–94) was also fairly evenly divided between these two influences, the liberalism of Montesquieu surviving until the crisis
of August 10, 1792; and the crypto-communism of Jean-Jacques
taking its place after that great upheaval.

In their turn, these two giants of eighteenth-century political
thinking had been indebted to precursors. Ever since the bloodless
revolution of 1688, Great Britain had offered the French a tantaliz-
ing contrast with their own system. Across the narrow Straits of
Dover lay a happy land of free men, endowed with excellent parliamentary institutions characterized by division and balance of
power. Like Voltaire, but without suggesting that it could be
imported successfully, Montesquieu stressed the advantages of the
British system and his compatriots had taken note of what he
wrote. Another fecund source was classical thought. Trained by
the Oratorians, Montesquieu was familiar with Greece and Rome;
so was the largely self-educated Rousseau, because this was the
very stuff of contemporary instruction, however it was acquired.
Thus both these writers knew about the Spartan legislator,
Lycurgus, who provided his country with a constitution and a
senate, redistributed the land amongst deserving citizenry,

imposed severe social and military discipline, launched compulsory public education, and instituted fraternal diversions resembling love-feasts. Such a man appealed to the eighteenth century—and especially after 1750—because he had opposed profligacy, injustice and absolutism and afforded visions of virtuous democracy.

Distilled through the imagination of recent Frenchmen, the classics turned up in another way too. One thinks particularly of novelist-theorists like Fénelon, whose *Télémaque* had supplied the last years of the seventeenth century with a primer in the art of ruling, in which he had promoted hatred of despotism, love of simplicity and economic liberalism. This combination appealed directly to Robespierre, who once remarked that he himself desired to found a Salentum. He thus paid tribute to the former Archbishop of Cambrai,[1] in whose *magnum opus* the hero's return to Salente is the crowning moment, when Telemachus is astonished to discover that the display of opulence he knew before has given way to austere simplicity and that cultivation of the soil has now become an honourable pursuit. These ideals, reinterpreted and revived in the Troglodyte episodes of Montesquieu's *Lettres persanes* and to some extent in Rousseau's first *Discours*, were to become the very foundation of the Robespierrist political primitivism.

It was natural, after all, that Maximilien should esteem much about his great predecessor, the *châtelain* of La Brède—the definition of democracy, opposition to atheism as a viable State system, notions of punishment and equitable judgement and the precedence of ethics over metaphysics. Furthermore, Montesquieu had in his day most clearly stated that republics depend upon virtue, a seminal idea which brought forth much fruit in Robespierre's political garden.[2] The acknowledged proof of Montesquieu's influence is Maximilien's first published work, his *Discours sur les peines infamantes*, in which we learn of the basic characteristics of the three forms of government, despotism, monarchy and republic. We note also that Robespierre has mentioned the *Esprit des lois*, but has not forgotten Persia, or *le droit naturel*,[3] which effectively provides the climax to his *Lettres persanes*; and, when he borrows from this great precursor the notion of ridicule pointed by a foreign visitor, he even lapses into the style of those letters.[4] In more general terms, it should be pointed out that long before

Maximilien, Montesquieu had argued that if virtue lapses, ambition and avarice take over; that if citizens seek their freedom against the legal system (rather than within it), anarchy will ensue. Moreover, in anticipatory contrast to Rousseau, Montesquieu had decided that it is impracticable for people to represent themselves in parliament. We recall young Robespierre putting up a stern struggle against war, partly because it might ruin the Revolution as conceived by the best minds, but also because it could lead to a military dictatorship. This too Montesquieu had warned against in the *Esprit des lois* of 1748.[5]

On the other side of the balance-sheet we must set the disadvantages of Montesquieu. First, he was undeniably an aristocrat, a little suspicious of the common people and convinced that the best solution to the French constitutional problem lay in a resolute monarchy, tempered by intermediate powers, consisting of nobles and *parlementaires*. This Maximilien was to dismiss after Varennes as pure moonshine, just as he had opposed the royal veto on the grounds that France needed only one master, the General Will.[6] Certainly the Committee of Public Safety adopted little or nothing from Montesquieu on the subject of executive power.

The alternative was, of course, that other expert on statecraft, with whom Robespierre had found easy identification, since he too had lost his mother at an early age and been cast upon the untender mercies of a feckless father. Since identification was in fact almost total, Rousseau deserves mention at several places in our study and especially at this point.

The Genevan thinker was not quite as tradition has imagined him to be. For example, contrary to popular opinion, this 'emotional' writer was at the same time very much a logician, preferring to argue in theorems which still bewilder many readers who expect him to mean what he says. Rousseau's 'natural man' was not necessarily a primitive savage or indeed a primitive man. Purely and simply, he was someone who was fulfilling the requirements of his nature. He was living according to his own lights. Unnatural man was man living with his lights dimmed, and as such was worse off than the savage, since ignorance was preferable to error. So Rousseau commended natural man, who used his reason to rediscover his true nature. In this sense—and Maximilien agreed completely—Rousseau admired the stoic who had eschewed the easy life, which was basically unnatural. The quest for nature was consequently the quest for some measure of austerity and self-control, so that self-love, which was natural, might not develop into pride, which was a character-defect. So, relying upon very little direct observation and thus attempting to do for eighteenth-century politics what Descartes had done for seventeenth-century philosophy, Rousseau had proceeded by deductive steps until he had met his 'natural man', not in the backwoods, but in a logical stance which defied over-civilization.

Possessing a spontaneous regard for morality, this natural man enjoyed the freedom to choose between good and evil. Anything less would have amounted to automatism and have led to apathy and immorality. Thus, in Rousseau's view, natural man was perfectible through reason and should struggle towards the goal of greater goodness; and in this sense, he was the man of tomorrow as well as today and was free to choose. (Robespierre was to accept the idea of struggle as very salutary to public morality, but was not at all convinced about freewill.) Paradoxically, when this ethical notion was transferred to the political arena, liberty was one of the things which reluctantly Rousseau had to sacrifice on the altar of equality. So, just as the Revolution confused classicism and romanticism, it failed to resolve this dilemma concerning the rival claims of individualism and collectivism or of liberty versus equality. Let us see how this strange contradiction came about. First of all, Jean-Jacques would have us believe in the inalienable and sovereign will of the people. The 'General Will' (as he calls it) is infallible, since it cannot fail to choose the good of the commonweal. Republics are best for smaller States. If the monarchy is preserved in larger States, then it should be made clear to the king that he is subject to the corporate will—that is, to the law. If he breaks this contract, then he becomes a traitor to the people; but, like the people, he is free within the limits of the law. It is the people who exercise the legislative functions, of course. Natural man must never renounce his birthright in this respect. Having surrendered to the State in order to safeguard his individual freedom a portion of that very freedom, by making the laws he must express the General Will, the organ of corporate self and in this way natural man is seen as the basis of natural society.

It all sounds very simple, but in politics apparent simplicity can be the bed-fellow of absolutism and inflexibility, because in fact human beings are complex. Facts tended to prove the point. Society at the time of the Revolution was certainly not natural and in this lay the first snag, the first rift between precept and practice. Secondly, there was the problem of representation. Influenced to some extent by British ideas acquired from Montesquieu, Robespierre accepted the idea of delegation of authority invested in deputies of the electorate; but Jean-Jacques had been rigidly opposed to such delegation of the General Will. However, since Rousseau thought that the best democratic system would be achieved by small States, and since France was certainly not a small State, Maximilien was bound to decline his mentor's advice on this point. Expressing the matter in modern terms, it was almost as though any sensible Rousseauist would have preferred the personal attention of the family grocery store, but was nevertheless obliged to use a large and impersonal supermarket, which paid less attention to individual requirements, because the business was too large for one man to supervise. So, between Rousseau's theory—influenced of necessity by his campaign against oligarchic control of republican Geneva—and the real situation faced by the Jacobin government of 1793, there was a tremendous difference and of this dichotomy Maximilien was clearly well aware. As a compromise, he suggested that Assembly debates should be held in a hall holding up to 12,000 citizens;[7] but he also declared that, if this proved impracticable, at least the agents of these citizens exercising their right to universal suffrage should be subject to checks in the form of petitions. Moreover, representatives should not automatically enjoy parliamentary privilege (for instance, immunity from legal proceedings), and should maintain lines of communication with the grass-roots, so that the people could be constantly informed of their deliberations. If things still went wrong, the people's right to insurrection as an antidote to misrepresentation or oppression could be invoked, and deputies be easily displaced at any time.

Robespierre and his colleagues of the Convention had also taken heed of the objections made to another consequence of Rousseauism. The Assemblée Constituante had been so anxious to separate the executive from the legislative power, that they had chosen ministers from outside parliament—men like Necker and Montmorin, for instance. This arrangement had proved unsatisfactory, so, realizing the advantages of the English method, according to which ministers were members of the House and answerable to it, the *Conventionnels* made sure that the two Committees of Public Safety and General Security were staffed with men from the parliamentary benches. In this way power was vested even more securely in the hands of the people's representatives, who supervised the work of their executive colleagues; but it must be added that neither Montesquieu nor Rousseau would have been happy to contemplate executive power vested in the two Committees.

In practice, several variations on the triple association between source, middleman and elected representatives seem to have been possible. For example, on one point the Convention agreed with Rousseau against Robespierre, who had been inclined to oppose the death penalty. In the *Contrat*, Jean-Jacques had unequivocally stated: 'The person who wishes to save his own life at the expense of others must also give it when necessary . . .: it is in order to avoid becoming the victim of an assassin that a man consents to die if he becomes an assassin himself.'[8] Yet another variation: just as under the pressure of reality Robespierre was obliged to deny his mentor, it is clear that on some issues Rousseau had condemned in advance the style of his enthusiastic acolyte, when, in his *Lettre à d'Alembert*, he had scorned precisely 'these puny law-scholars'[9]—of which Maximilien was to be the classic Revolutionary archetype—a judgement incidentally confirmed by Duport who spoke of him as having held 'an imaginary Chair in Natural Law'![10] Thirdly, the author of the *Contrat social* had expressed anticipatory disapproval of sectarian influence, which would, he thought, obstruct the expression of the General Will; and it is undeniable that Robespierre's Jacobin government was unfaithful to this article of Rousseauist canon. Finally, the Genevan had deplored in principle precisely the legislation which in Prairial 1794 was to cause so much indiscriminate suffering. In his view 'to sacrifice an innocent person for the safety of the multitude' was contradictory to the fundamental laws of society.[11]

Thus Rousseau would not have sanctioned the Terror.

We have seen how Maximilien diverged from both Montesquieu and Rousseau and that he did so partly because of circumstance; partly because of the multiple pressures from other quarters which, though less significant, cannot be overlooked in our assessment. For instance, speaking generally, if Jean-Jacques accounted for

60 per cent of the tribune's ideas and Montesquieu for another thirty, there remained a small margin for sappers like Voltaire, who had undermined the hegemony of Versailles and the Catholic Church. These characteristics were those of Robespierre also; they were inherent in the very context of his Revolutionary desperation; but it must be remembered that Voltaire, hater of the arrogant aristocrats who had humiliated him, was at the same time no lover of the common people, and in the Revolutionary political package appealed to the reactionary Girondins, not to the liberal Jacobins.

In concocting his peculiar brand of democracy, Robespierre was much more indebted to Mably who, whilst impressed by Rousseauist ideas, stamped them with a trade-mark which Robespierre and his friends were to copy as occasion demanded. For Mably, equality, even to excess, was a noble passion; private property was anathema, since it promoted inequality; laws (and here he concurred with Rousseau) should be made by the nation, although (and here he turned against Rousseau) it had to be admitted that representatives making up a national convention would have to do the job for the nation as a whole. Mably also argued that, if France was to be ruled by a constitutional monarchy, the sovereign should be deprived of the right to veto legislation; and, wary of despotic power, Mably at all times subjected the executive to the legislative. In these ways Mably looked forward to that remarkable Constitution of 1793 (and especially to its more markedly Robespierrist preamble), the nearest thing to a social contract produced by the leader and his team, who had no great appetite for a contract in Rousseau's airy-fairy sense—namely an ideal transaction, presumed to have existed in the past or, alternatively, envisaged as a future hope.

It will be recalled in this connexion that the sixth chapter of Jean-Jacques's *magnum opus* speaks of a pact that has never been clearly defined, but which apparently is universally recognized and everywhere consistent. This, then, is very much a case of the great Genevan paying silent tribute to that principal eighteenth-century shibboleth, natural law, but doing so in a way which is characteristic of his major writings (as distinct from his projects with specific aims)—namely, in a general, theoretical form, which is not readily adapted to urgent needs. In any case, did the Revolutionaries need a contract of the kind supposed to be outlined in the famous work of Rousseau? Was it not in reality true that since 1792 France had witnessed a unique *de facto* rule of the General Will, which meant that there were no longer any major conflicts to resolve in this domain? Even those who had considered popular sovereignty utopian had been forced to recognize that, for long periods during the French Revolution, the rule of the people had proved effective, especially through violence and demonstration, best illustrated by the famous *journées*. Thus, for propagandist and also for juristic purposes, what was needed most in 1793 was a declaration[12] outlining the liberties which these sovereign citizens might now enjoy *in time of peace*. Hence the following principles were laid down:

1. The aim of government is to provide for the rights of man, to be enjoyed equally.
2. Liberty is the power to exercise all his faculties at will; it is based on justice; the rights of others determine its limits; nature [or God] is its principle and the law its safeguard.
3. The rigour of the law reflects the needs of society and must not alienate the rights of man.
4. Property is the right of every citizen to enjoy what is guaranteed to him by law. It must be respected by others and must respect the rights of others.
5. Society is obliged to provide for the subsistence of citizens, either by work or social benefits.
6. Citizens who barely subsist will not pay taxes, which will be contributed by others in proportion to their means.
7. Society must provide education for all.
8. The law is the expression of the sovereign will of the people. The law must be equal for all.
9. Public officials must be paid by the State and those who serve the community must be compensated for loss of earnings.
10. Every citizen must obey just laws, but has the right of insurrection in the case of oppressive and unfair legislation.
11. Men of all nations are brothers and different peoples must help each other, as if they were citizens of the same State.

From this summary it becomes clear that Maximilien was concentrating attention upon social justice. If Rousseau's *Contrat* was intended either for fallen angels or for risen apes, Maximilien's declaration of rights was tailor-made for the poor of the capital, precisely at a moment when Girondism in the provinces needed to be obliterated by attractive notions from Paris. Thus it lay between

extremes and contained a minimum of theory to justify solid principle and attainable privilege. Rights rather than duties are the
keynote of the Declaration, which sets out to ensure that ordinary
citizens should be neither overgoverned nor preyed upon by
ambitious politicians. This built-in check on leaders—like
Robespierre himself—is a novel feature, betraying a shift to the
Left. Moreover, if we compare this Declaration with its predecessor of August 1789, which gave moral sanction to a revised
and restructured monarchy, set up according to the Constitution
of 1791, certain interesting conclusions emerge. Inspired partly by
Montesquieu's favourite *caveat* and partly by the British system,
the 1789 document lays stress upon *habeas corpus*, whilst, stemming
much more from French sources, the later document underlines
the truth that liberty depends on justice and nature and consequently upon natural law, which, as we have said, was Rousseau's
attitude too. Rousseau also prevails on the property issue to some
extent, for John Locke's ideas of sacred inviolability are now half-
forgotten, though property rights are still respected: in a propagandist document directed against Girondism it was essential not
to offend the middle classes.

Other details are quite striking. For instance, for the very first
time France is to have social services and universal suffrage
without property qualification. Hobbes and Locke may be said to
rear their ancient heads in prompting a strong encouragement to
protest by petition and insurrection and at all times to maintain
vigilance. In short, the 1793 statement reflected not only demo-
cratization during the course of the Revolution, but also Maximilien's growing identification with the man-in-the-street. For
instance, in 1793 all classes were to be subjected to the rule of law,
but in its application magistrates were to be made submissive to
the sovereign will of the populace, just as citizens were to legality.

The shift towards human rights was accentuated in the speech
which Robespierre made to the Convention on December 25.[13]
This masterly 'Christmas' homily—and the date was not casually
selected—followed close on the heels of the law which, on December 4, had constituted the Revolutionary government of the
French Republic. After some preliminaries, Robespierre established the true function of such a government, namely to guide
the moral and physical energies of the people of France. Since
revolution was warfare, circumstances could not possibly be

regarded as normal. For instance, a constitution crowns the edifice of freedom, once victory has been achieved; meanwhile it has to await that outcome, because a revolutionary government should allow itself more freedom of action than democratic, peace-time governments enjoy. Here Maximilien made a subtle distinction between civil liberty and public liberty, the first being principally the aim of constitutional, the latter, the concern of revolutionary government. In the first case, the citizen was to be defended against the State; in the second, against enemies at home and abroad.

Having broken free from his first mandate, Maximilien could now cultivate the social class he had idealistically sought at the very beginning of the Revolution, when we found him keeping company with three Artesian peasants during his early days at Versailles, a couple of years before he lodged in Paris with a master joiner. The people were his friends and he could trust them—so ran the argument, based on the sincere belief that the Revolution was aimed partly at restoring public opinion to its rightful place as the sanction for important national decisions. How could expression of popular opinion be anything but salutary, seeing that 'the evils of society never come from the people, but from the government'?[14] There was no suggestion here that the people get the government they deserve. 'The people are sublime!' declared the enraptured democrat.[15]

In this assessment, the people can do no wrong. It is unrealistic, because Robespierre has been guilty of exaggeration, and for another reason also. It will not have escaped the reader's notice that the word *people* has been used without any account being taken of its unfortunate ambiguity—an ambiguity best illustrated from Voltaire's *Lettres philosophiques*,[16] which define the people on one occasion as a part of society to be contrasted with *honnêtes gens* and with men of taste generally and, on another, as the most virtuous and the most respectable section of society, consisting of students of arts and science, businessmen and artisans (not journeymen). If the Sage of Ferney could do no better than that, what chance had men involved in very practical politics of finding a more precise or consistent definition? After all, at the end of a century which had become accustomed to dividing society into three orders and had seen the triumph of one, it was natural to forget that the Third Order consisted of bourgeoisie and manual workers, who were regrettably becoming more and more divergent in their policies and aims as the Revolution progressed. Faced with the impossibility of reconciling the two, Maximilien had to move with the times or be left behind. So, deciding like Rousseau that the least cultivated must necessarily be the least depraved, he opted for the workers. No longer did he stress the distinction between the *vulgaire* and the *penseur*, as he had done in 1784,[17] but the problem could not be swept under the carpet. Even the expert Rousseau had not been able to make it clear how ignorant, simple-minded folk could acquire enough intelligence to participate in government. He had not been able to do so, because the task was impossible. Working men were not at that time able to govern themselves and there was no sense in pretending that they were. Hence an opportunity arose to win their support for a resourceful compromise, by which the General Will would be canalized into controlled modes of self-expression. In such a system of indirect self-expression the trained lawyer was willing to be cast in the role of Legislator—playing the part of one sympathetic to the popular cause and therefore the ideal man to represent untrained minds; and, in case anyone noticed the snag in all this, in January 1792 he made this bold claim, anticipating Balzac's character, Vautrin: 'I am of the people!'[18]

Naturally a man with this vision of his own identity was likely to supply a socialist definition of democracy and one with which modern republics could scarcely quarrel: 'Democracy is a state of affairs in which the sovereign people, guided by laws it has made, achieves for itself what it can and through delegates what it cannot.'[19] So a delegate he would be, never unmindful of his mission or his mandate. To French journalists he still appeared as the 'faithful friend of the *sans-culottes*'[20] and the workers found in the Incorruptible a person to understand their fears in the political, if not in the economic sector.

The power of the working-class was a new factor in French politics and Robespierre was largely responsible for its full emergence and encouragement. Self-identification with the General Will afforded him access to that great source of power, which totalitarians turn to advantage in our own time. To oppose Maximilien and his popular government was to become an 'enemy of the people'. To diverge from the Committee of Public

Safety was to bring the whole *sans-culotte* organization against you. The definition was clear-cut now: 'people' meant *common* people.

So the workers became Maximilien's main sanction and chief shield—a shield increasingly necessary as his identification with the Left added to the army of royalist foes a new force of middle-class Frenchmen (mainly of provincial origin like himself), who regarded Robespierre as a traitor to his class. After the murder of Marat in July 1792 had brought home to him the realization that no Revolutionary tribune was safe from attack, Maximilien used the *sans-culottes* even more in his own defence; and, during this crucial period of his career, a cobbler from Arras slept like a watch-dog outside his bedroom door and the typographer, Nicolas, served as a permanent bodyguard. Indeed, more often than not, he employed three *sans-culottes* for personal security, three men armed to the teeth and ready for anything. If he dined away from home, he had pistols lined up with cutlery on each side of his plate and never ate anything unless someone else had tried it first.

Robespierre continued to enjoy the confidence of the *sans-culottes* almost until the end of his life. Even the harsh Prairial Law, which brought upon his head the opprobrium of the provinces, of Europe and of posterity, met with fairly general approval amongst the Paris workers, who feared prison breaks and royalist and clerical reprisals. The honeymoon continued in fact into mid-1794, when political ideals and economic realities could no longer be reconciled. Just as it was rash of the Girondins to assume that working-men were never fit to rule, it was equally silly of Robespierre to believe that they were always and in every case filled with virtue and fired with good intentions. The simple fact is that the Parisian rabble were a mixed pack of pitiable underdogs, unprincipled wolves and other assorted beasts of prey interested only in appetites, food and survival. To surround any class of society with a halo of moral rectitude was stupid[21]—just as stupid as the earlier eighteenth-century assumption that all shepherds and shepherdesses were delightful, gracious, sweet-smelling and elegant. It was clearly untrue to say that the rich were essentially egotistical and the poor essentially altruistic; it was also untrue that riches promoted corruption and privation provided moral benefits. The poor were insulted at the suggestion, claiming that poverty engendered crime rather than virtue; and, faced with the rising cost of a loaf, in the end they despatched to the guillotine this naïve roundsman who failed to deliver bread at the right price.

Poor Robespierre! He lacked the equipment with which to run a working-class movement. He needed a different background and education. He lacked the theories of a Marx or a Lenin and he knew little about trade unions, which existed only in reactionary, embryo form. He does not even appear to have been unduly concerned about workers' rights under the Le Chapelier Law, which made strikes illegal. The Reign of Virtue would solve all that, he mused. He was handicapped in other ways too. Politics gradually ceased to be politics and became religion. Immersed in rosy dreams and noble abstractions, he forgot what the man-in-the-street, for whom he was slaving so hard, really looked like. The classic type of gentleman lodger, he dressed unlike the people he represented. Madame Duplay did his shopping, waited upon him and saw to his laundry. In short, he never actually bought a loaf of bread—the root-cause of nearly all great disturbances.

Throughout history men remote from grim reality and real experience have been known to espouse the workers' cause and tell them how to run their lives. In the end they have nearly always reaped a harvest of angry disillusionment. So it was with Robespierre. The idealist who liked to consider himself 'The Voice of France' would one day have his vocal organ severed from his body by the same beloved French people he had so often flattered and who had proved quite different from the reasonable and intelligent Jacobins he knew best. So it transpired that the *peuple français* of reality were unlike the *peuple légal* who fitted so snugly into dreams, schemes and constitutions. The man who on February 25, 1793 had declared 'I have maintained . . . that the people are never wrong' and who on another occasion was heard to say 'I know of nothing great apart from the common people', must surely have changed his mind in his last hours when the 'virtuous' *sans-culottes* deserted and reviled him.[22]

Chapter 12

VIVE LA FRANCE!

'Le patriote n'est autre chose qu'un homme probe et
magnanime dans toute la force de ce terme'

ROBESPIERRE

It was the Scottish writer Smollett who said that 'true patriotism is
of no party'. In his last great speech to the Convention on July 26,
1794, Robespierre too argued that true patriotism, which he
taught by means of symbolic fêtes, is not a matter of sectarian
politics, but of the heart. Now cynics might well enlarge upon this
by observing that, in his case, the psyche was even more important
than the heart; that his patriotism was in reality an extension of
paranoia, a symptom of sickness rather than noble enthusiasm.

Patriotism can be positive or negative. Positively it can manifest
itself in love for the native land, in ardent zeal for a national cause,
in determination to erase defeat or celebrate a triumph. In this
respect Robespierre was lacking. Even when, on February 5, 1794,
he seemed to be defining patriotism more positively, it is clear that
the true patriot was envisaged chiefly in contrast with the hypo-
critical, argumentative 'false revolutionary'.[1] So, whilst he had
occasionally waxed eloquent ('I am a Frenchman . . . Oh, sublime
people!'),[2] he was never as effective as, say, Danton, especially after
military successes, in which he discerned disquieting prospects of
either complacency or dictatorship. So he was a sour, dour fellow,
this atrabilarian from Arras, this anaemic person almost without
patriotic emotion, since in times of stress he was never sure of the
fidelity of his compatriots.

Virtually alone, we recall, he had opposed the declaration of war
in 1792. He had done so because he felt that hostilities might benefit the enemy at home, the opponents of the Revolution itself, and
because it might advantage the external foes of France, who could
well overwhelm a nation so unprepared. War, he argued, is best
waged when men have their backs to the wall, defending their
homes or repelling invaders. Conversely, war waged by professionals or mercenaries, campaigning beyond the frontiers in the
cause of glory, were anathema to him.[3] Professionals he distrusted.

The best example of this is La Fayette,[4] who justified his suspicions by defecting. If forced to choose, he preferred private soldiers to officers. Time and again he defended other ranks against commanders. For example, when Bouillé took rigorous measures against the mutineers at Nancy, Robespierre gave passionate support to the rebels.[5] Fearful lest a military junta should seize power, he repeatedly demanded civil control of affairs and he who had once opposed conscription came to favour the National Guard as the lesser evil.

Compromise he urged on another occasion—the Nootka Sound incident.[6] In May 1790 a dispute had arisen between England and Spain for ownership of this strategic point on the Pacific coast of North America; and, when the French 'Foreign Minister' announced that the king had ordered the fleet to prepare for hostilities, Robespierre warned the Assembly to keep the reins of decision firmly in their own hands, whilst at the same time adopting a conciliatory attitude. The king, he affirmed, had no right to declare war, for he was merely a servant of the State. Finally, on May 22, the Assembly concurred: war could be declared only by a decree of the legislative body, still acting on a proposal from His Majesty and sanctioned by him—a victory for compromise and constitutional power.

Alas, it is difficult to maintain principles when your whole way of life is in jeopardy, and especially when you are in charge of a nation at risk. In 1793–94, involved willy-nilly in directing conflict, Maximilien did his best. For example, reluctantly he began to praise the army more than before, describing it as the glory of France and of humanity.[7] Consequently, although the real hey-day of the French army dawned after Thermidor, by the spring of 1794 it was obvious that the morale of the French forces had taken a turn for the better. The Austrian Ambassador, who now resided in Brussels, explained to his Foreign Minister in Vienna the resurgence of spirit in France, the enhanced authority of the Convention and the great Committee, and the essential unity of the nation. Above all, he pointed out that the *bleus'* devotion to their country was based on incentives such as freedom, promotion, reasonable pay, good food and the abolition of severe punishments. In particular, he mentioned that the bread ration was distributed on the evening before it was due, which meant that by European standards the supply position was quite enviable. The

Ambassador put his finger on the real advantage of service in the French army when he explained that in a citizen force the common man was the real leader and hero, the pampered darling of a Republic which would rather sacrifice a general than offend the susceptibilities of the plebeian patriots.[8] Thanks to these methods, the unwilling generalissimo won the war and by so doing helped both to make himself redundant and clear the way for his successor.

Whilst admiring some aspects of Robespierre's principles and later imitating a few himself, the successor whom the Incorruptible had feared most in imprecise prospect was a stern critic of his handling of action in the Revolution. As a gifted professional soldier himself, Bonaparte considered that Robespierre's failure to grasp the advantages of military power was the main cause of his undoing. The Corsican was indeed a shrewd judge of such things. The fatal flaw discerned by the future Emperor of France developed into a mighty fissure on the 8–9 Thermidor, when military operations were left to the drunken Henriot;[9] when time was lost and the slender forces of the Convention were unexpectedly allowed to prevail in Paris, the true home of the Commune and the *sans-culottes*. Had Maximilien cared to make appropriate use of force, what a different story might have been written about the month of July 1794! It was Madame de Staël who referred to Bonaparte as 'a Robespierre on horse-back',[10] but, as we have seen, that spirited mount made all the difference.

His trouble lay in shrinking from violence, hurting and from being hurt. How he would have detested 'the bomb'! He even rejected the design for a cannon designed to fire twenty-five shots a minute, since, in the hands of tyrants, it might help to subdue the populace.[11] Being of a sensitive, introspective disposition, he shrank from any but the inescapable aspects of the problem of violence in society; and he never completely stifled his natural aversion from a hateful necessity. The aversion was long-standing. At school he was the kind of boy who would rather spend his time composing verses than punching his contemporaries. Distaste crystallized into principle and we saw how, as a young lawyer, he went off his food for two days after passing the death sentence in the Bishop's Court; how the strain indeed became so great that he had to tender his resignation from a lucrative post—surely the acid test of sincerity. At heart completely anti-Draconian, Maximilien anticipated nineteenth-century thinkers and reformers (and, in particular, Bentham and Peel) in condemning capital punishment. May 30, 1791 found him stoutly maintaining that the new penal code of the constitutional monarchy should not include a death sentence and supporting his views by quoting examples from Greece, Rome, Russia and Japan.[12] So, borrowing Madame de Staël's expression, we conclude that, 'horseless' by nature, he was transformed into an unwilling chair-borne warrior, who kept away from the Front and refused to rejoice at military successes; or, as he himself said, 'I am one of the most suspicious and most melancholic patriots to emerge since the Revolution began'.[13]

The negative aspect of Robespierre's distorted patriotism emerges mainly in xenophobic distrust. Coming from the north of France, much-invaded and close to hostile territory, he began with a disadvantage in any case. To heighten a suspicious insularity, he travelled rarely and then only between Arras and Paris. This restricted view of the world supplied a fertile soil in which narrow-mindedness could flourish.[14] With the occasional exception of Americans and Swiss, he distrusted foreigners[15] in an age when cosmopolitanism was generally the accepted cult and he failed to live up to the international ideals of a proselytizing republicanism. In confirmation, Mathiez explained: 'He never fell prey to idle cosmopolitan day-dreams.'[16]

Worse than mistrust and insularity is hatred; and it was above all upon Britain that most of his distilled venom was poured. Few overseas statesmen have detested the British as much.[17] The British, he averred, were arrant Machiavellian hypocrites. The English parliament was corrupt. When it was suggested that Louis XVI might be replaced by the Duke of York, Maximilien's anger knew no bounds and he denounced the man who proposed this idea as a madman, intriguer and disguised Moderantist.[18] He considered, moreover, that he knew the real villain of the piece: the arch-enemy of the French was clearly William Pitt.[19] Pitt had struck particularly at the French economy. Not only was Robespierre furious that the English Premier had flooded France with forged bank-notes, but he deeply resented the commercial treaty of 1786, which had exposed the rustic French economy to the harsh competition of a relatively advanced industrial nation, ruled by the power of gold, the seat of which was the City.[20] This dour

northerner, who willingly introduced to the Jacobins a Man-
cunian Left-wing delegation seeking affiliation with that club
(April 13, 1792),[21] at the same time detested the capitalists of
London.

Though London was enemy number one, other monarchies had
much to answer for also. Of course, they were hostile to the
French Revolution; but Maximilien's chap-book imagination
embroidered on this simple fact, speculating that in such monarchies vice ruled the roost and that the courts of Europe were
spewing over France a horrid brood of well-paid rogues, intent
upon the ruin of the great cause.[22] For this reason his benevolence
did not extend to aliens currently resident in France.[23] In October
1793, when he feared the consequences of dechristianization,
Fabre d'Eglantine had therefore no difficulty in persuading him
that the growth of atheism and anarchy were traceable to the
foreign fifth-column;[24] and, in the margin of the execution-order
for Hébert, one notes the names of Momoro, De Kock, Proly,
Desfieux, Pereire, Clootz and Dubuisson—all men considered to
be in that category. He was thus clearing out the peregrine refuse
at last in the spring-clean of Germinal.

Just as it was patriotic to purify in this way, it was beneficial to
the Revolution to rid the Republic of an even more insidious
enemy, the wooden-horse represented by treacherous native-born
Frenchmen opposed to the present government and its leader. So
Maximilien became immeshed in a vast web of suspicion, made
up of numerous threads of intelligence spun by agents of many
kinds and of espionage applied to all important men of the Revolution and backed up with notes about habits, weaknesses and
opinions held or expressed since the Constituent Assembly.[25] On
this information he acted when it suited him, and one wonders
whether in fact Admiral, the man who fired at Robespierre's
current *bête noire*, Collot d'Herbois, did so as an agent for Robespierre himself.

The reports Robespierre received were numerous and informative.
Consider a good case. Naturally he did not trust Tallien, the rogue
who had been sent on mission to Bordeaux and was to marry
the delectable Thérèse Cabarrus, later 'Madame Thermidor'.[26]
Evidence to justify suspicions proved to be elaborate and detailed.
Here is one scrap of intelligence about this politician. Having left

the Jacobins at the end of the meeting of 6 Messidor, the suspect waited impatiently for a man with a thick stick at the side door of a house in the Rue (Saint-) Honoré. Finally the man arrived. obviously from the public gallery of the club. They went up the Rue (Saint-) Honoré, up the Rue de la Loi, past the open-air stalls into the right-hand arcade of the Palais-Egalité (Royal). Then they sat at the end of the garden, ordered a *bavaroise* each, came back under the arcades, grasping each other by the arm and speaking in whispers. At eleven they crossed the courtyard and, having reached the square, said good-bye until the morrow. When a cab arrived, the spy drew nearer to overhear what was said to the driver. He learned that Tallien was to be driven to the Rue de la Perle. The companion went to the Rue de Chartres on foot, but, having run towards the Seine, the spy was unable to catch up with him . . . So it continues, full of every fragment of information that could possibly be expected from an enthusiastic agent.

In addition to men used for espionage, it will be recalled that Robespierre had agents and representatives, sent on mission to various parts of France (but generally to trouble-spots), in order to perform some State function or supervise some vital aspect of central policy. To illustrate this, credible historical fiction proves helpful. In a memorable section of *Quatre-Vingt-Treize,*[27] Hugo has his reader visit a public house in the Rue du Paon, Paris, currently favoured by important political tycoons. The date was June 28, 1793. At a table were seated Marat, Danton and Robespierre, the latter dressed in a light-blue coat, nankeen breeches, white stockings, a high cravat, a pleated jabot and silver-buckled shoes— which apparel contrasted strikingly with the much less elegant costume of the other two. On the table was unfurled a map of the Republic and in front of Robespierre lay a pile of papers and despatches, for he never left his work for long. From these documents, he informed his colleagues that the Vendée district had now assumed an all-important role in France's political affairs and went on to substantiate the claim by supplying elaborate proof. He knew, for instance, that a certain captain had recently landed near Pontorson in the bay of the Mont-Saint-Michel. He knew also that guerrilla warfare was being organized in this province of Brittany to coincide with a projected English invasion.

At this juncture, the prospective cloak-and-dagger man entered and was greeted by Danton. Robespierre then plunged *in medias res*, describing the threat from the west and adding that 'The Vendée is more deadly than ten Germanies'. Informed that the new Vendean generalissimo was the Marquis de Lantenac, the agent, Cimourdain, remarked that he knew the man in question, but was surprised to learn through Robespierre's information-network that the Marquis had been in the Vendée for the past three weeks. The orders then delivered to Cimourdain were precise and businesslike. Lantenac was to be outlawed and subsequently guillotined. In order to accomplish this, Cimourdain was approved as delegate of the Committee of Public Safety.

In this scene, which continues with further details of the mission, Maximilien does all the talking, with only occasional and brief interruptions; yet he does not waste words. On the contrary what he says is precise and to the point, and above all, the impression left upon the reader is of Robespierre's superlative efficiency in secret-service matters. All this information stood him in good stead in struggles with awkward colleagues and political rivals. Many are the examples that could be cited, but the classic cat-and-mouse game was played out between a very feline Maximilien and a very sly rodent indeed, who came into the cat's field of vision twice, at the beginning and end of Robespierre's career and was to learn from the currently more powerful animal how to stalk other victims, when he in turn became the predator. We refer of course to Joseph Fouché, shortly to make use of Robespierre's police- and espionage-system under successive régimes. The last blows in the contest were desperately exciting. Just before his fall, Robespierre cleverly replied to one of his adversary's speeches, addressed to the Jacobins. On this occasion he threw into the ring reports from his emissaries about Fouché's sadism.

The future Duke of Otranto defended himself with stealth and insinuation, but Robespierre had not done with him yet, for he fully intended to consolidate temporary gains and advantages. Sending out his best spy, Guérin, he learned that, in the very corridors of the Convention, Fouché had been in close consulta-tion with Léonard Bourdon, Thuriot and Bréard. Had the foxy ex-schoolmaster not gone to earth at this point, it is unlikely that he would have lived long enough to unseat his rival. Luckily for him, he was in fact not present when his redoubtable foe (and former friend) named him several times at the Jacobins, who agreed to exclude from membership this inveterate intriguer.[28]

Expelled thus from the club of his choice, only Fouché's determination turned the tables and sealed Robespierre's fate instead of his own and that of his accomplices; and clearly, till the very last moment, the conspirators' victory could not be regarded as certain. They were playing with death, because they were up against such an accomplished super-sleuth, whose business it was to know all about his potential foes.

Indubitably, when the supreme crisis came, Maximilien's informers had done their work very well indeed. He knew who his opponents were and he knew a great deal about their past and present plans. The question was, however, how to act on this information. The fact that, so well documented by this army of investigators, Robespierre did not manage to save his own skin from the machinations of men like Barras, Tallien and Fouché is explained by his state of mind and by his deep desires at the time of supreme crisis. Like Hamlet, he failed to act because his will-power and determination had been eroded; and, like an even more important person, whom we must consider later, he had other intentions in any case.

Chapter 13

THE NOBLEST WORK OF GOD

'Per Robespierre, il principio dello stato che la Rivoluzione
deve costruire ha un carattere essenzialmente morale...'

CATTANEO

Mirabeau is reported to have remarked that the young orator,
Robespierre, would go a long way, because he believed what he
said[1]—obviously a rare quality in the Assembly. Though he had
toyed with esotericism in his Arras days, both as a Mason and
Rosarian, Maximilien was clearly inclined to sincerity, until, at the
time of the Fête de l'Etre Suprême, he could gaze at the vast multitude and soliloquize: 'This is the most interesting section of
humanity. Oh nature; how sublime and delicious is thy power!'[2]
This ejaculation, given beneath his breath, may be accounted the
more sincere because it was made for himself (but accidentally
overheard). Rhetorical, lyrical, ingenuous, high-flown, it was the
exclamation of the Man of Feeling obliged by a sudden effusion to
bare his heart as he envisaged the possibility of the Reign of
Virtue.

Paradoxically—the age was full of such contradictions—virtue
had been very popular throughout the permissive century initiated
by Fénelon, who had belaboured a supposedly future dauphin
with his exemplars. Preached initially by Madame de Lambert, it
had been consecrated by novelists like Marivaux, who had made
the female defending her honour into a best-seller long before
Richardson thought of it. The struggle was in fact the selling-
point. It is well known that virtue does not bring its own reward,
so realism ousts idealism. Society tires of the constant triumph of
good over evil, casts off the straitjacket and becomes as interested
in bad boys on the prowl as in good girls on the defensive. By the
end of the century the shocking novel was exceptionally attractive
to an epoch which filled a gloomy irreligious vacuum with magic,
pseudo-science and necromancy. Thus, without perhaps fully
realizing it, the Incorruptible was destined to defend the old-
fashioned author of the *Nouvelle Héloïse* (who told of a seducer
redeemed by love) against Laclos (whose *Liaisons dangereuses*

recounted the seduction and ruin of a good married lady); against even more lurid ideas expounded by a schoolfellow from Louis-le-Grand, Sade, whose 1791 *Justine* demonstrated how virtue may lead to disaster and vice to profit. So, in a Miltonian epic contest, Robespierre was to take sides in favour of the standards of Julie d'Etanges and her preceptor against the immoral attitudes of Valmont or Cœur-de-Fer.

He had cast down the gauntlet in the very first of his works, where he had proclaimed his guiding principle: 'Nothing is useful if it is not honourable.'[3] Maximilien's brand of ethics was indeed of the penny-plain variety. Pragmatism—that indeed was a thread that had run through the whole eighteenth-century intelligentsia, which, to a man, had proclaimed that metaphysics were to be eschewed or disdained. To a man also, the writers of the century had been fascinated by metaphysical problems and in this contradiction Robespierre looks back to the *Philosophes*, rather than forward to Victor Cousin. Interested, then, in morals first and foremost, he clung nevertheless to two basic beliefs: first, the existence of some sort of god; secondly, the fact of divine Providence. Not always sure about the soul, he often inclined to the doctrine of immortality—if only for the peace of society—and, in his latter days, came round to accepting it himself.

God, however, was really all that mattered; but what sort of god? As Montesquieu had observed, if triangles invented a deity, they would give him three sides, like themselves.[4] So, being a lawman, Robespierre made a god in his own professional likeness. The image-making had begun at the start of the ten-year period of productivity in Robespierre's life—in 1784, in fact, when in the same breath he spoke in the *Discours sur les peines infamantes*, at one point of the laws of the Supreme Being sanctioned by their natural consequences, and immediately after that, of *le droit naturel*.[5] In quasi-classical terminology the theme was continued in the *Eloge de la Rose*, where we find an image of the divinity 'engraved on our hearts'—the stock deist phrase in such cases[6]—and in the *Discours sur la nécessité de révoquer les décrets* of 1791, where the author spoke about an Eternal Legislator whose immutable decrees were 'deposited' in human reason and in the hearts of all men.[7] Later in the same year, the *Discours sur l'inviolabilité royale* revealed that natural laws were anterior to positive law and applied to mankind

as a whole.[8] On June 6, 1792, the author of this *Discours* spoke
again on the same subject—that is, of eternal laws engraved on
our hearts; and the following May found him arguing, in the
Discours sur la Constitution, that political tyranny disturbed both
nature and legality.[9] On February 5, 1794, Maximilien spoke on
les principes de morale.[10] This speech too contained a reference to
eternal justice, to laws engraved on our hearts—a theme which
was to be duly consecrated a few weeks later during the Fête de
l'Être Suprême, the consummation of a long struggle to create the
image of a deity uniting nature and law, the basic sanction for
legality, of which all men have concepts.

Undoubtedly, Robespierre's god was the god of most eighteenth-
century deists; but, though he resembled these *Philosophic* forebears in fundamentals, he parted company with them over
elaboration upon those fundamentals. They investigated and
speculated further; he did not and, by not bothering to go beyond
the most elementary beliefs, he avoided a number of nasty pitfalls.
For example, he did not share Voltaire's dismay at the 'divine'
Locke's uncomfortable and inconvenient claim that customs vary
throughout the world and that what can be considered good in
one country may be sinful in another. Secondly, by avoiding discussion of Lockian epistemology (that is, the denial of innate
ideas), Robespierre did not need to adopt the Voltairian compromise that notions of natural law are *not* innate ideas, but a
'disposition', later developed at about the age when we realize
that two and two make four! Thirdly, by failing to mention
Montesquieu's awkward doctrine of climatic determinism (according to which national character and even individual characters are
influenced by the latitude in which we live), he avoided an unfortunate contradiction implicit in the *Persian Letters* which end
with the apotheosis of universal, natural law, and yet suggest that
climate causes human variations. Finally, though he showed
determinist inclinations—for instance, when he said that 'No man
has the right either to arrest the working out of his destiny, or to
contradict its supreme will'[11]—he does not appear to have noticed,
or bothered about the dilemma in which true fatalists find themselves, namely that they leave no room for manœuvre and retain
no reason for struggle. In other words, fatalism inhibits choice
and effort. Of course, had he realized this contradiction, Robespierre would have brushed it aside, since his whole life's work was

directed towards spurring his fellows to reforming their way of life.

If he skirted dialectic difficulties in these directions, he invited trouble by adding theism to basic deism—in other words, by walking blindly into the problems raised by the special intervention of the deity in a universe regulated by rules of immutable nature. Pantheism and Providence are awkward bed-fellows. He did not realize this fact and, like Bossuet or Mézerai more than a century before, Maximilien was a Providentialist. This he revealed when he alluded in a speech to the death (on March 1, 1792) of the hated Emperor, Leopold. Having long considered that God created men to be equal and happy and therefore safe from the oppression of tyrants, the theistic politician gave his opinion to the Jacobins. God had removed one of France's outstanding enemies without the military taking a hand in the event. 'Providence, which watches over us much better than our own wisdom can do, by striking down Leopold appeared for a certain time to confound the projects of our enemies . . .'[12] As he further explained: 'I call providence what others will perhaps prefer to call chance, but the term providence accords better with my own sentiments'.[13] He believed in a personal God, therefore, but at the same time in the God of the People; for without divine support, they would not have been able to sustain the Revolution. Atheists never forgave him for this remark; rationalists derided such a countrified, Old-Testament approach to essentials. Voltairian Girondins smiled at this seventeenth-century *pastiche* in Revolutionary guise—Providence with a Phrygian cap, no less. Now they had him at a distinct disadvantage and were jubilant.

Though he knew that he was swimming against a current that might overwhelm and drown him, the Providentialist continued to defend his theism, arguing that to use the name of the Divinity was not to invoke servitude. Having been a 'bad Catholic' (even at school the Abbé Proyart reproved him for agnosticism), he was able hotly to deny that he had a clerical bias or a soft spot for the Roman Church.[14] Rather, he claimed, his views had been hammered out on a personal anvil of soul-searching and suffering. Rousseau had often argued that contact with divinity, coupled as it was with convictions about design and guidance, afforded the strength to carry on. Maximilien agreed wholeheartedly:

'Yes, to invoke the name of providence and postulate an idea of the Eternal Being, who essentially influences the destinies of nations and who appears to me to watch over the French Revolution in a very special way, is not a notion that is excessively rash, but a sentiment quite necessary to me ...'[15]

The convictions of the *Vicaire savoyard* also encouraged him to demand that the Jacobin Club should destroy the bust of an enemy of Jean-Jacques, the noted atheist, Helvétius;[16] and in December 1793 he risked the exasperation of the *enragés* by declaring that anti-clerical demonstrations were the work of foreign agents.[17]

A few days before that he had expounded the Government's religious policy as being: religious freedom and freedom of worship, provided that no disturbance of public order ensued; on the other hand, the right of French *communes* to suppress public worship in their areas; the necessity of belief in a Supreme Being.[18] The last item was the most important, because Robespierre considered the existence of a deity necessary to good government and because he was sincerely committed to making virtue prevail. He had not been called the Incorruptible for nothing and intended to live up to the title. He even said grace before meals and, at the risk of angering sophisticated decadents, the man who (thinking of Wolmar in *La Nouvelle Héloïse*) claimed, on November 21, 1793, that atheism was aristocratic but Providentialism democratic and even added the well-worn *Philosophic* tag: 'If God did not exist, we should have to invent Him',[19] persisted in refusing to imitate the *Philosophes* in all things. Indeed, he accused the Encyclopaedist enemies of Rousseau of reducing egoism to a system (and here once more he was tilting at the memory of Helvétius); of judging human society a mere battle of cunning; of regarding success as the touchstone for discrimination between just and unjust and honesty as a question of taste and decorum. In saying these things Robespierre was quite egregiously frank; and on May 7, 1794, went to suggest that this sect 'went far beyond the destruction of religious prejudice'.[20] What he obviously did not understand was that his idol Rousseau had equally gone much too far by launching the idea of an extreme, yet theoretical democracy which, in practice, was to produce illiberal, totalitarian régimes, with the regrettable consequence that the would-be promoter of happiness achieved widespread misery. Maximilien could not foresee this, because he was basically a religious, rather than a political, animal. The great Genevan precursor had disagreed with the *Philosophes* chiefly about religion. That was enough for Maximilien.

On December 5, 1793, he had reprimanded those who were attacking the Church;[21] and on the morrow the Committee of Public Safety had issued a decree about religious freedom which satisfied many unbelievers. Nevertheless, by believers and unbelievers alike it was much abused and led both to fanaticism and anti-clericalism; so further clarification of government policy was requested by agents entrusted with the job of applying that policy in the provinces. Thus it became imperative as quickly as possible to formulate a statement of principle, which, far from being worked out to please Robespierre alone, was drawn up largely to help *représentants en mission* in their relations with provincials.

The stages of the formulation of this new State religion follow logically. Mindful above all that he was a lawyer-moralist, on February 5, 1794, he provided a sketch of the new cult, based almost entirely on jurisprudence and ethics.[22] First, he claimed that the purpose of good laws was to suppress cruelty and to stimulate benevolence; thus, for instance, there was nothing wrong with ambition, provided that it led to public service; nothing wrong with distinctions, provided they arose from equality. Citizens should submit to magistrates and magistrates should be answerable to the people, who in their turn were answerable to officers of justice. It was the business of the State to ensure the welfare of all its citizens, and the duty of the citizens to make the country prosperous and glorious. The arts should serve the cause of liberty, which gave them dignity. Commerce should provide public, rather than private, opulence and luxury. Continuing similar themes culled partly from the pages of Montesquieu, he stressed that egoism was nationally ruinous. In the new order, selfishness was to give way to morality and honesty was to replace the old-fashioned aristocratic and monarchical notion of honour. Principles were to be more important now than habits, duty more precious than decorum, reason more powerful than tyrannical fashion. Vice was to be held in contempt, as were insolence and vanity. Instead of good company, Frenchmen were to prize good men; instead of intrigue, they were to esteem merit, preferring genius to wit, and truth to ostentation. The charm of happiness was to be accounted more precious than mere pleasure, which was boring. Recognition of man's true grandeur was to supersede respect for 'greatness', as previously defined. Thus the sermon can be summed up almost as a Rousseauist exercise. All men are born equal and free, but society corrupts. We must therefore return to nature, that is to natural goodness, since man is born good also. Then reason will no longer be obscured and we shall readily perceive the right road to follow. When we take that road, we shall rediscover natural equality and liberty.

This blazing beacon was intended to guide the nation away from self-indulgence and the agnostic hedonism of pre-Revolutionary aristocratic and bourgeois society towards the New Jerusalem of simple citizenship with its bright aspect and pure hearts. France was henceforth to be a model for other nations, a glorious paradigm of true democracy, striking fear into the hearts of oppressors and giving hope to underdogs.

In pursuit of these 'Troglodyte' ideals, as Montesquieu would have called them, it was essential to crush all enemies at home and abroad. Good people should be guided by reason and their enemies exterminated. Of course, as we have discovered already, under war conditions comfort had to give way to an amalgam of virtue and terror, the latter being nothing more than quick, inflexible justice and, therefore, in itself a promoter of virtue. So, whether or not he was the author of the *Eloge de Depaty*, Robespierre now aspired to emulate that *parlementaire*, referred to in the work as 'a man who was incorruptible, intrepid and fair-minded'.[23]

Maximilien then dealt a formidable blow at atheists: in March 1794 the Hébertists went to the guillotine; but atheism was not dead and, whilst its devotees could vaguely tolerate a form of deism, they would not accept pseudo-Christianity. The word is chosen deliberately for, despite denials, Robespierre had undoubtedly shown some un-revolutionary softness towards certain elements in the Church, the organization which had given him his chance in early life. In striking at atheists too, he was suspected of advocating a watered-down version of Christianity—the first step towards a Concordat. His critics need not have worried unduly on this account, however, for memories of a corrupt and decadent Church were too fresh in French minds to permit such a restoration yet. Indeed, there is really no solid reason to suspect that

Maximilien desired such a change. It was as a *secular* moralist that he persisted in his efforts to tidy up the Republic, for he was certain that otherwise it would perish, as surely as the decadent *Ancien Régime* had done; and it was also as a secular moralist that he completed the Germinal purge by striking at the Indulgents in April—another step in the creation of the Platonic State. However, this second onslaught upon the Augean stables was destined to be more Herculean than the first, since some very prominent democrats were involved. Moreover, if they were corrupt, they were now part of a vast network of wickedness.

It was extremely unusual to be pure and unsullied in 1793-94, when there were so many fat supply contracts for arms, for food and for uniform and so many possibilities of blackmailing trembling aristocrats and rich burghers, destined for the next list unless they 'greased' the appropriate palm. It was easy to profiteer and difficult to remain incorruptible, for, in the course of an upheaval. idealism wears thin or is stretched to utter tenuity; and many lose that first flush of enthusiasm for liberty familiar to students of Wordsworth in Blois. However, the fact is that a handful of leaders —Couthon, Marat and Robespierre, for example—retained their ideals and their standards, at the same time keeping an eye on colleagues and associates of dubious allegiance to the cause. Thus the guillotine, *Louison*—thus called after the king who helped to design its blade, only to become its victim—worked chiefly against turncoats, corrupt politicians and lapsed administrators. Some Government representatives and agents, encouraged to crime by self-indulgent, predatory mistresses, as Tallien was, were behaving worse than the *aristos* they had come to obliterate; and, with men like Fabre and Danton in it, the Government itself was not much better. The bucolic Fabre d'Eglantine was a light-weight and a coward. There was not much to worry about there; for the public would understand that he was involved in the Indies Company Scandal and condemn him readily; but popular, eloquent Danton was an entirely different matter and, as the trial showed, was capable of exciting approval to such an extent that the case nearly went the wrong way. Nor was his crime quite so obviously heinous. For, though his private budget revealed undisclosed sources of income to sustain a lavish expenditure beyond the means of one in his position, it could be argued that it had been on the whole patriotic to arrange, via Dumouriez and other Masons, that the Duke of Brunswick should 'lose' the Battle of Valmy in exchange for the Blue Diamond of the Golden Fleece, 'stolen' from the royal *garde-meuble* in the Place de la Révolution and conveyed to the German Freemason at precisely the right moment to make him change his mind.[24]

If clean hands were uncommon amongst such men, so were clean minds, and this angered Maximilien just as much. It was surely truly Gallic of Danton to insist that the best expression of virtue was the nightly act with his new spouse.[25] The average Latin could understand that remark, but the puritanical northerner could not. Rabelais had not been raised in his part of the world. We have seen already that in fact Robespierre disapproved of sex jokes and had perceived in Danton's salacious flippancy a jibe at the very basis of Robespierrist politics. On this issue the two leaders divided most sharply. For Danton virtue was sex: for Maximilien it was terror. These attitudes were irreconcilable. Ironically, Danton perished, yet prevailed; for counter-revolution was being prepared during Robespierre's rule, by unprincipled, pleasure-loving, self-indulgent scoundrels against dedicated men who had risked their necks and sacrificed their comfort to the cause. But in the spring of 1794 the virtuous few were holding on to precarious superiority and continuing the crusade against sin.

Robespierre's report on the relationship between religious and moral ideas on the one hand, and republican precepts on the other, was presented to the Convention on May 7, 1794 and it restated several basic principles.[26]

The author began by discussing the thorny question of progress—a topic very dear to eighteenth-century audiences. Pointing out that civilization is an accomplished fact, he claimed that man had changed the face of nature by his developing technology—for instance, crops had replaced forests, to the benefit of mankind—but progress had not been uniform over the whole spectrum of human activity. Taking a cue from the arch-enemy of *Philosophic* atheists, he affirmed that, though the arts and sciences had made marked advances, man's nature had remained undeveloped and even brutish. This was particularly true in the realm of ethics and made it difficult to tell people about their rights and duties. That was the fault of heads of State who, in their selfish desire for power, had deliberately denied influence to those who would have helped most—the true philosophers and thinkers, as opposed to geometers, poets and painters. The moral nostrum of February 5 had obviously not been taken by those patients who needed it most, so he repeated the dose with slight modifications. The remedy for all this delinquency and misguidance lay in substituting the pursuit of education and enlightenment for the pursuit of luxury and pleasure. It lay also in creating good institutions which would aid mankind in its quest for social morality.

This vehement saline was followed by the vital decree setting up the Worship of the Supreme Being, couched in simple formulae. First, the French people recognized the existence of a Supreme Being and the immortality of the soul. Secondly, they acknowledged that the kind of worship best suited to this Supreme Being consisted in doing one's various duties. Thirdly, these duties amounted to hating bad faith and tyranny, punishing tyrants and traitors, relieving the victims of misfortune, respecting the weak, defending the oppressed, doing good to one's neighbour and being unjust to no man. Fourthly, it was decreed that fêtes should be instituted to keep these ideals before mankind and remind man of God and his own dignity. Fifthly, these festivals were to take their names from the glorious events of the Revolution, from virtues dear and beneficial to men and from the great bounties of nature. Sixthly, the main dates to be celebrated in this way were to be July 14, 1789, August 10, 1792, January 21, 1793 and May 31, 1793. Seventhly, *décadis*, replacing Sundays, would celebrate a whole list of ideas and ideals—for instance, the human race, equality, liberty, patriotism, truth, justice, friendship, maternal tenderness, heroism and so on.

Article Eight invited projects for the organization of such festivals. Article Nine requested the submission of hymns and civic songs specially composed to beautify the proposed ceremonies. Article Ten duly promised rewards for authors of suitable contributions of this sort. Article Eleven was very important, since it confirmed freedom of worship, as laid down in a decree of 18 Frimaire; conversely, Article Twelve banned meetings of aristocrats or anyone else coming together to disturb public order; and the next item promised punishment for fanatics or counterrevolutionaries provoking acts of violence. The last two articles dealt solely with detailed arrangements and set a date for the Fête de l'Être Suprême, the centre-piece of which was to be the symbolic destruction of that effigy representing atheism; after which the apotheosis would be enacted high above workaday Paris. This lofty (and now familiar) setting was backed by ample precedent and noble sanction, quite independent of that which we studied in the chapter on Freemasonry.

Not only does this final tableau in Robespierre's religious pageant betray the influence of the *Contrat social* and the more personal outpourings of the *Vicaire savoyard* on his hillside;[27] another of Rousseau's writings lies behind it. Reminding us that Thomas Jefferson named his dream-house Monticello, the *Lettre à D'Alembert* provides this personal souvenir:

> 'I recall in my youth having seen near Neuchâtel a view which is fairly attractive and perhaps unique on earth—an entire mountain covered with houses, each one lying at the centre of its own plot of land; so that these houses, spaced apart at distances which are equal, like the resources of their owners, afford the many mountain-dwellers both the peace of seclusion and the pleasures of society.[28]

Could Rousseau-loving Robespierre and his obedient slave, David, have resisted the temptation to construct a Rousseauist tribute in the heart of Revolutionary France? Surely they could not, and the results justified their choice. In the inferior aesthetic context of its age, the Fête was quite an artistic triumph and was certainly David's greatest work in the unusual *genre* forced upon him by the Revolution. Indeed, the mound was not unlike some of his own paintings—crowded with detail, resolutely classical and terribly artificial.

Its didactic purpose was recalling citizens to the straight and narrow, at a time when morals were running out; and, borrowed partly from Chaumette's suggestions, like Napoleon's Concordat of some years later the Fête was intended to seal a gap in France's moral sea-walls and to restore unity in an important sector of national life. In order to achieve some sort of harmony, it was necessary to find a mean term between orthodoxy and atheism. It was thought that such a compromise would be best effected by adopting the universal cult, which had already been given currency and respectability by Voltaire, Rousseau and Montesquieu. If their social and political ideas had proved seminal in the Revolution, then it would be reasonable to suppose that their religious ideas would also find favour with the majority of citizens of the Republic, because it was the cult which divided Frenchmen least.

Political motives were much outweighed in Robespierre's table of values by sheer idealism, for, as we have said before, he was moralist above all things. As we saw, Masonic symbolism was largely rustic as well. Remembering the vogue enjoyed in the early Revolution by Trees of Liberty, Maximilien had his mountain adorned with these emblems and numerous other bucolic insignia. Nor did he forget that the Revolutionary calendar drawn up by Fabre d'Eglantine contained a great deal of idealistic symbolism with Physiocratic associations. Humble folk, who had named their daughters Vache, Carotte and Rhubarbe and their sons Chiendent, Canard and Pissenlit without needing to have their tongues firmly in their cheeks, would surely accept the Mountain's adornments. Indeed, it is this incredible ingenuousness and complete absence of Gallic cynicism that helps to explain Maximilien's confidence in the Fête. Like his mentor, Rousseau, he had no sense of humour; and, again like Rousseau, he was an enthusiast for improving people. Thus the famous object-lessons found their way from the pages of *Emile* into the Cult and Feast of the Supreme Being, just as surely as the Bible had found its way into the proceedings of the English Long Parliament.

But Rousseau did not in fact supply the really crucial doctrinal inspiration. Dwarfing all other messages in 1794, was this one: 'The idea of the Supreme Being and the immortality of the soul is a constant recall to the notion of justice.'[29] The highest aim of this midsummer's-dream-of-a-harvest-festival was consequently to renew the spirit of the laws, as this was conceived in Montesquieu's *Esprit des lois* and in the earlier *Lettres persanes*, at the end of which, amid chaos and disorder, the leading lady, Roxane, exclaims: 'I have reformed your laws on the pattern of Nature's laws.'[30] Maximilien's positive moralizing was directed overwhelmingly to this end, for, as a lawyer, he was intent on renewing the law by returning to the essential spirit of law. In this respect, then, the man from Arras was faithful to his other main precursor, the man from La Brède.

Success should have been assured on the dialectic, as well as on the aesthetic plane, since so many citizens were glad that Robespierre afforded them the vision of a way of life different from that of corrupt, cynical, cloacal Versailles. Thousands trusted him and cherished his mammoth integrity. No other politician had his immaculate approach or lived what he taught. For his part, Maximilien alone, the idealist and moralist, was sure that good would triumph over evil in the end: he, alone amongst the surviving foremost politicians of the Revolution, considered man in society redeemable and perfectible; and yet the day was disastrous.

We are told that the Feast was the culmination of a whole year's effort; that it evoked such responses as 'Protector of patriots, incorruptible genius . . . You are my supreme godhead. I regard you as my guardian angel!'[31], but these were by no means general. The difficulty was one of personality and more than that. Every professional man attempts a projection suitable to his status and occupation. Thus we have the doctor-image, the teacher-image, the judge-image and so on. It was in this aspect of his job that Maximilien had failed. The politician's status depends so much on imagery that sheer idealism is not enough. Images have to be carefully drawn, and tenderly preserved, because they are so easily erased; and Robespierre's northern predilection for cheap *images d'Epinal* had not only failed to convert, but actually invited ridicule and hostility. The Fête de l'Etre Suprême did harm also to Maximilien's God and the stark inadequacy of the new cult was now shown up clearly to the French people. The Legislator's authority could not, via the Cult and the Fête, replace that of the abandoned Church. They were not on the same plane, and citizens knew it. There were also those who sensed that it was stupid to hark back to the eighteenth-century cult of a Supreme Being, which appeared to be not only old-fashioned but also counter-revolutionary. Furthermore, there were many who recalled that Robespierre had argued against Cambon's attempt to withdraw financial support from the Constitutional clergy[32] and, seeing that Republican France was not yet ready to deal with the Church again, this fact too was used against him. The substitution of mumbo-jumbo in the Tuileries and on the Champ de Mars for sermons in stone at Chartres or on the portals of Notre-Dame had failed.

Above all, the ostensible glorification of one who was by profession a democrat, but in this new setting apparently a proud dictator, was infinitely damaging to Robespierre's popularity.

Behind the pomp and circumstance of June 8 lurked the menace of repression.

In revolution, it is fitting that a minority should tremble. It is, by the same token, highly perilous to terrify the majority of citizens in order to make them good. In his ivory tower, Maximilien does not appear to have realized that men and women prefer to be happy rather than virtuous. For, in an imperfect world that does not live by absolutes, the two things are not synonymous. People would rather be entertained, flattered and amused, than purged and saved. It was therefore short-sighted of the Incorruptible to imagine that rigid value-judgements can be imposed on a whole nation. The very idea of imposition was, in itself, dangerous. If the Fête achieved anything, it helped to promote the Concordat of 1801, which became the foundation of another brand of tyranny.

Chapter 14

THE GREAT DICTATOR

'Il faudrait ... voir en lui ... un grand homme d'Etat.
Richelieu aurait fait plus que Robespierre s'il se fût
trouvé dans une position semblable'

LOUIS XVIII

The political leader who writes: 'We need one will and one only!'[1]
is bound to arouse the suspicions of liberal democrats; and there
were many less liberal who saw in Robespierre a new Cromwell.
As early as 1792, the opposition were accusing him of such aspirations. On May 3, Marat reported how Guadet had charged the
Incorruptible with having inspired in the *Ami du peuple* an article
calling for dictatorship on the fashionable Roman model.[2] Marat
went on to counter this by rejecting the idea that he was controlled
by this up-and-coming tribune from Arras, and by recounting
how Robespierre had paled in horror at Marat's suggestion that
the workers should have reacted to the Massacre du Champ de
Mars by butchering their attackers and their masters. This timidity
and revulsion were taken by the more resolute politician as clear
proof that the other lacked vision and audacity; but it is also
evidence against Guadet's accusation. Later Robespierre himself
denied the charge, claiming that it was Marat and Marat alone
who had favoured such a course.[3] Furthermore, in self-defence he
maintained that he, Robespierre, had repeatedly demanded a
weaker executive and a stronger legislative; that he had constantly
incited the public to be vigilant about their interests, imperilled by
tyrants, bureaucrats and over-zealous administrators—which was
true, but convinced few people.

After the mini-revolution of August 1792, the Girondins singled
out for their counter-offensive targets men like Robespierre, who
was accused of using the illegal Paris Commune and the extra-
ordinary criminal tribunal to pave the way for personal power. The
arguments taking shape in Louvet's mind since the beginning of
1792 were now poured out before the new Convention. Louvet
accused Robespierre on October 29, and on November 5 Maxi-

milien refuted Louvet's allegation that he had wielded a 'despotisme d'opinion' at the Jacobins:[4]

> 'I know not what is meant by the despotism of opinion, especially
> in a society of free men . . ., unless it is the natural dominion of
> principle. Now, this dominion is not personal . . .; it belongs to
> universal reason and to all men willing to harken to its voice.'[5]

Of course, Maximilien's critics pointed out (and still maintain)
that denial is easy, but that facts cannot be dismissed so glibly. For
four months, from April until July 1794, Robespierre's Committee
ruled France and Robespierre ruled the Committee. Like those
Romans of old he had always lionized, the leader was more faithful to principles than to friends. There was no accepted opposition
now and the guillotine awaited those who impeded the Will of the
People. Despite this convenient tag, there was no direct appeal to
the people or to public opinion: and the Convention's only check
on its dominant Committee consisted in the right of proscription
and arrest and theoretically of refusing to re-elect members to that
body. Whilst it was just possible to maintain that Marat began it
all by launching the September Massacres in 1792, it is impossible
to dismiss with an apologetic shrug the repressive legislation of
the Committee under Robespierre. For example, the Law of
Suspects of September 1793[6] was a thoroughly frightful affair.
Individual freedom vanished overnight. Immediately on publication of the decree, all suspect persons residing in France were to
be arrested and sent before the Tribunal which found itself very
busy. *Les suspects* were defined as those who by their conduct, their
associations, their remarks or their writings were proving to be
supporters of tyranny or federalism and therefore the enemies of
freedom; those who could not, in the manner outlined in a decree
of March 21, 1793, justify their means of subsistence and prove
that they had duly performed their civic duties; those who had
been refused civic certificates by the appropriate board. Suspect
also were civil servants who had been suspended from their functions by the Convention or its commissioners and not subsequently
reinstated, especially those who had been affected by the decree of
August 14, 1793; former nobles, their families and agents of the
émigré aristocrats who had not constantly shown their devotion to
the Revolutionary cause; those who had emigrated from France

between July 1, 1789 and March 30—April 8, 1792, even though they had come back to France within the period fixed or earlier. Yet all this was organized to ensure the 'despotism of freedom' in its struggle against tyranny. Strange as it may appear, the Robespierrist faction did not find the situation ironical.

Even more terrifying was the legislation which on June 10, 1794, followed the Fête de l'Etre Suprême.[7] Spreading the net more widely, the Prairial Law intensified the Reign of Terror. Classified as enemies of the people were all those persons who spread false rumours or confused public opinion and by so doing interfered with the morale of the French nation or sullied the purity of republican principles. Included in this category were those who had praised tyranny or supported federalism by word or deed or by their social contacts. Designated too were former officials dismissed from their posts, all nobles either at home or in voluntary exile and those who had not found useful work to do. Incompetent officials and those who had exposed the nation to danger, as well as those who had impeded the war effort by demoralizing or starving the people, were included in this general category of guilty persons. Worst of all, we have already noted that even members of the Convention were liable to be arrested and condemned; for, though their parliamentary immunity was not specifically at risk, colleagues recalled Robespierre's opposition in 1793 to that immunity and trembled accordingly.

Some of the provisions of this terrible law smacked of total dictatorship. Citizens were encouraged to denounce conspirators and counter-revolutionaries and in addition to the Public Prosecutor, the Committees of Public Safety and General Security and the *Commissaires* of the Convention could bring suspects before the tribunal without further formality. In due course Paris became the headquarters for proceedings and central abattoir for victims. Suspect persons were denied the elementary right of having a lawyer to defend them, a detail which is at first sight strange, when we consider that Robespierre (who drafted some of the clauses in this bill and approved the rest) was a trained lawyer, and inveterate champion of victims of injustice. In time of war, however, it was apparently natural to deny the accused his rights, since by exercising them he might spread royalist propaganda. The further pretext that lawyers cost money (therefore, a defence counsel was an aristocratic luxury and an unfair privilege of the rich) will hardly stand up to scrutiny. Evidence acceptable to 'reasonable' people in itself constituted proof of guilt. Juries did not retire to consider their verdict, but voted openly for or against the accused—for or against death—the only alternative to 'not guilty'! There was no right of appeal. By this legislation the Terror was intensified and some 1,400 victims faced the guillotine between Prairial and the death of Robespierre. The prolonged series of hecatombs in 1794 was the natural consequence of this dreadful law, which may be regarded as unnecessary and anachronistic and which, in final form, had not been submitted in advance to the higher Committee or disclosed to the other one at all.

Prairial was cruel, but it was not the work of Maximilien alone. We have suggested that one might consider that the Terror was launched in September 1792, but officially it was put 'on the day's agenda' by the Convention precisely one year later; so the entire Committee of Public Safety could claim that they were acting as agents of the sovereign legislative body (representing the sovereign General Will). So responsibility could be handed down to the workers themselves; or it could be argued that essentially under democracy terror came from below. There is no doubt that Couthon presented the Law and had much to do with its terms, which incidentally applied effectively only to Paris. Furthermore the legislation had several supporters in high places. For instance, similar definitions of enemies of the State are found in speeches from Carnot (who none the less accused Maximilien of dictatorial aspirations), from Barère and from Saint-Just.[8]

Secondly, it is a mistake to think that Robespierre's absence from the Convention immediately prior to his crisis of 8–9 Thermidor was due mainly to controversy surrounding Prairial. During three weeks succeeding the law, Maximilien's attendances were fairly regular, and it was precisely when the *religious* controversy surrounding the Théot Affair burst upon him on June 15 that Robespierre began to be ill and stay away frequently from the Convention which, since he had by this time saved Cathérine Théot from the guillotine, was now regarding him still more as aspiring to arbitrary rule. The furore was followed closely by that aroused by Robespierre's henchman, Saint-Just, who now accused Carnot of ordering troop movements without consulting the on-the-spot representative of the Committee of Public Safety, Saint-Just himself, and then of making blunders.

In the third place, the text of Robespierre's speech defending the Committee's Prairial Law makes it quite clear that the leader of that Committee regarded the new legislation as less severe than that which the Convention had been demanding for the past two months and that the compelling motive for that legislation was the 'assassin's blade' against which no deputy was safe. If he had not left the initial attack upon the Girondins to the redoubtable Marat, he might have taken the latter's place as victim to Mademoiselle Corday. He talked now about nothing but daggers and, since Marat's murder, had been visibly obsessed by the imminence of violent death, making such comments as this one: 'the honours of the assassin's dagger are reserved for me too ... Priority has been determined by pure chance.'[9] So he had a very good motive for sowing more deterrent seeds of terror.

Robespierre never indulged in terrorism for its own sake, which is another way of saying that he was not a sadist; and the man who dared to be in minority in the great Committee which had such ruthless power over France during the last year of its greatest upheaval could hardly be called a personal dictator. Indeed, he had precisely guaranteed his country against such a development. 'What a strange dictator, this man who had arrayed against himself the principal State powers!', Mathiez claims.[10] In fact, the virtuous leader who executed so many alleged enemies of the people and so many counter-revolutionaries, had the noblest of slogans. 'It is terror concerning crime which guarantees the security of the innocent,'[11] he explained on 8 Thermidor, the very day before he was hurled from the uncomfortable position he had reluctantly occupied for a few brief months.

So we must be fair to Robespierre. Many who had little reason to love him seem to have made the effort. For example, even Madame de Staël remarked that he did not amass riches and, above all, that he did not do what every successful tyrant must do, namely make sure that the military were on his side.[12] Marat, whom the other politician had reproached with talking too much in his columns about ropes and daggers, had doubted this squeamish democrat's qualifications for a totalitarian role, and claimed that Maximilien in fact paled when he saw a sabre.[13] The weapon is not without significance, for, in the hands of the military, it decides the fate of empires ... and republics; but, as we have seen, the Incorruptible

relied on the Word rather than the Sword—another rare characteristic in dictators. The highly critical Le Bon added in 1912 that
amongst tyrants in history, Robespierre was different, because he
was a tyrant without soldiers.[14] Even Anouilh, who is generally
far from sympathetic, concedes that Robespierre wished his awe-
inspiring system of justice to be automatic and impersonal; and,
from the dialogue between this character and Saint-Just in the
second act, it is clear that the leader derived no personal satisfaction from rooting out crime and punishing it. We are in fact
back to the situation in Arras, when he lost his appetite at the
prospect of pronouncing the death sentence. By nature an intro-
vert (unlike Saint-Just and Danton, who loved to be up there at
the Front), this semi-pacifist showed little interest in the armies
for which he was responsible and upon which might ultimately
depend the fate of his régime. On the other hand, in spite of his
natural inclinations, he recognized that they were necessary, just
as he was bound to admit that a dose of terror could be salutary;
and when conscience assailed him, he could always repeat to himself this passage from the *Contrat social*: 'if peril is such that the
apparatus of law may be a stumbling-block to avoid, then a supreme
leader is appointed, who silences the laws . . .[15] Even Rousseau had
authorized emergency measures of this sort for his Legislator.

We return, then, to the question: Was he a dictator? Three
times (July 1, 9 and 11, 1794)[16] this eighteenth-century Shakespearean character—more like Hamlet than Julius Caesar—had
protested that he did not seek absolute power. On numerous
occasions he had observed that he disliked Cromwell as much as
he disliked Charles I,[17] and with obvious sincerity reproved in
others the very traits with which he himself was charged. The
dictator type does not encourage the electorate to be vigilant about
the Establishment and to defend its rights; he does not leave for
posterity a vast heritage of democratic institutions and ideas,[18]
especially that contained in Article XIX of the 1793 Declaration of
Rights, which states: 'law must first and foremost defend public
and individual freedom against the abuse of authority by those
who govern'[19]—surely most undictatorial language.

Other evidence of what we assert is not difficult to unearth. For
instance, his attitude to direct, popular election of the executive
authority, as recommended by Chabot, is thoroughly democratic.
Claiming that he feared the swamping of the legislative body by an

to the men with the big stick.[20] Again, an aspiring dictator would
have acted very differently. Nor does the dictator type allow his
personal and political fate to be tied up with that of a helpless
paraplegic condemned to a wheel-chair or to be carried about by
a gendarme. In emergency a supporter like Couthon could be a
terrible embarrassment. Any ruthless leader would have jettisoned
him long ago.

Always he feared that the Revolution might end in military
dictatorship; so he warned his compatriots about Kellermann and
Westermann, but such sentiments were mild compared with the
strictures prompted by the defection of La Fayette.[21] Anticipating
the developments that were bound to follow and foreseeing the
Brunswick Manifesto, he wrote to Couchon at a time when
intrigues in preparation for the events of August 10, 1792 were
going on around him:

'We are here coming close to the most momentous events. Yesterday
the Assembly exonerated La Fayette; indignantly the people have
pursued several members as they came out from the parliamentary
session . . . ferment is at its height and all seems to foretell for this
very night the greatest commotion in the City of Paris. We are now
at the *dénouement* of the constitutional drama. The Revolution will
move more speedily, if it does not founder in military and dictatorial
despotism.'[22]

His successor had already been unknowingly designated by
Augustin, who, in correspondence with his elder brother,
remarked that 'The citizen Bonaparte has outstanding merit'[23];
but then, Augustin always had more good red blood in his veins
and had criteria different from those of his brother who, for
instance, lacked enthusiasm after the victory of Fleurus, when he
himself was still virtually supreme but feared a coup or *putsch*
initiated by others. Though capable of putting thoughts into
words, he was unable to translate words into action; that was
Robespierre's deficiency and it explains why the Revolution
needed two men, and not one, to steer it into the nineteenth
century.

The deficiency was real and long-standing. The child who was
grateful for the present of canaries, who cried at the loss of a tame

dove, who hated fishing because it involved killing things,[24] would hardly turn out to be the *buveur de sang* of defamatory legend. As he grew up, he did not change much in this respect. There is no record of his attending an execution: he was notably absent when Louis XVI and Danton met their deaths, and he complained to his brother about the violent and bloody methods used by representatives sent to the provinces.[25] The provinces responded in a predictable way. For instance, in November 1793, royalists from Vendée appealed to him to have the plundering of their lands stopped.[26] They did so because he was regarded as fair-minded and the least cruel of the influential statesmen of his time. He himself was proud to be thought so. When the Terror proved to be appalling in its manifestations—for instance, at Lyons and Nantes, where respectively Fouché and Carrier distinguished themselves as bestial sadists—the leader expressed disgust and disapproval, for basically he was anxious to temper justice with as much mercy as was feasible under prevailing conditions. So, with indignation Robespierre protested against charges of cruelty levelled against him personally, and with reason; for he had shown clemency to certain patriots in prison and had pursued representatives and proconsuls who abused their power.

Most significant of all, he had tried to save his enemies, the Girondins, from the worst fate which the *sans-culottes* were demanding.[27] Rising from his sick-bed, Maximilien had spoken in favour of clemency to the Convention, who changed their minds and spared the Girondins from the most extreme penalties; and, when Parisian fanatics had on another occasion demanded the death of 28,000 people who, in 1792, had signed a petition to save the monarch, Maximilien had impeded the progress of immediate retribution.[28] He had done these things at his own peril. What, for example, did Billaud-Varenne and Collot d'Herbois, the *enragé* duo on the supreme Committee, think about these signs of weakness: of his defence of Madame Elizabeth (the king's sister); of the rescue from the scaffold of Louis XV's illegitimate son, the Abbé le Duc; of the kindness he showed towards Marie-Antoinette; of his initial opposition to the proposed judicial murder of Danton?[29] By these actions Robespierre gradually put himself into the position of lagging behind and tending towards reaction. But he could not have behaved otherwise, since even the idea of galley-slaves made him shudder or glow with righteous indignation about injustices. The same feelings assailed him when he thought of underprivileged sections of the community—actors and Jews,[30] for example, who were his special concern because he knew that liberty cannot survive without its Siamese twin, toleration. So when, in December 1789, Maury claimed that French Jews were foreigners, Maximilien protested about anti-Semitism in a State moving towards democracy and equality. French Jews, he maintained, had been turned into the people they were purely by ill-treatment. Treat them well, and they would respond to decency: 'They will behave properly when they find some advantage in being good.'

A most outstanding and meritorious example of Robespierre's kindliness and humanity is furnished by his progressive and advanced views on the colour question, which was beginning to be discussed in more than one European country. For instance, British liberals had said much on the matter. In 1787 Clarkson, Wilberforce and Dilwyn had founded the 'Society for the Suppression of the Slave Trade' and the matter had been debated in parliament. Along with Brissot and the Abbé Gregoire, Robespierre was one of the most eloquent partisans of the French Société des Amis des Noirs and, by 1791, was waging a vehement campaign in favour of the West-Indian Negroes. On September 24 he asked:

'But who is the man, or who are the men, capable of saying to another class of men: I have restored to you the rights of a fully-fledged citizen; I have not withdrawn your political rights, but I am to cast you at the feet of your tyrannical masters!'[31]

In this way Robespierre took sides against white colonial plantation bosses and at the same time reproved Frenchmen like Barnave for going back on their previous decree of May 15, 1791, regarding political and polling rights to be accorded to coloured people in the West Indies—rights which were now to be withdrawn by abrogation of the decree. Unfortunately, in May Robespierre had only been able to persuade the Assembly to give citizenship to Negroes born of free parents;[32] and by September the colonists had organized their opposition to the whole liberal trend, so, after three vehement speeches, Maximilien had to admit that he could not prevail against the conservative and capitalist elements in parliament, for Barnave succeeded in putting mulattoes as well as freed slaves at the mercy of the colonists.[33] Robespierre was proved right, however. Civil war and oppression, accompanied by savage brutality, followed this reactionary move in Paris; and, however unsuccessful the campaign waged by the resolute reformer from Arras, his ideas rang around France. They also justify our claim that he was naturally inclined to justice and tolerance, not to cruelty. His own utterances on colour-prejudice speak for themselves:

'But I, whose idol will be liberty and who know not happiness, prosperity or morality for mankind or for nations divorced from freedom, declare that I abhor such systems and invoke your justice and humanity, justice and national interest, in favour of free coloured men.'[34]

These sentiments were very warmly received in some parts of the House and in all sections of the nation where toleration was appreciated.

Consider finally what happened to the crazy visionary, Cathérine Théot.[35] Surely it would have been wiser to have this old lady guillotined and thus both to silence her wagging tongue and prove that the Incorruptible had no regard for her. Instead, he resorted to mildness and clemency. This took great courage at this particular moment of danger and crisis; a real terrorist or dictator does not behave in this manner. Consequently, Jean Anouilh misunderstands Robespierre on this issue of cruelty; for the Revolutionary leader did not guillotine principally because of his own incapacity for life and for enjoyment; but rather to ensure that ordinary people would have life and have it abundantly. It was in fact to stem the flood which threatened to overwhelm his Republic of Virtue—which was calculated to promote happiness via social justice—that Maximilien was obliged to be tough.

Thus, exposed to impartial scrutiny and subjected to common sense, the great-dictator myth explodes. Subsequent history provides the crowning evidence. The road to Empire was littered with shattered democratic hopes. An executive of twenty-four envisaged in the Robespierrist Constitution of 1793, was reduced to five, then three and finally to one. One year, stipulated in that same document, became five, ten, life and finally an hereditary mandate. That is, *par excellence*, what we expect from régimes and countries slipping into tyranny and dictatorship. The man who held high office *under a Committee*, and *for a mere four months* of hegemony, was clearly not a serious contender for the title of dictator. Even Barras, the crafty one who was to survive and profit by Maximilien's fall, could not escape the truth: that fall was due largely to an attempt to arrest the Terror and mitigate its horrors:

'He opposed the arrest of several members of parliament, of a great many reputable citizens; he paid his respects to God, he spoke of clemency, he perished like Camille Desmoulins and many others for having returned to the principles of justice.'[36]

Other politicians in history have stifled their natural aversion and, had *he* been prepared to do so, the road to dictatorship would have been open. He could have seized control of the thousands of armed men assembled in front of the Hôtel de Ville on the night of 9–10 Thermidor, after which it would have been fairly easy to take over the two State Committees. Once in control of them, Robespierre could have ordered domiciliary arrest of unreliable deputies. With the two Committees in his pocket, the trained lawyer could have manipulated legality in order to rally the Convention, which he knew to be full of cowards delighted to put themselves into a favourable position in case he needed them in his government. With this mass of deputies on his side, the Incorruptible would then have passed laws under the guise of representative government, laws which would have confirmed his totalitarian stranglehold on France. In short, he could have done what Bonaparte was to do, when he saw how Robespierre's native kindliness and concern for law had precipitated the downfall of the Jacobin republic. Yet it was this very difference between the two leaders and their methods which provided history with one of its most dramatic transitions.

If we may borrow a few frames from the typical Hollywood Western, we could imagine that the small, conscientious, be-spectacled lawman, unwillingly created sheriff, was gunned down along with his deputies. Then the town was taken over by a gang of unscrupulous men, whose boss, a ruthless Corsican immigrant,

The *Cabaret* in the *Rue du Paon.*

From left to right, Danton, Robespierre, Marat. Drawing by Herkomer (see p. 135)

Cartoon showing Robespierre guillotining the executioner
because he has run out of victims

(see p. 155)

seized the badge of office and pinned it to his own proud breast. The facts speak for themselves. After the death of the Incorruptible, the symbolic Hydra of Tyranny spawned a vast brood of most horrid offspring, plus one very frightening monster of the species *tyrannus triumphans*.

Chapter 15

THE NON-ECONOMIST

'La dottrina economica di Robespierre è basata sulla visione
essenzialmente morale della società e della politica'

CATTANEO

Was the French Revolution going communist after 1792? It often
looked as though it was. For example, in the early days one had
heard a middle-class slogan, 'Liberté, égalité, propriétés', but the
third panel of the triptych was changed later to the more familiar
'fraternité'. Small details of this sort signposted the road to
socialism and made the bourgeois apprehensive. Many of their
fears were, however, either unfounded or premature, for, though
pre-Marxist statements were already beginning to be made in
some quarters (for instance, amongst the *enragés*), in 1793–94
Babeuf's more specifically communist doctrines were still being
adumbrated and in any case represented a tiny minority view of
society and economics.

Robespierre was at no time a convinced communist, for his ill-
defined socialism did not extend to enforced redistribution of
wealth or nationalization of property and he favoured State control only under war conditions. In assuming this stance, he
undoubtedly represented the majority opinion; yet at the same
time it must be admitted that his view was illogical and short-
sighted. It was illogical, because, fighting for better conditions for
the common man, he must have realized that the unfair distribution of wealth was a fundamental problem and crucial grievance;
it was short-sighted because he should have seen already the
shadow of the Industrial Revolution, with its sweat-shops, dark
satanic mills and heavy emphasis upon economic power—the key
to popular support and social progress. Although he may well
have understood that the French Revolution had been launched
largely by the capitalists and merchants for economic gain, he does
not seem to have realized that his conception of a virtuous Legislator was out of kilter with the principal motivation behind the
social landslide he was trying to direct.

The trouble was that Robespierre was out of date because, as we have said, he was inhibited by his mentor Rousseau, who, unlike the contemporary Adam Smith, had paid more attention to moral than to economic forces, and, on the issue of property and equality, had been irritatingly ambivalent. For, whereas in his second *Discours* Rousseau had argued that contemporary society enshrined inequality, which was unnatural and arose from land-ownership, the article *Economie politique* of the *Encyclopédie* declared unequivocally the sacred right to the possession of property.

Thus Robespierre was, in a sense, still Rousseauist in protecting property-owners. At the same time, he was opposing single-minded extremists like Morelly, whose 1755 *Code de la nature* had alarmed French *bourgeois* with an utopian formula for human happiness centred especially around the problem of equality. The true natural laws, claimed Morelly, had been neglected by legisla-tors since the beginnings of civilized time. That was the first and basic error. It had always been supposed that coercive legislation was necessary to curb human obliquity, but that was not true. Man was sinful because governments had made him so, by encouraging and admitting the idea of property, which was not a fundamental right at all but an illusion. Inequality was therefore barbarous and could easily be abolished by a good government, which would turn to account men's benevolent affection for each other and for society. In order to give this generous emotion practical expression, Morelly proposed community of goods.

In the 'fifties, this partly early-Christian, partly pagan, extrava-ganza had been considered pure moonshine; but, by the time the Revolution had entered its wild and anarchistic phase, the question could no longer be treated so lightly. Communism was a small but growing threat to private property and current talk about an agrarian law crystallized these fears. Robespierre was quite aware of these apprehensions and he reacted as well as a bewildered Rousseauist knew how, because he had to perform a balancing act which involved utopian reformers like himself and realistic proprietors and capitalists, whose support he needed for winning the war. Alas, equilibrium is no substitute for economic expertise, which neither he nor his contemporaries had acquired at college, where they had learned a good deal about rhetoric and ethics—poor equipment indeed for dealing with the dreadful burdens imposed by the nascent age.

The problems were long-standing and daunting. For example,

before Maximilien entered the great Committee, matters had first come to a head after that successful mini-revolution of August 10, 1792, when the *sans-culottes*, who had by their exertions overthrown the monarchy, demanded payment in kind, namely a higher standard of living. As a sop, the moribund Legislative Assembly offered some semblance of universal suffrage, but of a kind more limited than that advocated by Robespierre—who was a devoted partisan of the one-man-one-vote idea. It also allowed them to serve in the National Guard, hitherto the exclusive province of the middle classes. All this was nevertheless immediately irrelevant to starving workers and their families. As Maximilien had admitted in opposition, when he discussed the subject of voting qualifications:

'Yes, the coarse raiment covering me, the humble abode where I earn the right to withdraw and to live in peace; the modest wage with which I feed my wife and children; all these are, I admit, neither lands, castles nor carriages; all these are perhaps accounted nothing compared with luxury and opulence . . . but they represent something for humanity.'[1]

At the end of its tenure the Legislative's most energetic agents had made matters worse, when they exceeded their terms of reference in hounding grain monopolists.[2] In the case of Momoro and Dufour, sent to the Eure and Calvados, a general egalitarian attack upon property-rights ensued, which unsettled the peasant farmers of these western regions, remote from Parisian Left-wing agitation. Momoro was particularly disturbing because of his advanced ideas on the new Constitution-to-be, including the suggestion that the nation should guarantee possession only of industrial, and not agricultural property. The embarrassment of the central authority can be judged by the fact that the Legislative were sufficiently relieved to have private property stripped of feudal limitations and to opt for a system which would guarantee some rights.

Came the Convention. Sniping at the Girondins from the opposition benches, Maximilien spoke his mind,[3] maintaining that bread is more basically important than property; that economic liberalism on the pre-Revolutionary Turgot model had failed in respect of grain supplies; that action was called for in the emergency. As a prerequisite for discovering a cure, the orator distinguished, therefore, between essential and non-essential commodities, citing as an example of the latter the dye indigo; and, against the conservative Girondins, stated that no man had the right to amass stocks of food whilst his fellows died of hunger—that was the first social law, which made hoarding morally wicked. (Here he was back on familiar moralist territory and more at home with his theme.) Consequently only a surplus over and above subsistence requirements could be considered as legitimate private property. In adopting this attitude, Robespierre was clearly not restating the ideas expressed by Saint-Just a few days earlier, when the younger statesman had blamed the whole trouble on inflationary pressures, thus proving that his grasp of elementary economics was more secure than his master's!

On the question of communism, Maximilien wavered again and as usual talked morals instead of economics. Thus, when the Abbé Dolivier claimed that the nation ought to own the land of France, the Artesian politician omitted to mention the more revolutionary sentiments expressed by this fiery *curé* from Étampes and, illogically dismissing equal distribution and collective ownership as fairy-tales, argued that in any case riches harm those who possess them—an irritation to the poor and needy, and no help to the very people whose sufferings he felt so acutely. So at the end of 1792, facing two ways, Maximilien was fighting for the poor, whilst admitting the justifiability of some forms of private property and, to salve his conscience, had endeavoured to make a distinction between essentials and non-essentials. So, when we read in his *Opinion sur les subsistances* the injunction: 'Learn how to enjoy the charms of equality!',[4] we also note the title of this monograph. He was talking about *subsistances*, not about money or real estate, about which he continued to be cautious.

Apparently equivocation was a necessity for those in power. Even under the Montagnard Convention, Danton was at pains to reassure small landowners and, whereas Momoro and Dufour had once announced that only industrial property would remain inviolate, parliament hastened to add agricultural property to this exemption. Later, when, discussing the 1793 Constitution, a deputy called Harmand denied the absolute right of citizens to private property, Robespierre felt obliged to assert his favourite compromise.[5] Property, he argued, was the right to dispose of that part of one's goods guaranteed by the law and, in the *Discours sur la Nouvelle Déclaration des Droits*, continued his own particular tight-rope performance on this issue. So, whilst objecting to constitutional proposals calculated to promote narrow bourgeois interests, he once more endeavoured to dispel disquiet. Thinking, principally about land-ownership, he declared that 'equality of possessions is an idle dream', adding: 'it is more important to make poverty respectable than to proscribe opulence'.[6] This compromise, which pleased no one completely, was the result again of interest in ethics. The Incorruptible was once more trying to live up to his title, and the formula he favoured was carried forward into the constitutional documents themselves. The rich were still unsettled, of course, because revolution brings compulsion and requisitioning, and war against other nations had made the necessity more imminent than ever.

War, in fact, justified anything, since so many economic difficulties arose from the fact of being at war and since time was at a premium. Labour too was in short supply, so salaries rose and inflation stalked the land. Even more bewildered by economics than their leaders, the French people displayed fantastic energy because they were afraid. Like Germans and Japanese in the 'fifties and 'sixties of this century, they were spurred on towards salvation by adversity and defeat. For example, their ship-building effort outstripped that of the 'wave-rulers' across the Channel, and they accepted conscription on a large scale and made it work. The *levée-en-masse* of August 23, 1793[7]—a most comprehensive affair—was destined to become the pattern for similar undertakings in Napoleonic and modern times. All resources and people were theoretically called up or requisitioned for the war effort, but their employment and deployment had to be staggered and phased to avoid confusion. Since, as the relevant decree declared, liberty had become the 'creditor' of French citizens, all owed something to its maintenance, whether it was work, wealth or life and limb. The main thing was that, in one way or another, every person should help to defend essential freedoms; that all physical and moral faculties, that all political and industrial means, that all metals and all elements should be monopolized for the duration. Some citizens were to turn out munitions, others were to help feed hungry troops, others were to make the uniforms they needed; some might even hand over their own garments for this purpose. The young men would soon be up in the forces; married men would, for the time being, manufacture arms for their comrades in the fourteen armies that cried out for supplies. The women had their part to play too. Their duties were set out as sewing clothes and tents for the brave men at the Front; whilst their children would not remain idle, but would make lint out of waste cloth. Finally, the old men would be busy as unofficial recruiting sergeants, speaking in the market-places of France, as old men had done in Greek and Roman cities.

Though it was generally successful, as we have said, this colossal and classic requisitioning which smacked of absolutism was not accepted without some protest by the French. Still determined to maintain newly-won freedom in the private, personal domain, they constantly turned away from controls and were, on the whole, unwilling to adopt socialist measures. With memories of the *Ancien Régime* still fresh in many minds, citizens viewed all ministers of State with suspicion, so for some time there was no interference with the natural processes of supply and demand. Then, in the spring of 1794, ministries were abandoned in favour of what we would call civil-service departments, responsible to the Committee of Public Safety and therefore indirectly to the Convention. Some nationalization of vital sectors of industry was reluctantly introduced. For example, the supply of cannon, labour and raw materials called for more determined State control. In Paris national workshops began turning out muskets in a most efficient manner. Saltpetre was diligently scraped off the walls of outhouses and coal-cellars. At the same time the war gradually squeezed out of existence luxury trades and a ban was imposed on the export of essential commodities and supplies, whilst the Committee of Public Safety controlled movement of bullion. The British navy under Howe was busy trying to intercept convoys of essential imports; therefore foreign trading was very limited during this period and so consequently was choice. The commodity which affected the ordinary man was food. So grain was requisitioned, sometimes with difficulty, sometimes with unfortunate consequences for the housewife. As we have seen, agents were despatched to ensure that the towns were properly victualled, especially with cereal products. Yet, despite these ferrets, black markets flourished everywhere and often disputes arose between two towns claiming the same catchment-area for supplies. Bread was so expensive that most working men were spending half their wage on that alone. The demand for wheat and rye was enormous during the Revolutionary wars. Farmers were asked to concentrate on growing grain, since such a large part of their labour force was now in the army. This concentration led in its turn to a shortage of beasts and, in April 1794, meat had to be rationed, but butchers found ways and means of imposing additional conditions upon their customers, conditions which partly defeated the Government's intentions. As in all comparable emergencies, money was the *sine qua non*. But money is a token. Its value is relative to purchasing-power, so price-levels had to be fixed.

The Jacobins had promoted their first price-control, the initial *Maximum des Prix*, in May 1793—that is, before Robespierre joined the great Committee. They had done so partly in order to gain support of the Parisian *sans-culottes* in their struggle against the conservative Girondins. This first price-control measure was a worker-orientated decree, in that it applied only to the supply of flour and therefore to the poor man's staff of life. Although the decline in value of bank-notes was temporarily arrested, the results did not come up to expectations. Suppliers preferred not to sell at the reduced prices. Grain was kept in store by *accapareurs*, who were far from patriotic; so a series of decrees ensued prohibiting hoarding of grain, and, by being allowed to retain a third of discovered loot, spies were encouraged to unmask evaders of the new laws.

As this was obviously going to be a fairly haphazard process, a second *Maximum* on prices was brought into operation in the autumn of the same year, 1793. Now a list of about forty priority items was added—clothing, shoes, foods (other than grain), drink and fuel being included in this *Maximum-Général*. Prices were fixed at a third more than they had been in 1790, whilst wages were pegged at the rate of one half above the 1790 level. In Paris this increased wages, but in the provincial areas the reverse was often the case. The price *Maximum* of September 29, 1793, was intended to cure the worst malady in the economic sector; yet it had the opposite effect and its results were quite disastrous. For instance, before the *Maximum*, even though prices were exorbitant, it was possible to buy a coat with about a month's wages. Once the decree had been passed by the Convention, such things were not to be had at all. Nothing now was bought or sold, except on the black market. Paris suffered most. Bread, fuel, and other basic necessities seemed to disappear from the shops, whilst the country-side could not dispose of a good harvest. As in Britain in 1946, bread was such a precious commodity, that when you called on your friends, you were expected to take it with you. White bread was so rare that secret parties were held to consume it surrepti-tiously, for most bread was made from peas, vetches or chestnuts issued from government stores—the 'national loaf', as it was called in the Second World War. As in occupied France in 1940, long queues formed outside food shops. Sometimes wages were sacri-ficed in this time-consuming manner just to acquire sustenance. In the Revolution, moreover, if you did not join the queue, you might well be suspected of hoarding or trading on the black market.

Poor Maximilien, who in his *Opinion sur les subsistances* had sighed: 'if . . . all rich people were to consider themselves . . . as brothers of the poor',[8] was faced with the bankruptcy of fraternity. Alas, he sighed again, so very few citizens had that essential, patriotic virtue which enabled the best of them to put country before self. To make matters worse, like their customers, trades-men detested a government regulation declaring that all trans-actions should be made in the Revolutionary bank-notes, *assignats*, which regularly declined in real value. For instance, taking the exchange value of the Revolutionary bank-note, on the basis of the value in *livres* metal compared with the value of 100 *livres* paper, it appears that, whereas at the end of 1792 that value was running at 70, in April 1793 it had fallen to 44 and in August to 22. During the same period the price of sugar rose from 3 *sous* to 3 *livres* a pound. With the currency reduced to a quarter of its nominal value, it was inevitable that sterner measures should be con-templated.

Robespierre was almost alone in welcoming this, for, as a life-long puritan, he had long wished to have economic virtue imposed from above, if it could not emerge from below. In the spring of 1794 a new price structure had to be worked out to take account of depraved and egotistical human nature. Failing regeneration, only compulsion would meet the case. But compulsion alone did not seem to work either, so to the stick was added the carrot.

Guaranteed profits of 5 per cent for wholesalers and of 10 per cent for retailers, plus a transport allowance, were decreed. But this new scheme was brought into effect very slowly and, in the six months needed by the planners, city-dwellers were making more and more trips to purchase food on the rural black market. In Paris itself, since 1790 the price of veal had risen by 70 per cent and sugar by 116 per cent. On the whole, wage-earners were much worse off than they had been in 1790. Where, they inquired, was the reward for destroying the Bourbon tyrants and rooting out so many other undesirables? To counter this profound disillusionment, the Paris Commune issued a proclamation in May 1794. Scapegoats were required and found. First, it was announced that the Convention and the Committee of Public Safety had taken steps to make certain that Paris would be fed. Then the Commune deplored obstreperous gatherings outside butchers' and grocers' shops. Such scandalous behaviour, it was asserted, suited *aristos*, traitors and foreign agents, who were opposed to the new liberty acquired by the French nation, and who loved to see authority defied in this way. Indeed, secret agents often instigated refractory assemblies and should be denounced.

But economics could not be replaced by patriotic finger-wagging, any more than it could be replaced by ethics. Workers continued to be grasping and selfish; so Robespierre and his colleagues decided to impose a *Maximum* on wages on 5 Thermidor. They were driven to do this by a series of stern events. First, the tobacco workers, demanding increases, were told that they themselves had been requisitioned for the war effort; the apprentice-bakers followed suit and were threatened with the Loi des Suspects. As if this was not enough trouble, pork-butchers and munition-workers clamoured for more money. Despite pep-talks and threats, no section of the workers appeared satisfied with the new wage-structures announced on July 2 and revised three weeks later. Furthermore, everyone resented the Le Chapelier Law forbidding strikes. In despair, Maximilien surveyed the desolation of his hopes: after all, the beloved *sans-culotte* section of French society, the virtuous 'have-nots', the well-intentioned and honest underdogs, were proving just as selfish as all the rest. They would have to be taught a further, sharp lesson.

Clearly, the ivory-tower dweller failed to understand that, since Germinal, when the Dantonists and Hébertists had paid the supreme penalty, the uneasy alliance between the educated middle-class Jacobins and the rough, sturdy *sans-culottes*—an alliance loosely within the framework of the notion of a 'government revolutionary until peace'—had placed the workers in a ridiculous position. Workers do not relish being on the other side of the counter; their position demands of them a constant opposition to authority. Traditionally determined and aggressive, they were now regarded as acquiescent; and the Revolution began to falter when members of *comités révolutionnaires* were turned into salaried functionaries, deserting their Sections, who naturally resented this high-handed transfer of personnel. Thus, in a sense, the Revolution froze up when fiery *sans-culotte* leaders were transformed into respectable, but chilly, *agents nationaux*. Their job was so thorny with ambiguity. Consider the case of Payan, whom Robespierre had made *agent* in the Paris Commune. Now Payan felt obliged to report to his master that the Paris Sections were ready to break out in rebellion against the Government. So, in order to clip their wings, Robespierre decided to withhold the 40 sous payment made to those attending Section meetings, to close down some popular societies and to stop the open-air love feasts on the Mably model, at which patriots were wont to share their bread and wine—a surprise-party, with a reminder of Jean-Jacques, if not of the Eucharist.

As the recent *Maximum des Salaires* had effectively reduced Parisian wages to about half their former value, this final straw was enough to break the proverbial camel's back. A vast movement of revulsion against controls surged up, engulfing the non-economist committed to a task for which he was unfitted, not only by lack of professional training and lack of expertise, but also by haunting memories which warped his judgement. For instance, he could not forget the 'Jean-Farine' bread riots of 1775, directed against Turgot's régime and generally understood to have been organized by royal princes and aristocrats wishing to settle a score with the reformer, whom they finally brought down by forged evidence. Consequently, over-estimating the threat of a counter-revolutionary conspiracy, Robespierre missed the point. More important still: remembering what he himself had said to the Girondins from the opposition side of the House;[9] remembering also that in reality the price of bread had precipitated most of the great *journées*, he should have moralized less and thought more about economics. For, by lacking economic policy, Robespierre alienated all his former and potential supporters at one and the same time. The workers were angered at the restriction of purchasing-power. The middle classes hated him for favouring Parisian workers, for destroying their own freedom of action and for moral strictures about selfish businessmen. They cared little for his tales of aristocratic plots. They had grievances in sufficiency without such preoccupations.

In March 1794, apparently with Maximilien's approval, willingly or unwillingly extracted, Saint-Just was to outline the famous Laws of Ventôse, relating to redistribution of the property of condemned persons amongst the deserving poor; for the ambitious and ruthless young politician had realized the power of sequestration in binding men to a new régime—that same power which, in recent history, has been so devastatingly used against defenceless Jewish traders, Christian priests and Tibetan monks; that compelling magic conjured up by stolen property distributed as perquisites amongst the greedy sycophants of the new leaders. Public opinion in this nation of devoted property-owners was quick to reject the Saint-Just formula. Some even feared that Robespierre himself was going communist, but they were wrong. His attitude on this issue could best be compared with that of Thomas Jefferson, because his ideal was that of a society of virtuous citizens, equal before the law and owning a small-holding.

Chapter 16

SCHOOLS FOR CITIZENSHIP

'Après le pain, l'instruction est le premier besoin du peuple'
DANTON

Education was to have a key role to play in making French citizens rational and articulate enough to contribute to the expression of the General Will. Education, which was so fundamentally important, had nevertheless been much neglected until the time of Robespierre. Before the Revolution, it had been largely in the hands of the Church, elementary schools being staffed chiefly with secular clergy and the colleges depending on regular clerics. Oratorians, Doctrinaires, Dominicans, and especially Jesuits, continued to be prominent in teaching until 1762, when the last-named were expelled from the country's schools and lay teachers like Billaud-Varenne and Joseph Fouché took their places with profound effects on the moral climate. Of 562 colleges (the best secondary institutions), Paris had ten, outstanding among which was Louis-le-Grand, where Maximilien was educated. Out of 73,000 pupils in these colleges, about 13,000 were accepted without fees; but democratic concessions did not suit the reformers. In particular, the *Philosophes* of the *Encyclopaedia* had led a campaign for entirely secular education and that cry had been taken up above all by a Breton nobleman called La Chalotais, who demanded a State system. In education, undoubtedly the most important reformative notions stemmed from Rousseau's 1762 *Emile*, where the author had maintained that the child should develop by virtue largely of his own experience. Thus, despite civilization, he hoped to re-create natural man, by renewing moral qualities such as honesty, virtue and sound judgement; and he recommended that the tutor should allow the child to follow natural evolution, not imposing bookish education when the pupil was unready for it. He also advised methods dependent upon experience and calculated to arouse natural curiosity without appearing to do so.

That was still the situation on the eve of the Revolution, which took great interest in the subject. Talleyrand made a report to the Constituent Assembly concerning primary education; Condorcet did the same thing to the Legislative Assembly. The Convention discussed the Romme project of 1793, proposing a primary school for each village of 400 inhabitants, and the Bouguier plan of the same year, suggesting compulsory and free elementary instruction. On June 26, 1793, Lakanal presented a proposal for State education and the session of July 3 was partly devoted by parliament to this subject. At which point it was announced that the brother of the late Lepeletier wished to read out to the Convention his brother's educational scheme. This the Convention refused to allow,[1] but publication of the text was granted and Robespierre rose to propose a government commission to examine all such projects. He did so with enthusiasm, first, because he was convinced that the *Ancien Régime* had bred generations of vain egoists pursuing purely nugatory values; secondly, as we noted at the outset, because education was the foundation-stone upon which citizenship was to be built. Lepeletier's scheme to provide republican education was expounded on July 13, 1793.[2]

Since Maximilien not only sponsored, but presented to the Convention this project of Lepeletier, we can assume that he approved of its provisions. He did so largely because Lepeletier had faithfully followed some of the leads provided by the divine Jean-Jacques. The whole emphasis in the new document of 1793 was upon democratic ideas, for both Lepeletier and Robespierre had realized that France's political future depended upon the creation of a fair and equal system of instruction. Indeed Lepeletier's scheme was conceived to some extent as a reply to ideas expressed by Moderantists in the Convention, men like Sieyès and Daunou, for example. Their report had appeared on June 26, 1793 and was considered by the Left to contain suggestions too close to those of the Girondin, Condorcet, who had been in charge of the steering committee until May 30. When Robespierre discharged the counterblast of Lepeletier's ideas, he had not yet entered the Committee of Public Safety, but was close to doing so. As we suggested, Lepeletier was unfortunately unable to present his own report, since he had been stabbed to death by a former royal guard on January 20, 1793, the day before the king's execution. Thus his project appeared as a martyr's last will and testament in support of the new Republic and this enhanced its emotional and topical appeal.

Separating 'instruction' and 'education', Lepeletier had claimed that the former was concerned with propagating knowledge, the latter with forming human beings. Instruction was limited to the few who could profit: education was for all citizens. Despite this obvious fact, the committee sitting on this subject had so far neglected 'education' altogether, he argued. It had suggested four different types of establishment—primary schools, secondary schools, institutes and *lycées*. Lepeletier accepted the last three, but insisted that they were a minority concern compared with primary education, everyone's birthright. Lepeletier was sorry to note that, until the age of six, children were to be left to wallow in prejudice and error; moreover, if primary schools were not built quickly, there would not be enough to go round. In particular, country children would be at a disadvantage, because, obliged to work for their keep, they were deprived of part of their education. Another complaint which Lepeletier had made against the Moderantists' plan related to physical training. In his view, a modicum of gymnastic exercise was insufficient; for his part, he favoured more regular physical exercise, sustained by nourishing diet.

Viewing the system as a whole, then, it is clear that primary schools were the important levelling and democratizing institutions. In towns like Paris, there should be at least one such school per *Section* and, in the country, one per *canton*. The aim was that primary schools should contain between 400 and 600 pupils and should be closely integrated with the communities from which they were drawn, thus permitting parents to keep in touch with their children's interests. Should there be compulsion? In the long run, the answer could only be, yes; but for the moment France would have to be content with setting up the system and providing the premises. In four years' time the Government could proceed to making primary instruction compulsory; meanwhile, strictly as an emergency measure, church buildings and castles could be pressed into service to accommodate the new schools. After the age of eleven or twelve, it would prove impossible to educate children comprehensively, because of orientation towards chosen professions and occupations. Obviously it was not feasible to make everyone become apprentices in the same trade, so careers necessarily had to diverge at that point. Thus the continued education of the adolescent in school often appeared to be less desirable than a period of probationary service in studios, workshops or farms. As for teachers, Lepeletier suggested that there should be one per fifty pupils (rather more than Rousseau's lonely *précepteur*, of course!), some of the older pupils helping the staff as student-teachers. Classes should be mixed in respect of age; and each member of staff should have the same number of charges, for whose welfare he would be responsible only to the administration and a special body set up to supervise him.

In ethics he found deplorable inadequacy. Between brief spells of moral instruction, the child was left to the soft life of luxury, pride and vanity, which engendered coarseness and delinquency. To remedy this defect and, at the same time, to promote equality, he proposed a national, democratic system, open to all and aimed at improving both physical and moral qualities. Taking a leaf literally from Rousseau's book, Lepeletier was of the opinion that one should commence with the physical, in order to form a good strong body and fine temperament. In order to toughen the little citizen, school should ban luxuries expected at home. This was a great advantage of boarding-school, with full-time professional supervision, again analagous with the incredible devotion of Jean-Jacques' *précepteur*. Boys from five to twelve should be brought up together at the Republic's expense. All should dress in the same way and eat the same food, the cost of all this being met by tax-payers according to their resources—an arrangement conveying the additional benefit of reducing inequality of fortunes. Solid beds, plain fare, hardwearing clothes—these became symbolic of a Spartan republicanism.

Lepeletier considered that the public should have vital contact with such institutions. First, he was in favour of publishing the programme of studies. Then he proposed annual prizes for citizens who had made the most useful suggestions for improving the system. Thirdly, he wished fathers to be more closely associated with their sons' education. In this connexion he planned the formation of councils, each consisting of fifty-two fathers, elected for a year, during the course of which each father would spend a week resident in the primary school 'to observe the conduct, both of pupils and masters'—a rather daunting thought for the teachers, one would suppose! From this fifty-two-man council would be constituted a finance sub-committee, consisting of four members charged with the duties of *intendant* or *économe*—that is, with out-

Rue St. Honoré, where Robespierre resided with the Duplays.
The courtyard entrance is currently covered by the restaurant
awning of 'Le Robespierre' (see pp. 28 and 204)

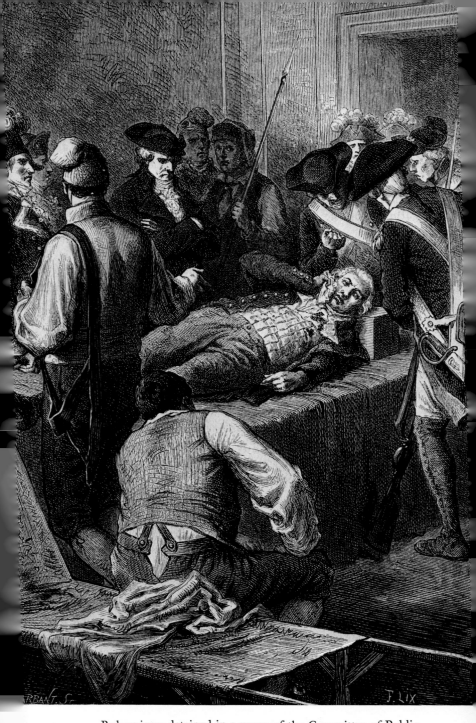

Robespierre detained in a room of the Committee of Public
Safety, following his arrest (see p. 212)

goings and receipts, the ordering of food and the upkeep of the fabric. Again, Lepeletier desired that older children should take the place of domestics, helping younger ones with menial tasks. This aspect of education, in the widest sense of the word, was intended to promote self-sufficiency.

This self-sufficiency was aimed to some extent at the influence of the family. It was one thing to invite family cooperation, but another to allow a child to be under family influence. The family could have access to the school, but the school was to exert the dominant formative influence. In future, loyalty should be first to the State and second to the family. This sort of pedagogic totalitarianism was likely to be unpopular in practice precisely because, as a people, the French attach such importance to the family unit and naturally resisted the idea of sending their children to boarding-schools for the good of the Republic; so Robespierre later advised his colleagues that this aspect of the Lepeletier scheme was to be modified.[3]

Puritan zeal was, however, far from expended yet. Children were to undertake farm-work, construct roads and develop mind and body in the school's workshops, where useful articles would be made. 'Useful' was another key word in the system, since, by virtue of this stern effort, the nation's productivity would also benefit, crime would be reduced, poverty would disappear and adult citizens too would learn to be more self-reliant. Though in itself this was a kind of religion, the subject itself was not neglected in the curriculum; but it was to be presented in very general terms, so that at the age of twelve the young tiro could make up his own mind. In short, education was for life, the whole of life, physical and moral, irrespective of narrow professional ambitions.

In this way, though aware that difficulties beset the would-be educator at all stages, Maximilien contemplated the total renovation of society in such a way that the *mores* of the nation would be worthy of new institutions. This would take time, of course, and the Incorruptible was quite satisfied to receive pencilled-in the ground bass for the new symphony, part of which concerned adult citizens. In adult education, working for the moral and civic good of the Republic meant taking all opportunities to point a moral, to give object-lessons in the Rousseau manner. Utilization from Ancient sources of examples of duty and virtue; the close investigation of human rights; the realization that good laws were made

to help people to fulfil their destiny as human beings; the staging
of plays calculated to teach rectitude and patriotism; the mounting
of festivals laced with didactic symbolism—such were the methods
he proposed to employ with mature members of Revolutionary
society, a society which could only flourish collectively if each
individual felt free, and therefore happy, within that society. This
appears, therefore, to be one more attempt to instruct in *citizenship*—an idea so successfully launched by Montesquieu and Diderot in the first half of the century and reinforced by the Physiocrats, that after 1779 men were speaking more and more naturally
about the 'nation' and looking forward to the Abbé Sieyès and his
constitutional drafts.

An urgent practical sequel to Robespierre's promotions on the
subject of adult education was provided by a collective report of
the Committee of Public Safety, dated June 1, 1794—that is before
Fleurus, which transformed the military situation and reduced the
political head of steam. The purpose of this memorandum was
clearly set out at the beginning—namely to rear truly republican
members of the armed forces, and to do so with all possible
expedition. A crash course in citizenship and military art is a tall
order; so there was no time to waste in weighing one method
against another and talking at great length about principles. Yet
Maximilien's régime rested upon ideals, which had to be declared
in advance. The chief principle in fact concerned the use of reason,
for it was only when an adult began to be truly enlightened that
his native land should take him under its wing and give him a
republican education. The best ages for this were considered to be
16, 17 or $17\frac{1}{2}$, at which stage in his development the citizen should
be asked to serve the State by defending its unity, its laws, its
territory and its independence. An *Ecole de Mars* was therefore
to open its doors to these young fellows—3,000 of the strongest,
the most intelligent and the best behaved, who would devote
themselves to common tasks and make themselves ready for army
service.

In the course of an important speech on religious and moral ideas,
on May 7, 1794 Maximilien referred to an eighteenth-century
Philosophe who, 'by his lofty soul and greatness of character,
showed himself worthy of his ministry as tutor to the human
race',[4] and, in the light of the scheme for primary education,

sponsored by Robespierre, it is interesting to consider and assess the importance of Rousseau as a source and background. Admittedly, in the article *Economie politique*, written before the *Emile*, Rousseau had stated that the object of education was the formation of citizens, but later he had changed his mind. The author of the *Emile* disagreed from the very start with the idea of republican education for citizenship, an attitude stemming from his almost religious belief in natural equality. In his opinion, the aim of education was to make a man, rather than a citizen, but he would have agreed with Lepeletier that the main task of the educator is to teach a person to live successfully rather than to labour at a particular trade. Secondly, it will be recalled that Emile was to be brought up privately by a tutor and thus deprived of school; so, when considering common primary education in State schools, Lepeletier was true to the Rousseau of 1745 rather than the author of the *Emile* who considered that, in an essentially corrupt society, public instruction would partake of that corruption. Formulating practical schemes for a whole nation, he could not suggest that all should live, like the little Emile, in a country setting; nor could he postulate that one had to reform society before the ideal system of education could be put into operation. On the contrary, it was precisely to achieve as much as possible in that direction that Lepeletier and Robespierre had ventured into the field at all.

Furthermore, whilst the legislators of 1793–94 could perhaps agree that primary education should be mainly what Rousseau calls 'negative'—that is, allowing the individual to develop according to his own nature and not be tied to 'subjects' at an early age—with classes of fifty, too much freedom and too much 'negative' approach could not be entertained. On the other hand, we have seen that the whole of French society was to be exposed in Revolutionary times to Rousseau's favourite object-lessons with a useful or moral purpose; and the idea that the first stage of education should end at twelve was entirely consistent with Rousseau's treatise of 1762. At that age Emile is healthy, vigorous, open-minded, loyal and strong; he is sensible, proud in the best sense of the word, and possesses a will of his own—all qualities which Lepeletier was trying to develop by his two-fold scheme of physical training and moral indoctrination. Above all, Lepeletier was practical and sensible. This physical and moral bias did not exclude traditional scholarship, so he did not ban the use of books, as Rousseau tended to do. In short, the theoretical Emile, who had read next to nothing until, at twelve, he was handed *Robinson Crusoe*, would not do entirely as a model for the children of the new Republic. Nor was religious instruction to be delayed until the age of sixteen; for pragmatic politicians were quite content if their offspring in the five to twelve group followed the deistic nonsectarianism of Jean-Jacques himself. It would do them nothing but good and make police work easier.

In general, then, the inspiration of Jean-Jacques was substantially evident, but modifications in the direction of realism and adaptation had been made. After all, Rousseau himself had varied a great deal between one work and another, since to legislate for Poland was different from pure speculation. The first had to be pragmatic whereas the second could remain paradigmatic. Therefore, whilst remaining fundamentally faithful to their master, Lepeletier and his sponsor adapted to the urgent needs of the moment the most helpful ideas they had culled from all Rousseau's educational writings.

Some of Lepeletier's suggestions bore immediate fruit. Almost exactly a year after his assassination, an education act dated January 6, 1794, decreed three years of free and compulsory primary education. The speed with which this was decided proves how enthusiastic Robespierre was for his friend's schemes; unfortunately, it was still a pious hope and, after the fall of the great leader, primary education remained still in private hands and the compulsory principle was abandoned. As usual, lack of funds and staff were blamed for this lamentable state of affairs!

PART IV
FORTUNE AND FAME

'Comment est-il arrivé . . . qu'un homme sans nom, sans talent, sans courage, sans fortune et d'une figure hideuse, soit parvenu dans l'espace de six mois à consommer l'anéantissement de la plus ancienne monarchie de l'Europe?

B. DE MOLLEVILLE

Chapter 17

THE FORCE OF CIRCUMSTANCE

'J'ai gagé . . . que Robespierre ne méritait pas tout le mal qu'on dit de lui. Les temps fera voir si j'ai raison . . . Il faut que Robespierre soit bien changé s'il est tel que le représentent certain journalistes'

AN ARRAS FRIEND

It was that forceful young disciple, Saint-Just, who expressed the opinion that 'Perhaps the force of circumstance leads us on to results we had not anticipated';[1] and he was right. At any other period in history Maximilien could easily have remained what he was trained to be—a small-time lawyer defending provincial clients. Yet Saint-Just's remark is merely a half-truth, for people are conditioned and determined by themselves as well as by things. Indeed, moving from one position to another, Maximilien was sometimes driven from within and without at the same time.

His attitude to his king supplies a good example of this. We recall the confidence he expressed that an early work of his would not be useless to the monarch and would not escape his notice. We recall too the gradual evolution that ensued. Despite the schoolboy's humiliations in that rain-soaked encounter, the sovereign remained for a long while symbolic of hope of a peaceful solution to constitutional problems; hope that democratic desiderata might be promoted by this sexless artisan-of-a-monarch, so unlike all the others in French history and for these reasons a man after Robespierre's own heart. There was something more personal still. Perhaps Louis had been for Maximilien a father-figure preferable to his own shifty parent; and it is significant that he used the word *cher* when speaking of the king in early days. On one occasion he had even gone so far as to speak of the king as 'l'homme providentiel'[2]—a remark having important undertones in the light of subsequent religious development. The monarch was also the sanction for legality via the 1791 Constitution and the young lawyer naturally favoured strengthening the law. Then the stupendous impact of Varennes![3] The father-figure had run true to form, after all, and repeated the flabby performance of Robespierre *père*; consequently, the young man's confidence in this maverick monarch was shattered. He felt hurt. Having agreed to a legal bargain with the people, Louis should not even have used the veto to save reactionaries from the due processes of law;[4] above all, he should not have made contact with the enemies of his people in order to break his legal bargain. Such considerations naturally altered the lawman's attitude to the 'providential man' of yore; disgust with one half of the constitutional arrangement threw him into the arms of the other. Even before the Convention, Maximilien was a *Conventionnel*.

Personal and professional reasons fused together in bitterness. Gradually the bitterness gave place to the memory of a much better father-figure from the past—that of Jean-Jacques. The idea of a monarch yielded to that of the Legislator; and none could better play the filial role than Robespierre, the educated commoner endowed as he was with an unusual sense of duty and public-spiritedness, the new 'providential man'. When the Girondins had departed to exile or to death, the way ahead became clearer than ever. No one was better placed than he to accept the inheritance of power. Already, in the Constituent Assembly, he had been ahead of his contemporaries, for there he had expressed ideas which were to give the Convention some aspects of its distinctive character, for, as we have seen, Robespierre had helped to plan the Convention and its committees. In early days, he had more than moved with the times, whilst others had been left by the wayside, out of date like old Raynal. Socially he had turned, and been turned, from sympathy with the bourgeois to concern for the artisan, the shop-keeper, and the urban working class. Thus, in cadence with political evolution, Maximilien had run down the social scale of Third Estate, endeavouring to enlarge the spectrum of support, failing sometimes and losing some partisans on the way, but numerically more than making up for the losses.

In the course of this development, which factor mattered and counted more—the man or the unfolding pattern of events? It would be difficult to supply a categorical answer to that question. For one thing, in an earlier chapter we had occasion to note the fantastic effects of events upon health and, conversely, were led to speculate how different events might have been if Robespierre had been fit, physically and mentally, to carry the burdens of office in times of acute strain. Health is not the same thing as personality, yet who can say that one is not a part of the other? The two obviously interact; but so also do character and events, further complicating a difficult assessment.[5]

Critics have tended to emphasize one at the expense of the other, which can be misleading. Here are some examples. In his judgements Taine ignored circumstance; in Aulard's it assumed prime importance; and, whilst Rudé maintained that Robespierre submerged his principles deliberately—sometimes with regret too—to meet the needs of a new situation, Renier considered that his character was moulded by events that were bigger than he was. For and against, so it goes on.

To make matters very much worse, Robespierre the man is not an easy book to decipher. Indeed, his sheer inconsistency and variability have bewildered historians and critics alike. In his short study of the Incorruptible, Mornand refers to the 'the immense contradictions in Maximilien's character',[6] thereby confirming the impression we receive when considering the various facets of this strange personality. If, like Beaulieu and Michaud, joint authors of that highly critical nineteenth-century *vignette*, we regard him as a 'a political Tartuffe' or if, like Marat, we sum him up as a 'cowardly hypocrite',[7] there is clearly no mystery to unravel and nothing more to be said; but, of course, both strictures are the consequence of bias and oversimplification. Complication is best treated precisely as it is. Unity, consistency are rare indeed and, in the case of our subject, virtually non-existent.

The Revolution witnessed such staggering changes in this idealist from Arras. For example, the young fellow who praised the writer Gresset for declining the office of perpetual president of the Académie d'Amiens on the grounds that this would have led to a sort of dictatorship,[8] was forced into masterful stances under pressure from the activities of hostile manipulators and schemers. Having become virtually prime minister, the liberal agitator hardened into an authoritarian, whose moral teachings now took on more dogmatic form and became an excuse for witch-hunting. The speaker renowned for liberal opinions was now considered a tyrant; and men who remembered with gratitude his opposition to a decrease in pensions, to the maintenance of a tobacco monopoly, to the censorship of mail, to anti-emigration laws, to unfair tax methods, hardly recognized him in this new guise. Nor could the leader of a Committee prosecuting a savage war be identified with the pristine opponent of martial law, the champion of the common soldier against his officers, or the kind of pacifist who had opposed war in the first place and, in the context of 1792—and it is an incredible thought—he must have appeared on this issue a counter-revolutionary.

Contradictions all along the line: in June 1790 he had spoken up for parliamentary privilege and inviolability in the Toulouse-Lautrec Affair;[9] yet the Prairial Law of 1794 was virtually to nullify this exemption. Still more inconsistency: the deputy who, in his early days, had been keen on regionalism, devolution and provincial autonomy was to be the chief partisan of centralization under the banner of unity. We noted his probable inclination towards regional devolution at the time of the Rosati Society. In 1791 when in opposition, his attacks on ministers were so frequent that Beaumetz accused him of federalism and, amazing as this charge may appear in the light of subsequent orientation, it was supported by the British Embassy, which reported that Robespierre was one of three leaders bent on annihilation of the monarchy and opposed to the centralized government.[10] Later, of course, he hounded down the Girondins largely on the grounds that they were federalists encouraging provincial autonomy. This marks a striking change of attitude. Here, after all, was a man who in 1792 had favoured the division of the City of Paris into *Sections*—that is, small local government units, which could on occasion exert pressure on the Paris Commune, or central municipal authority; yet he frowned upon the same kind of division of France into regional units already provided for to some extent by the *départements*. Could it be wrong for Deux-Sèvres to disagree with Paris, if the local Section des Piques could disagree with the Commune?

So it goes on and diligent Robespierrists have been able to make quite a list of such contradictions. Gallo[11] indicates inconsistencies in Maximilien's reactions, showing how he disliked petitions in theory but approved of one in fact; how he disclaimed a Regency in principle, but may have temporarily favoured Orléanist schemes to this very end; how he feared anarchy yet fostered it by his own public pronouncements. Thus Gallo adds to the list drawn up many years ago by Clauzel; who gave this *résumé* of the most blatant incongruities: 'He writes ... against calumny whilst slandering others; he invokes freedom in order to promote tyranny, justice and humanity in order to achieve murder!'[12]

Clauzel's stress on the clash between justice and injustice is of paramount importance in such a list. For it is here that the most crucial inconsistencies emerge. Undoubtedly, as Gallo says, Robespierre's fall was due partly to betrayal of principles which he understood better than most—to rabble-rousing, which he knew to be the reverse of legality. Even if we attempt to excuse the Incorruptible for changing his views when in power; even if we claim that, after Varennes, this trained lawyer still tried to prevent citizens from being unjustly condemned and insisted that juries should consist of the accused's social equals, it must be admitted that the Prairial Law of 1794 denied the elementary rights of man.[13] We may perhaps be able to explain why the politician who, after his friend Lepeletier had been assassinated, spoke against the death penalty for the miscreant and yet on another occasion required that the Tribunal be reorganized so that General Custine could be sent to his death for a lesser offence.[14] We may even try to understand how the opponent of capital punishment could excuse the Terror. In the end we may find ourselves inquiring with Edouard Herriot whether this Revolutionary politician was a mere sophist after all—a lawyer, blinded to logic by his own verbiage.[15]

Certainly his conduct is difficult to understand, especially when religious undertones were involved. Consider his strange behaviour in the Théot case. Vadier had wound up by proposing that, as members of a conspiracy, the group should be referred to the public prosecutor, but, when Fouquier approached him to implement the decision, Robespierre seized the relevant papers and had the case dropped. When Fouquier reported this to the Committee of General Security, they could hardly believe their eyes. Indeed, they could hardly believe their luck, for this was precisely the kind of loop-hole they were seeking to avenge their humiliations since April 1794, when the other Committee had usurped some of their police functions. They reacted by stacking the tumbrils to the fatal discredit of Robespierre. The outstanding example (it will be recalled) is the batch of fifty-four victims sent to the guillotine with Mademoiselle Renault in what came to be called *La Messe Rouge*—in itself a subtle criticism of the god-like leader, who appeared to require so many sacrificial lambs for an alleged *attentat*. The result was that Parisians no longer trusted Robespierre's sense of fair play. He also lost the respect of middle-of-the-road deputies. The man who had once declared: 'It is better to spare a hundred guilty men than to sacrifice a single innocent person' now personified cruel government power.[16] The image of the Legislator, the Incorruptible lawman, was defaced for all time. Justice had been sent to the guillotine with Mademoiselle Renault and her pathetic little band.

Where had he gone wrong? Precisely by allowing it to appear that he was conditioned by his own ego. The intervention to save Madame Théot seemed to fall into this category and ego was beginning to give the old platitudes on the subject of the General Will of the people a hollow ring now. Madame de Staël saw this clearly when she observed that, once he was suspected of having personal views, Robespierre's fate was sealed.[17] The comment was indeed perceptive, because errors of judgement may be traced to private defects projected on a public screen for all to see. For instance, as a terrorist he was too hesitant and too timid to succeed. In a cruel world, truculence is more useful than conscience. Marat spotted this fatal flaw, when he judged his reformist colleague deficient in ruthlessness and audacity.[18] Certainly, Maximilien could never have made the famous speech on this subject which became Danton's enduring glory. To be half bold is to lose the battle and Robespierre's vague accusations against colleagues in the Convention did him far more harm than good; in July 1794, the Incorruptible had drifted temporarily into the counter-revolutionary camp. It was Napoleon's opinion that Robespierre had indeed wished to curtail the Terror, for Cambacérès had told him that Robespierre had made a speech to this effect—a speech which was in fact never printed, but must have accelerated his downfall.[19] To have appeared to be hesitant about violence in 1792 had been bad enough; to appear counter-revolutionary when in charge of the Revolution was much more risky.

Revolution is a funnel down which leaders of opinion are driven ineluctably by virtue of their position and interests. The stream runs inevitably on, for no active revolution stands still for long. Continue it must, for a certain time. What is that 'certain time'? That is the really difficult question. To surge forward at the wrong moment is dangerous, especially if public opinion has decided that, for a complex of reasons, it is opportune to call a halt. To hang back is equally dangerous, for the political leader may then be dubbed a counter-revolutionary and be cut down by the determined minority who have made up their minds that it will go on. Indeed, no matter how many purges he may have carried out, at any moment this leader may be struck down by ultra-revolutionaries or by counter-revolutionaries who disagree with his way of handling things. Now the situation in which Robespierre found himself in 1794 by virtue of temperamental defects was comparable with that of a nervous person crossing a busy street, dragged forward by an eager, resolute younger person (Saint-Just), but at the same time held back by natural timidity and conscience—a highly dangerous state of affairs. So, when it came to the point of no return, he found he had not moved quickly enough; that he was incapable of travelling in unfamiliar territory. Motionless in irresolution, he was fated to be dragged down with his small band of henchmen, disunity having contributed to his fall. The person who hangs back in this way lacks attack, judgement and vision. It was this latter characteristic which Marat had found most reprehensible.[20] Robespierre lacked the clairvoyance which ensures continued and *enduring* success; for Rousseau's jargon was no substitute for genius. Thus he failed to seize the opportunity for complete domination of his own Committee, of parliament and therefore of France; thus, at a crucial moment in July 1794, the *sans-culottes*, who should have been his soundest supporters, obeyed the Convention rather than their eloquent champion. Indeed, in this very eloquence lay another pitfall. After the Fête de l'Etre Suprême, the agent Payan had tried to persuade his master to fight his enemies by hurling the Paris mob at them in the streets; but, accustomed to reasoned arguments in the courts and over-confident in his own oratorical skill, Robespierre was foolish enough to think that rhetoric would prevail. Once again time was lost, when it was most precious. Once more, he had proved that he lacked political foresight.

Lacking vision, this highly suspicious politician trusted the most unreliable of people on some important occasions. Consider the case of the commander of the National Guard, the drunken and stupid Henriot, upon whom Maximilien was to depend in his supreme hour of trial. Being less easily swayed by considerations of loyalty, the younger Robespierre, Augustin, had never cared very much for Henriot and, in fact, had looked elsewhere. Having travelled in the south during stirring months of the Revolution, he had tried to persuade young Bonaparte to accept the command of the Paris armed forces, so that the Convention might not prevail in a future struggle against the Committee or Commune. Needless to say, the future Napoleon was no fumbling idiot, though he was one day to be imprisoned by the Thermidoreans for Robespierrist sympathies.[21] The irony is that on the occasion under discussion, deciding that he could not support a person as idealistic as Maximilien, he replied that he would take over the Paris command later, when it suited his programme.[22]

The incident leaves us with a highly arresting speculation about possibilities: for if Bonaparte had agreed, things might have turned out very differently. Alas, the two men were fated not to like each other, because their respective personalities were totally different. It was a case of the man of action against the man of scruple. As we have seen already, Napoleon was also to deride his precursor precisely for his inability to cut the Gordian knot when the situation required him to do so. Napoleon's timing was much superior to that of Robespierre.

Lacking political vision, the short-sighted Maximilien made mistakes in deciding when to act. After all, history is an experiment with time. Maximilien never mastered this aspect of his destiny as a political scientist and it is not surprising that he was punished for his bad timing. No man can have revolution on his own terms, even if he is in charge of it. The one and only constant in any revolutionary context is the fact of change, but how quickly will change occur—that is another question. It is simply true that few can foresee the speed at which, once set in motion, events will be enacted. In 1794 events galloped along. *Ego* could not cope, because procrastination upset timing. For instance, the Prairial Law appeared to many to be redundant, since it had been introduced *after* the Germinal purges, that is, *after* factions had been virtually eliminated and political unity and victory assured for Robespierre and his group. To add to the perils of the moment, anachronistically Robespierre felt attached to that very legality which the Prairial Law had set at naught. So he maintained vestigial confidence in the Tribunal and apparently failed to act on his own behalf.

He lacked vision too in his handling of religious matters. Here too, timing was at fault. Even Robespierre's Masonic friends were incensed at the revival of deism in the Culte de l'Etre Suprême since *by now* they were no longer deists and resented an *untimely* revival. Mornand explains: 'by proclaiming the Supreme Being, Robespierre had ceased to follow the line of Revolutionary Masonry. His fate was sealed. Fouché was able to profit by the situation.'[23] The tribune's Masonic colleagues was soon to take advantage of his former friend's anachronistic cult. Vengeance was at hand. Charlotte's pristine boy-friend was about to ruin Charlotte's nauseating brother and in this connexion the religious issue was to prove a boon to Fouché. When July came, the leader could no longer move with the times or foresee the next move in this deadly chess game. The decree of 5 Thermidor, restricting wages at a time when prices were soaring, dragged him down *a mere four days later* and, on the way to the guillotine, his supporters were assailed with popular shouts about the 'bloody Maximum!' Politics follow economic vicissitudes and vicissitudes are another aspect of the problem of time. If a politician is not in rhythm with changes of emphasis, he is not fully in charge and tends to panic. Robespierre's next move was dictated by the impulse of fear and, like the golfer whose timidity allows the club to slip from his grip at the crucial moment, Maximilien lost control of the situation. To change the figure of speech: finding himself on a political limb, he proceeded to saw it off by alienating parliament. In that surprising oration of 8 Thermidor, he virtually announced the end of the current party-system.[24] Saying good-bye to the Montagne, he spoke as usual about wickedness and thus alerted politicians of all parties, who in any case were aware that Robespierre had recently been impelled by one younger and more uncompromising than himself.

The dummy was beginning to take over the act. Saint-Just, that 'Archangel of the Terror', was now outstripping his master. This would not have mattered so much had he really been like his master, a mere reinforcement or prop, but parliament knew full well that the two were so different that one could suspect a ventriloquial act. The facts were notorious. Whereas Maximilien had been a hard-working, good-living pupil at school, Louis-Antoine had a long criminal record, for this confirmed delinquent had started his career as a gang-leader; had been dubbed a future villain by his schoolmaster; had played the rake in Paris and the seducer in Blérancourt; had stolen jewels and plate from his own widowed mother before absconding and, having been arrested and locked up, had amused himself by writing an erotic piece which Taine subsequently described as filthy. This was the rogue, turned grey eminence, who had thought up that Ventôse communist pipe dream, causing much alarm to Right and Centre and losing for his master the last shreds of bourgeois support. In the Year II the Convention sensed that things were very wrong, since they now realized that a sorcerer's apprentice,[25] much more ruthless than his master, had gained the upper hand. And, for his part, the Racinian enthusiast from Arras was now afraid of this terrible young Narcisse, whose statement that men are impelled by the force of circumstance to action they would not otherwise contemplate was proving to be true.

Chapter 18

HOW TO MAKE ENEMIES
AND INFLUENCE PEOPLE

'Le seul tourment du juste, à son heure dernière,
Et le seul dont alors je serai déchiré,
C'est de voir, en mourant, la pâle et sombre envie
Distiller sur mon front l'approbre et l'infamie,
De mourir pour le peuple et d'en être abhorré'

ROBESPIERRE

Although he was subject to the circumstantial forces to which we referred in the last chapter, within the limits of free will Robespierre was able to exercise crucial influence on the course of the Revolution. Renier, who maintains that he had little effect on events,[1] would not agree with this view. On the other hand, Poperen believes that 'the personal intervention of Robespierre is, at each stage, decisive'.[2] This last opinion appears to be partly supported by fact. After all, here was a man who, though unlike the man-in-the-street whom he defended and idealized, typified more than one aspect of the times and, if in minority, held significant views, which proved to be either valid or of prophetic importance. Indeed, it was one of his sternest critics, Madame de Staël, who remarked that his was the only name from the period that posterity would recall[3] and, in case we feel that Staëlian optics were distorted by proximity, we may find in J. M. Thompson the remark that Robespierre's five years in politics were more important than Bonaparte's fifteen.[4] The Incorruptible contributed much not only to the politization of Third-Estate France but also to its institutions, and when, on July 27, 1793, Robespierre joined the Committee of Public Safety, he was supremely valuable, because he was 'the one deputy who had the necessary influence at the Jacobin club and at the Commune to effect an alliance with the popular revolution'.[5] Thus, as a link-man and because he was trusted by more than one faction in the political struggle currently in progress, Robespierre was unique at a momentous stage in the Revolution.

The moment was ripe, because willy-nilly during this Great Year the modern socialist State was born, with its price-controls, its scientific and technocratic bias, its citizen army of conscripts, its centralization of power; and welfare services, which above all else are to its eternal credit and glory. Still ringing in our ears is the *Déclaration des Droits*, which proclaims that

> 'Society is obliged to provide subsistence for all its members, either by finding them work or by giving assistance to those who are unable to work. The provision of the basic essentials for those who lack them is a debt upon those who have more than they need.'[6]

Lloyd George, Roosevelt and Beveridge carried on from there. Indeed, Mathiez would have us believe that Robespierre stood at the fountain-head of British and French socialism and mentions his influence on the English Chartist movement.[7] Mornand stresses his contributions to Lenin's communism and modern *Etatisme* in the more general sense.[8] Agreeing with the latter, Rudé finds in Robespierre's application of the doctrine of the General Will a precedent for Napoleon's hegemony.[9] On the Left again, many commentators see Robespierre as the middle-man between Rousseau's nebulous collectivism and Babeuf's orthodox communism, the fruits of which are prolific in the current political field, whilst the nineteenth-century Louis Blanc and the modern Lefebvre regard the Incorruptible as the source of political and social democracy.[10]

Other critics have taken account of the importance of Robespierre's fall. Describing him as the keystone of the French Revolution, Thomas Carlyle, who certainly had no love for the Incorruptible, nevertheless pointed out that after his death the whole *sans-culotte* movement collapsed, proving that the personality of the man had been almost essential to the maintenance of this form of Parisian democracy.[11] In his *Études*, Albert Mathiez speculated about the vilification of Robespierre in his last months on earth and concluded that, had the would-be assassin, Admiral, succeeded in gunning down the right man instead of just missing the wrong one, Maximilien's reputation would have stood much higher and provoked less controversy.[12] In this sense, it is possible to argue that, brief as was his career, Robespierre lived just a little too long and survived his immediate usefulness. In other words, until the eleventh hour he was the Man-of-the-Hour; during the twelfth, he was outstripped by opinion and circumstance together.

Otherwise he might have survived to posterity as the greatest of them all.

He missed this general distinction by a short head, because the times were so confused, so complex, so difficult to gauge; in saying that, we hark back once more to our Cultural Mule. The era in which Fate had located this man from Arras presented such a curious mixture of buoyant heroism and heavy sadness, portrayed in the 'Emperor' Concerto by a contrast between the military pomp of the finale and the pre-Chopinesque mood of the slow movement. Thus the Revolution found it possible to reconcile, on the one hand, the tenderness of Vigée-Lebrun's portraits and the sentimental urbanity of the musical evenings spent at the Duplays, with, on the other, the martial brutality of armies sweeping to victory at Fleurus and whirling on again to Austerlitz.

There had to be a second Man-of-the-Hour, simply because the first was not equipped to perform the exacting midwifery needed to bring the nineteenth century into existence. Temperamentally too he was happier with older ways. Often imprecise about his aims or his projected means of attaining them in the military sphere, Maximilien was at home with a Rousseau, who had earned his living copying music. By the same token, he felt more secure in the bucolic eighteenth-century world of the *Devin du village*, than in the impatient nineteenth, with its steam-engines, factories, telegraph or the observation-balloon at the Battle of Fleurus. The scientific notions of Lavoisier, Berthellot and Lamarck; the medical discoveries of Pinel or Cabanis; the linguistic theories of the Ideologues were not for him; and he detested the swarm of materialistic *nouveaux-riches* with their amoral money-making and hoarding. Robespierre's belief in virtue and reason; in the identity of public and private interests; in the influence of the environment upon the individual; in the validity of comparisons between modern France and ancient Greece and Rome; in the sentimentality of Rousseau, stamps him indelibly with the mark of an age that was now over. The gallant, peaceful, scrupulous man was finished at the end of the eighteenth century. The soldier-gangster, the man of violence, the ruthless technocrat, arrived to presage our own unhappy times.

The situation in 1794 was even more complex than our own, for the leader was brought down by disaffected *enragés* and by counter-revolutionaries masquerading as super-democrats, hypocritically demanding freedom from the Terror and from 'dictatorship'. These two groups, Leftists and opportunists alike, were lucky enough to find an electorate that was either apathetic or refractory in respect of the Committee's rule. That is why Napoleon was to describe Robespierre as the scapegoat of the Montagnard Convention, sacrificed because he had been let down by former colleagues and electorate alike. How different it might have been if Robespierre had not been driven by that Varennes-induced traumatic agony to fall in love with the commoners! The Corsican had learned his lesson, and, faced with the crisis of imminent abdication, the Emperor knew what *not* to do. If he agreed to resist, the Saint-Antoine district offered to support him; but, spurning a pact with the fickle *plebs*, Napoleon refused. It is more likely that, under similar circumstances, the oversentimental Maximilien could not have rejected the outstretched plebeian hand; yet, in the light of harsh reality, Napoleon was right, for the people did not give their affection for nothing and could withdraw support at the drop of the proverbial hat. This Robespierre discovered too late, as he discovered most things too late in 1794. As we have seen, the time factor was all-important in critical emergencies.

The climate of French opinion changed quite rapidly during and after the winter of 1793–94. People of all classes had had enough suffering for one lifetime and were beginning to wish it were all over. Already in 1793, the *jeunesse dorée*, the extravagantly dressed *muscadins*, were parading their counter-revolutionary costume and threatening democrats with their cudgels. Alongside of the teenage delinquents there emerged, from the shadows of austerity and from assorted funk-holes in the wainscotting, an ever-lurking swarm of war-time profiteers, now intent upon a return to traditional gaiety and gain. The poor man's Revolution was finished and so was its sponsor. Now the beloved workers of the capital had a bleak prospect, for privation rather than pleasure awaited them.

Maximilien had been too busy winning the war to cope with the pressing social mutations besetting France in 1794; yet their consequences and manifestations were now everywhere apparent. Because monarchy and religion had traditionally maintained the supremacy of the family and therefore had safeguarded parental authority, the smashing of the *Ancien Régime* and the establishment of the secular Republic had engendered a decline in respect for authority of all kinds. Gilded Youth was already obstreperous and rebellious. To tiros of the new age, Robespierrist ethics were archaic and ludicrous. He had not taken enough precautions and had failed to look ahead to future developments and, though he had been able to acquire supreme power, he was totally ignorant of the means of sustaining that power. Of this his fall is the conclusive proof. In his last days on earth, the well-meaning dodo laboured on, whilst the more accommodating Tallien and his friends profited by the very changes in the moral climate which worried Robespierre, secretly laughing at the sober Legislator, who believed in virtue in times of cruelty and depravity, and in self-discipline when permissiveness was on the rampage. Legal men recognize what they term the law of talion, that is, revenge by retaliation. If we may be excused a terrible play on words, we can say that the Artesian lawyer was subject to the 'Law of Tallien', the revenge of the unscrupulous.

The attitude of Robespierre to the French Revolution reminds us of the old-fashioned Christmas spectacle, known as pantomime. Enthusiasts who attended these annual shows invariably had faith that virtue would triumph. As we saw in discussing the French novel, something of this simple confidence characterized the utterances of Maximilien. He honestly believed that virtue could and would win through. Just as the Girondist, Condorcet, expressed belief in progress a few weeks before he became the victim of a new age and cheated the technical marvel in the Place de la Révolution by taking another civilized refinement, poison in a handy dispenser, a more important victim of the Revolution kept his faith intact almost to the end of his life and certainly much longer than twentieth-century man would have done—he, who is never to go to the gallows and enjoys great expectancy of life, but is nevertheless depressed about everything. Eighteenth-century man anticipated his posterity of the nineteenth by adhering to the doctrine of inevitable progress. Robespierre clung to the illusion almost to the bitter end. It was only when at last the fairy scene was transformed by harsh reality that he collapsed into disillusionment, realizing now that no longer would pious hopes, stirring exhortations or idealistic planning stem the tide of obliquity sweeping across France, like a *mascaret* on the River Somme.

Inspired all his life by a pantomime morality, on May 7, 1794, Maximilien described his black-and-white universe in these terms: 'Vice and virtue are responsible for fate here on earth; they are two rival genies who fight each other for possession of our planet.'[13] When the evil genie prevails, the man of honour has no wish to live. Maximilien gave up the ghost. The triumph of 'Prince Thermidor' (as Tallien came to be called) was indeed the triumph of the Demon King. After obliterating the Indulgents in the second holocaust of Germinal, it was a terrible shock to be beaten by the 'Self-Indulgents'.

Yet the smart scene-stealers who had upset stage morality were themselves soon to be shocked. Having worsted the candle-bearing Fairy-Queen from Arras who had been watching them too closely for comfort, Tallien, Barras and the man whom Robespierre had latterly recognized as the leading conspirator, Joseph Fouché, were surprised at the reaction of the French people to this turn of events. It had never occurred to them that the day-long guillotining would be abandoned so soon, or that the Terror might now officially end. However, once they saw that the French were actually keen to get rid of these hateful things, the conspirators hastened to reinforce their new popularity by spreading the rumour that they were humanitarians. In order to prop up this more than dubious claim, the Thermidoreans began to blame all the bloodshed on the tyrant Robespierre; to seize every opportunity to blacken his memory and to impute to the Incorruptible all the crimes perpetrated during the Reign of Terror. So the men of Thermidor, delighted to find that virtue threatened them no more, indulged in the caddish pursuit of striking down the already dead leader. *De mortuis nil nisi bonum* not figuring in their repertoire of Latin tags, these reactionaries had a field-day. Robespierre's old associates suddenly discovered like Roederer that their former acquaintance was a 'blood-thirsty mountebank lacking courage and ability'; Dubois-Crancé posthumously accused him of having 'endeavoured to corrupt public virtue within its very sanctuary'; Courtois added his own seasoning of caddish accusations, including 'casting into irons both talent and wit' and 'imposing terror on all'. Montjoye spoke luridly of this rather timid man's 'orgies' and prostitutes—both in fact grossly out of character. Not to be outdone, Le Blond de Neuvéglise raved on about the 'roasted flesh of priests' and even 'a tannery using human skins'—a strange anticipation of Second World War propaganda.[14] Since it was fashionable to vilify Robespierre and present him as the great bogyman of the Revolution, herds of porcine hacks and disreputable scribblers had the time of their lives, rooting out filth, real or imaginary.

The restoration of the Bourbon monarchy in 1814 and 1815 made it certain that until 1830 France would be busy rehabilitating the regretted Louis XVI and his Austrian queen, digging up their supposed remains and hallowing their memory by acts of historic vandalism such as transforming Marie-Antoinette's cell at the Conciergerie into a hideous chapel of atonement. Maximilien still remained the villain of the piece. After the Revolution of 1830, France turned to the Orleanist branch in the person of Louis-Philippe, a fairly modest middle-class monarch reminiscent of Louis XVI in these respects. As if to underline the consequences of this similarity, 1848 was to witness a political, Left-wing revolt rather like that of 1789, except of course that it was more short-lived. In the years 1834–38, already Buchez and Roux's *Histoire parlementaire de la Révolution française* had cleared the ground for a fairer judgement and Lamartine and Louis Blanc took up the challenge. The 1848 Revolution itself provided an opportunity for Robespierre's admirers to reassert his worth and echo his revolutionary sentiments, for his was precisely the brand of oratorical fervour that appealed to their late-romantic tastes. So Michelet was able to provide a balanced opinion, located half-way between idolatry and condemnation, and his *Histoire de la Révolution française* is the starting point for more realistic appreciation of the great Revolutionary leader; and, whilst across the Channel Thomas Carlyle disapproved of almost anything French, on the other hand J. W. Croker, the great collector of Revolutionary pamphlets, produced a more reliable study which appeared in 1835. Though he detested many of the leaders of the Revolution, the English savant had a soft spot for Robespierre, who, in his considered view, came to grief precisely because he favoured decency, mercy and religion.

The twentieth century has been more scholarly, and therefore fairer still. M. Aulard's fantastic taste for documentation enabled him, in his *Histoire politique de la Révolution française* of 1901, to examine Maximilien's role in the light of the political difficulties and newly-acquired confidence of leaders of the Third Republic. Clearly, for him the First Republic had been an initial attempt to realize certain dreams and Robespierre was considered the most sincere dreamer of them all. Mathiez and Lefebvre continued the good work. In 1907 the former founded the excellent society to which we referred earlier and which set on a permanent basis the rehabilitation of the great tribune. Encouraged by this new enthusiasm for Robespierre, in 1961 Walter published the best biography in French, whilst Thompson's two volumes remain the fairest and most adequate English study. Though the 'man's man', Danton, is often preferred in our own day—witness Christophe's fascinating book—Robespierre is now appreciated by radicals and liberals for the part he played in laying foundations. At the same time, as Marxists blame him for favouring the bourgeoisie and therefore ensuring their triumph in 1815, the Right still see him as a vile demagogue. We remember, for example, the division of opinion on these issues in 1958, when a bi-centenary called for some recognition of Maximilien by the City of Paris he had served with such devotion. No street or statue, however, commemorates his career in a city which invented the Commune. In a France which cannot be sure whether he was really the friend of the workers or the middle classes, his memory is still ambiguous, because he failed to carve out a clear-cut, unified social democracy from what was essentially a social revolution.

Yet, in another sense, he triumphed for all time: reviewing his fortunes, we noted that he could never at any time be completely and definitively overlooked, neglected or forgotten. As we have seen already, he had a significant following in his own day and his passing left its impression on friend and foe alike, as is proved by the diversity and variety of tributes and strictures.[15] For example, the Comte de Montgaillard, who had no reason to like him, explained that the Incorruptible's popularity was due to his modesty, even in moments of triumph, and to the thrift and obscurity which were characteristic of his private life. Ginguené declared that his appeal was greater than that of any member of the upper Committee and, surprisingly enough, the arch-enemy Fouché went much beyond that simple statement when he averred that 'only one man in the Convention appeared to enjoy unassailable popularity; that was the Man from Artois, Robespierre.' In saying this, he concurred with another great personality of the Revolutionary period, the orator Barnave, in whose *Réflexions politiques* we learn that 'Robespierre engages public attention more than ever ... those who compose the history of our Revolution cannot avoid making known this singular person.' From an opponent like Barnave that epithet is surely striking, and we may well inquire in what way he was exceptional.

Danton and Marat had both been exceptional men; both had enjoyed a good following. Indeed, there are those who would maintain that Robespierre had less forcefulness than Danton and less instinctive sympathy with the electorate than Marat. Nor, as we said earlier, was Maximilien personally lovable. So we must seek elsewhere the reason for his hidden charisma and his enduring vogue. Danton and Marat, we have said, were exceptional men. Above all, they were men. They were supremely human and endowed with natural appetites. Without being either inhuman or superhuman, Robespierre was less obviously human than the other two. He was 'singular' and that fact accounts for much of the interest he has aroused over the years.

More than that, his fascination probably lies in a largely unconscious association of ideas, of which we must now take account.

Chapter 19

THE WOODEN EAGLE

'La doctrine sublime et touchante de la vertu et de l'égalité
que le fils de Marie enseigna jadis à ses concitoyens'

ROBESPIERRE

A Rosicrucian symbol daily confronted the carpenter (and Mason?) and his famous tenant. On the yard-wall of the Duplay house and almost beneath the room in which Maximilien prepared his speeches, there was affixed an eagle. It was not the bronze, gold or silver eagle of Rome or the Holy Roman Empire: nor was it the gilded eagle of the Napoleonic campaigns. It was a plain, unvarnished eagle, carved from common wood by the master craftsman with whom Robespierre lodged, Maurice Duplay, and could be considered an apt emblem for the down-to-earth, thrifty, hard-working lodger, whose life was destined to be associated with more than one carpenter.

Let us explain. After the Revolution, Madame Lebas, the widow of one of his stoutest disciples and daughter of his former land-lord, Duplay, owned a parrot, which, when asked 'Where is Saint-Maximilien?' was wont to reply: 'In heaven, next to Jesus-Christ!'[1] If this tit-bit appears not only to anticipate in some details the end of Flaubert's *Un cœur simple*, but also to border on the irreverent, perhaps a more serious example will serve our purpose better. A few weeks before the Incorruptible's fall, an old soldier came up to him and said: 'I consider you, citizen, to be the Messiah, whom the Supreme Being promised us to reform the world!'[2] Therein lie precious clues.

Certain similarities between the careers of Robespierre and Christ were inescapable. In the first place, their births presented irregularities of one sort or another. The new Messiah had been deprived of his parents at a tender age; Christ appears to have lost his father at the age of ten or twelve.

It is also a felicitous coincidence that both men passed thirty years before beginning a brief spell of proselytizing; that both had precursors of sorts, the Baptist and Jean Marat, who, like the other John, was to meet an untimely and dramatic death. Other

204

coincidental similarities spring to mind as we ponder the parallel. In Hebrew lore, the title 'Son of Man' is of northern origin. Nazareth is in the north of Palestine; Arras in northern France. Both men were apparently uninterested in travel beyond the confines of their own lands. Both went into retirement when they had to make major decisions. The 'End of the Days', the forty days in the wilderness, were paralleled by Maximilien's retirement for precisely forty days before the events that were to end his life. From busy turmoil and labour, both found innocent solace and comfort in the company of certain families. Just as Jesus sought out Martha, Mary and Lazarus at Bethany, so Maximilien spent happy *soirées* with the Desmoulins and the Duplays. Neither man appears to have formed attachments that went beyond the platonic.

More important still, however, were conceptions of the purpose of their lives. Both followed out a grand design, either calculated, or likely to end on the scaffold. Imbued with mystic dynamism and fired by a mixture of apprehension and determination (the one alternating with the other), both lived out their destiny amalgamating politics and religion in a special way. People of all persuasions and opinions were not slow to sense the 'holiness' of 'Saint-Maximilien'. A fellow politician, Rabut de Saint-Etienne, was heard to remark: 'He is a priest, who wishes to become God!'[3] and the strange Théot woman claimed that her 'Son' was fulfilling a mission foretold by Ezekiel, just as Jesus had fulfilled the prophecies of Isaiah. Both reformers, the Jew and the Frenchman who championed the Jews, believing in a special kind of Providence, took the stage precisely when they were needed—that is, when rebellion against tyranny was afoot. Democrats (some have said, almost communists), they led mankind towards liberty and were almost irresistible in their moment of time, because their ethics were uncompromising.

Paying sincere tribute in a *Lettre à mes commettans* to 'the sublimely moving doctrine of virtue and equality, taught in former times to his fellow-citizens by the Son of Mary'[4] and underlining by this very choice of words the fact that Jesus had held dear *the very values to which he had devoted his own life,* Robespierre quite clearly saw the point and seized upon it, so that one begins to wonder if his own forty days in the wilderness of his sick-bed were purely coinciden-tal. However that may be, it is certain that, travelling under the colours of a greater preacher than he was, before this withdrawal he had already disclosed his indebtedness:

	St Matthew, 5–7	*Feb. 5, 1794*
Change	Ye have heard that it was said by them of old time . . . But I say unto you . . .	'In our country, we wish to substitute morality for egoism and probity for honour . . .'
Legality	Think not that I am come to destroy the law . . . but to fulfil.	'We seek an order . . . in which the people are subjected to the magistrate, the magistrate to the people and the people to justice.'
Wealth	Lay not up for yourselves treasures upon earth . . . But lay up for yourselves treasures in heaven . . .	'We seek to substitute . . . the love of glory for the love of money.'
Hypocrisy	Beware of false prophets, which come to you in sheep's clothing . . .	'The false revolutionary is perhaps more often lagging behind, than outstripping the Revolution . . . He is madly patriotic . . .'
Proof of Hypocrisy	Ye shall know them by their fruits.	'Do you desire to put them to the test? Instead of assurances and declamations, ask them for real service.'

Here the similarities are arresting, in tone as well as in topic. The conviction that this imitation was deliberate grows when we consider a second case, the speech of May 7, 1794, directed against hypocrisy:

	St Matthew, 5–7	*May 7, 1974*
Patriotic compliment	Ye are the salt of the earth . . .	'Oh, my native land! . . . Oh, sublime people!'

	St Matthew, 5–7	May 7, 1974
Proselytism	Let your light so shine before men, that they may see your good works . . .	'The art of ruling . . . must be none other than enlightening and improving people'
Denigration of priests	except your righteousness shall exceed the righteousness of the scribes and Pharisees . . .	'Priests are to ethics as quacks are to medicine.'
Old v. New	Ye have heard that it was said by them of old time . . . But I say unto you . . .	'Immorality is the foundation of despotism as virtue is the essence a republic'.
Hypocrisy reproved	thou shalt not be as the hypocrites are . . .	'You have alerted patriots of good faith, who could be led astray by the dangerous example offered by the hypocritical architects of this plot.'
Stoicism	strait is the gate and narrow is the way . . .	'Stoicism saved the honour of human nature . . .'
The Universal moral contest	Ye cannot serve God and Mammon.	'Vice and virtue are responsible for fate here on earth; they are two rival genies who fight each other for possession of our planet.'

The pacifists' charter, the Sermon on the Mount, has served as model in both cases. Maximilien clearly prefers the new to the old, Jesus to Moses.

Retiring, non-violent like priests who are non-combatants in war; distinct from other citizens in their refusal to amass riches (Maximilien left about £100), Jesus and Maximilien visited righteous strictures on rogues and exploiters and, as teachers of righteousness, were spurned by sinful mankind. During the ethical crusade, both gathered around themselves a little band of disciples. There were twelve in the Committee of Public Safety. Though surely this is pure coincidence, nevertheless, that Committee contained its Iscariots. On the other hand, it had its intense loyalists: we think chiefly of Saint-Just, who identified Maximilien with God; and of the unfortunate Couthon, who worshipped his master with servile devotion to the end. Just as the disciples of the New Testament acted to some extent as a body-guard for their Master, so the Incorruptible had a circle of defenders, consisting of humble citizens who showed great devotion and, had not the Incorruptible's blustering 'Simon Peter', Henriot, betrayed his trust by being drunk when he should have been acting on his master's behalf, the leader's life might have been saved.

So the coincidences multiply impressively. Veronica brought children to Our Lord. They were even brought to be blessed by Maximilien too. He did not rebuke the adoring females who paid him this compliment. On the contrary, he *did* rebuke Merlin de Thionville for forbidding one woman to shout 'Vive Robespierre' instead of 'Vive la République'.[5] In pseudo-Christian vein the Revolutionary politician asked: 'Why do you ill-treat this poor woman?', and the critic retired in confusion. Furthermore, by deliberate exploitation of the state of celibacy, which to many females is a mystic challenge, Maximilien appears to have taken advantage of the deeply-rooted feelings which longed to blossom forth anew; and, in Robespierre's incorruptibility, in his un-compromising championship of the popular cause, in his immense sympathy for the underprivileged, in his simple life, spent, like Christ's, in a carpenter's establishment, the good folk perceived an echo of their deep need to worship—perhaps even an answer to that need. This fact too he understood and used to advantage on a very special occasion.

Two biblical events may have been recalled by this Feast of the Supreme Being. First, Robespierre may have sensed that ascent of the Sacred Mountain would remind his supporters (who had also been reared on the Scriptures) of the Transfiguration of Jesus in the presence of Peter, James and John, and might help his followers to regard him in a new light. The second possibility is more fascinating still. In an earlier chapter, we noted how he chose Christmas Day of the old calendar for a homily on statecraft. For the same reason, the Fête de l'Etre Suprême was almost certainly planned to coincide with old Whit Sunday, when Christians recall the descent of the Holy Spirit, repent for their sins and turn again to righteousness. Realizing that the Scriptures spoke of 3,000 souls converted on that first Day of Pentecost, Robespierre may have hoped that association of ideas would help him to direct men's ambitions away from self-seeking, lust and greed. The very choice of what had once been a Sunday is not without significance, for it was on a Sunday in the previous November that the Feast of Reason, against which the new Feast was directed, had taken place in Notre-Dame Cathedral. Thus it would appear that both dechristianizers and their critics hoped to turn old reverence to account. The Day of Pentecost would be doubly suited to Maximilien's purpose—and its potentialities did not stop there. His hopes extended to even more exciting prospects.

Like a catalyst, the moral character which had given Maximilien self-confidence when defending the right, helped to precipitate good and evil in the world around him. In George Büchner's play about Danton, the hero reproaches Robespierre with being *intolerably* virtuous, with not having stolen money, incurred debts, slept with women, neglected his appearance or taken to drink. That was the spirit that spilled over into the warmer, increasingly permissive months of 1794, and had once prompted one of Robespierre's enemies to refer derisively to him as the 'Holy Ark' which no one dared to touch for fear of being struck down.[6] Supplemented by hatred and envy, derision spelt extreme danger for the Incorruptible Legislator. What had happened in recent times to Lepeletier and Marat could happen again. How many more aspiring Cordays, Admirals and Renaults lurked in the shadows, behind symbolic mountains and allegorical figures; how many more (as perhaps on July 17, 1791) were hiding beneath platforms ready to pounce? He could never be sure, but, knowing that the pack of plotters was ever on his heels, Robespierre foresaw that (as Christ deliberately fulfilled the prophecies at the Passover) he might make a truly significant departure from this world by being assassinated on that great day of personal achievement, which was also a triumph for his God. Assassination seemed the most likely outcome of the growing conflict between the unique Incorruptible and the Corruptible many. An open confrontation would be less decisive. For the gangsters had the advantage of initiative, and Maximilien knew that, on this occasion, to use his own considerable power would not solve anything finally and completely, for, like the apprentice's broomsticks in the well-known fable, unlimited numbers of Corruptibles would spring forward to replace the present crowd. So it would only be a matter of time before he was up against the same danger once more. A missionary after his own fashion, and convinced that the Revolution could represent basic neo-Christianity in action, Maximilien sensed that by mid-1794 his effective work would have been accomplished. At college he had read his Racine carefully and had admired Andromache's *innocent stratagème*, an heroic suicide planned by a virtuous person in trouble. Why not plan something analagous in 1794? Since precept and example had to a large extent failed, conversion by shock might result from planned immolation and the desired moral revolution might thus be launched. The more he thought about it, the more satisfying this idea appeared. Furthermore, if assassination seemed the most effective alternative to public execution, it would be better to have it happen at a moment when the event would signify something to all those religious folk who hated sin.

The day chosen for the apotheosized demise of the great leader would have to coincide with the feast of his own deity, for at that point in time the ethical importance of his mission would be most evident. A 'religious' ceremony directed against dechristianizers and atheists would suit the case very well. So, a Flaubert ahead of his time, the ailing Maximilien planned his last chapter to coincide with a holy day in the old calendar, and, just as the nineteenth-century *conteur* would one day contrive that Félicité should die accompanied by the sounds and odours of processions, by choirs of young maidens in white and by the public spectacle itself, so the hero of the Revolutionary Montagne sought to end it all in appropriate surroundings.

Trembling and timid, Maximilien put on his best suit. Though the Duplays admired it and considered it only worthy of one so famous, they must have had their doubts about its appropriateness to the occasion, for, as we have suggested, sartorial ostentation could be accounted a bad error in one professing to represent the workers. But there was compelling reason why that suit had to be worn. Was he not in fact specially attired for immolation? Was he not arrayed in a gaudy costume, so unlike the sombre black of his fellows, in order to be absolutely conspicuous and therefore the perfect target? Whatever the truth, bearing in clammy hands bouquets of assorted blooms, he climbed the symbolic eminence that, symbolically again, was to bring him closer to his god. On the way, thoughts assailed him. Clutching with the flowers the manuscript he had used a few minutes ago, he recalled how he had done the same whilst waiting for his king in the rain. His head was swimming. Black spots danced before his tired eyes. That awful twitching of his facial muscles was beginning again. He hoped that the multitude would not notice the convulsions in his shoulders. He was very sure that his enemies were ready to strike him down, and murmurings on all sides confirmed this. He hoped it would happen today.

Alas, assassination did not come on that most significant of occasions. Though this was an anticlimax, he knew he would not have long to wait. A friend commented: 'For far too long he had been known as the Incorruptible.'[7] That put it in a nutshell. It was merely a question of time and right and proper that it should be so. The lamb had lain on the altar, but the knife had not fallen when expected, so, unlike the 'Passover Plot', Maximilien's scheme had temporarily aborted. No matter; the lamb would die before very long and thus fulfil a whole series of predictions.

So much of what was happening and was imminent had been foretold. Already in 1791, Robespierre had observed: 'I am called to a stormy destiny. I must follow out its course until I have made the ultimate sacrifice for my country.'[8] As if to stress the point again, in the following year, 1792, he had remarked:

'Heaven, which furnished me with a soul eager for freedom and arranged that I should be born under tyranny . . ., may well be calling upon me to trace out with my life's blood the path my country must follow if it is to achieve happiness and freedom. Rapturously I accept such a sweet and glorious destiny.'[9]

General de Gaulle could not have bettered that! His last words to the Jacobins are even more appealing:

'the speech you have just heard is my last will and testament. I saw the facts clearly today: the league of villains is so strong that I cannot hope to escape them. Without regret I succumb. I leave behind a memory of myself and you will vindicate it . . .'[10]

Thus his departure from this life was merely postponed and the parallels between his agony and that of Our Lord multiplied again. For instance, when, following his arrest, Maximilien and his disciples were briefly detained at the Tuileries before being taken to their various prisons, it transpired that a clap of thunder was heard, reminiscent of sympathetic climatic or sidereal manifestations in the Bible. Superstitious followers noted this divine pathetic fallacy and were thereby reassured on the issue of holiness. Other details seemed to justify this assurance. 'I leave unto them the terrible truth . . . and death', had declared the Incorruptible in truly biblical vein.[11] In response, the third issue of the *Vieux Cordelier* had given Desmoulins the opportunity to speak of Maximilien's imminent 'Calvary'; and, though *calvaire* often means nothing more than 'tribulation', the fact that there were to be three leading victims (the 'Triumvirate') on 10 Thermidor was to add some slight credibility to the association.[12] Another friend, Buonarotti, had mentioned his resemblance to Our Lord; as if to signal acceptance of the comparison, Robespierre had spoken of his own 'Gethsemane', which, as he saw things, was to be located on the side of that apocalyptic Mountain on the Champ de Mars.[13] The similarity continued to the end. At one point in his agony, Maximilien was taken into a room with a green-covered table used by the Committee. There, lying stretched out, with an old ammunition-box serving as a pillow and with his clothing dishevelled and dirty, he was reviled by guards with such remarks as 'Sire! Your Majesty appears to be suffering'; or 'Have you lost your powers of speech?' and similar indignities, reminiscent of the New Testament. Both Jesus and Maximilien made that humiliating journey along a *via dolorosa*—in the Incorruptible's case carried across a mocking Paris, by way of the Hôtel-Dieu to the Conciergerie on a filthy litter, with his shattered jaw draped in a dirty handkerchief, his shaking body insulted by passers-by. And it is an appalling coincidence that in their agony both were offered sour wine on a sponge.[14] Wounds, outrage, sarcasm—these were the background to the last journey, for on the morrow Maximilien had to traverse part of that grievous itinerary in reverse—this time in an open tumbril, through jeering crowds. Those who witnessed it could never forget one 'station' along this road of death. Outside Duplay's place the procession stopped, whilst some practical joker, having taken advantage of the proximity of Les Halles, flung at the carpenter's door a bucket of animal's blood.

How very reminiscent in spirit of that first Good Friday! Hunted down by the enemies of righteousness, both reformers had foreseen their deaths and both *may* have committed symbolic suicide, in the first case at thirty-three, in the second at thirty-five and, in both cases, after three years of active 'ministry'.

Wardens of children's homes are well aware that a child rejected by a parent never renounces the quest to find him again. So it was with Maximilien. It is also said that the great Racine passed through a period in his development when the father-figure dominated his interest and aspirations. In Robespierre's case, it would be truer to say that every period was dominated by this search and by this ideal: first, Robespierre *père* and disillusionment; then, Louis XVI and still more disillusionment; then, shades of the divine Jean-Jacques Rousseau, followed by considerable satisfaction; finally, and most significant of all, a desire for beatific identification with the Heavenly Father, incarnated by the Man of Sorrows.

The coincidences were many, as we have seen, but they remained either pure coincidences or similarities arising from sincere respect or devoted imitation. So we need hardly stress the point. The imperfect cannot be compared with the All-Perfect. Robespierre was *not* a late-eighteenth-century Christ, though he may have planned to become one; and throughout his political career, because of largely accidental parallels, a kind of spiritual hypnosis had been at work on the unsuspecting public, compelling response to contiguous imagery. 'Christ recrucified', murmured some as the blade fell, almost unaware of what they were saying. Yet this thread of cognition was to become an associative strand ensuring that posterity would never fail to be fascinated by this strangely familiar martyr.

REFERENCES

(See Code under *Printed Works* Section)

FOREWORD

1. (T.1), 1
2. (W.2), II, 325 sq.
3. (R.7), VI, 168; VII, 739
4. (R.7), II, 412
5. (R.7), I, 43
6. (R.7), VII, 432
7. (R.7), X, 388

INTRODUCTION

1. (R.5), I, 259–273

CHAPTER 1

1. (R.7), III, 98
2. (M.9), 40
3. (R.7), I, 45
4. (T.3), I, 9
5. (R.7), I, 211
6. (T.3), II, 150
7. (R.7), II, 129–224
8. (R.7), II, 181 and 195
9. See (R.7), III, 29
10. (R.7), II, 226–72
11. (R.5), I, 275–98
12. (W.2), I, 77
13. (R.5), I, 265

CHAPTER 2

1. (K.1), 708
2. (T.4), 235–36
3. (R.7), III, 46 and VI, 38–39
4. (W.2), I, 136–37
5. (W.2), I, 134
6. (R.7), I, 241–43
7. (R.7), VI, 39–43
8. (R.7), III, 87–88
9. (R.7), VII, 659–63
10. (R.7), VII, 514–39
11. (R.7), VII, 553–58
12. (R.7), VII, 601
13. (R.7), VIII, 15–23
14. (R.7), VIII, 308

CHAPTER 3

1. (R.7), VII, 383–93
2. (R.7), VII, 404–12
3. (R.7), VI, 131
4. (R.7), VIII, 47–64
5. (R.7), VII, 132–52 and VIII, 291
6. (R.7), VII, 432–37
7. (R.7), IV, 324

REFERENCES

8. (R.7), VIII, 427–28
9. (C.9), 193
10. (R.7), VIII, 458
11. (R.7), V, 56–64; IX, 183–202 and 228–30
12. (R.7), IX, 350–52
13. (R.7), IX, 295–300; 314–19 and 344–50
14. (R.7), IX, 419–21
15. (R.7), IX, 454–75
16. (R.7), IX, 495–513
17. (R.7), IX, 529
18. (R.7), IX, 358

CHAPTER 4

1. (R.7), X, 9–10
2. (M.9), 234
3. (R.7), X, 75–81
4. (R.7), X, 98
5. (R.7), X, 375 and 412
6. (R.7), X, 412
7. (R.7), X, 413

CHAPTER 5

1. (R.7), X, 479–482
2. (R.7), X, 469; III, 288 and 303
3. (R.7), X, 504–505; III 300–301
4. (R.7), X, 542–76
5. (R.7), X, 588–95
6. (R.7), X, 599 (n.1) and 600
7. (L.6), 296 (n.3)
8. (R.7), X, 596–600

CHAPTER 6

1. (R.11), 106
2. (R.7), I, 206
3. (L.6), 40
4. (R.7), III, 22
5. (W.2), I, 482 and (A.1), 21
6. (G.1), 154
7. (S.3), 75
8. (J.2), II, 57–58
9. (S.3), 80
10. (M.12), 261
11. (C.9), 190–93
12. (C.9), 195
13. (W.2), II, 21 and 344
14. (R.6), I, 30
15. (W.2), II, 345
16. (A.1), 15
17. (L.6), 212
18. (R.7), IX, 428–30
19. (C.9), 29–30
20. (L.5), 27–28
21. (L.5), 25
22. (R.7), III, 138
23. (G.1), 124
24. (R.7), III, 121
25. (W.2), II, 346
26. (L.5), 24–25
27. (R.7), IX, 206
28. (W.2), II, 367
29. (L.5), 29–30
30. (L.6), 124
31. (R.7), III, 49, 71 and 147
32. (R.7), III, 23, and 99–100
33. (R.7), I, 223
34. (L.5), 20
35. (G.1), 188
36. (M.12), 161
37. (G.1), 289
38. (R.7), III, 100

39. (R.1), 85
40. (R.3), 37
41. (C.9), 97
42. (A.1), 21
43. (M.12), 94

44. (M.12), 23
45. (G.1), 161
46. (N.2), 86
47. (M.9), 276
48. (M.12), 37–38 and (T.3), I, 31

CHAPTER 7

1. (R.3), 22
2. (M.12), 63, 84 and 157
3. (R.7), IX, 62–77
4. (R.7), IX, 559
5. (G.1), 89
6. (T.3), II, 218
7. (R.7), I, 242
8. (R.1), 24
9. (R.6), III, 131 and 184

10. (R.7), VIII, 447
11. (A.1), 14
12. (M.12), 195
13. (R.7), IX, 523
14. (R.6), II, 99
15. (R.7), X, 453
16. (L.6), 192
17. (L.6), 260

CHAPTER 8

1. (A.1), 210
2. (M.12), 41
3. (R.1), 24
4. (B.9), 198
5. (M.12), 45
6. (T.3), I, 125
7. (M2), 130–51
8. (M.2), 171
9. (M.9), 258: (M.12), 72–73
10. (B.8), 84 and n.15
11. See French school history textbooks, e.g. Malet et Isaac Classe de IIe, 145

12. (L.2), 34–35
13. (R.7), I, 193
14. (R.7), I, 188
15. (R.7), I, 194
16. (R.5), I, 173
17. (R.7), I, 220
18. *Lettres persanes*, XLVI
19. (R.7), I, 220
20. (M.9), 42–43; (M.12), 73
21. (R.7), I, 230–32
22. (R.7), I, 97
23. (R.7), I, 235–40

CHAPTER 9

1. (R.3), 109–10
2. (T.3), I, 180–81
3. (R.7), I, 103
4. (R.5), I, 41
5. (R.7), X, 455
6. (W.2), II, 141–42
7. (R.7), IV, 26–27

8. (W.2), II, 335
9. (W.2), II, 375
10. (R.7), IV, 37–64
11. (R.7), IV, 161–79
12. (R.7), IV, 173–75
13. (R.7), IV, 567–83

REFERENCES

CHAPTER 10

1. (R.11), 128
2. (M.9), 51
3. (M.9), 60
4. (A.1), 229
5. (K.1), 710
6. (R.7), I, 46
7. (M.12), 39
8. (R.7), IV, 39–42
9. (R.7), VI, 385–96
10. (R.7), VII, 377–423
11. (R.7), VII, 446–58
12. (R.7), VIII, 235
13. (R.7), IX, 120–42
14. (R.7), IX, 123–24 and 130
15. (W.2), II, 341
16. (R.7), IX, 356–71
17. (M.9), 59–60;
18. (R.7), IX, 460–61
19. (R.7), IX, 495
20. (R.7), 169–70
21. (C.9), 256–57

CHAPTER 11

1. (M.8), 40
2. (R.7), X, 353
3. (R.7), I, 22–24 and 31
4. (R.7), I, 35–36
5. Chaps. X and XV
6. (B.10), 47 and (R.7), VI, 87
7. (B.9), 25
8. Book II, Chapter V
9. (C.9), 87
10. (C.7), 81–82
11. (C.7), 79
12. (R.7), IX, 463–69
13. (R.7), X, 272–81
14. (C.9), 65 and (G.1), 191
15. (R.7), IX, 559 and (R.11), 136
16. IX and XIX
17. (R.7), I, 41
18. (G.1), 145 and (B.10), 412
19. (R.7), X, 353
20. (R.7), VIII, 351
21. (R.7), IX, 274–76
22. (R.7), IX, 274 and (C.9), 67

CHAPTER 12

1. (R.7), X, 353 and X, 462
2. (R.7), X, 445
3. (R.7), VIII, 74–92 and 132–52
4. (T.3), I, 219
5. (R.7), VI, 527–30
6. (R.7), VI, 356–62
7. (R.7), X, 281
8. (S.3), 327
9. (A.1), 38
10. (A.1), 35
11. (R.7), VIII, 262–63
12. (R.7), VII, 431–46
13. (R.7), IX, 560
14. (M.9), 102 and (M.12), 208
15. (R.7), IX, 546–47
16. (M.9), 99
17. (R.6), II, 99 and (R.3), 151
18. (T.3), I, 233; (R.6), I, 69 and II, 99
19. (R.7), III, 147; (R.6), II, 117
20. (R.7), IX, 624 and X, 168
21. (R.7), VIII, 272–73
22. (R.7), X, 278
23. (R.7), IX, 546–47
24. (W.3), 81
25. (W.2), II, 349–50

26. (R.7), III, 296 and (L.5), 30–31
27. Chap. IV
28. (R.7), X, 524–30

CHAPTER 13

1. (M.12), 80
2. (L.6), 156
3. (R.7), I, 31
4. *Lettres persanes*, LIX
5. (R.7), I, 31
6. (R.7), I, 190
7. (R.7), VII, 172–73
8. (R.7), VII, 554–56
9. (G.1), 163 and (R.7), IX, 495
10. (R.7), X, 350–67
11. (R.7), VII, 695
12. (R.7), VIII, 230
13. (R.7), VIII, 235
14. (M.9), 46 and (C.9), 105
15. (R.7), VIII, 234
16. (C.9), 106–07
17. (R.7), X, 233–37
18. (R.7), X, 193–201
19. (R.7), X, 197
20. (R.7), X, 455
21. (R.7), X, 229
22. (R.7), X, 350–67
23. (R.7), I, 156
24. (C.8), 268–87
25. (T.3), II, 154
26. (R.7), X, 442–65
27. *Emile*, Book IV
28. Chap. III
29. (R.7), X. 452
30. *Lettres persanes*, CLX
31. (R.1), 107
32. (A.1), 199 and (R.7), V, 116–21

CHAPTER 14

1. (R.6), II, 40
2. (R.7), VIII, 326
3. (R.7), VIII, 322–27 and IX, 14–22
4. (R.7), IX, 67–77, 104
5. (R.7), IX, 83–84
6. (R.7), X, 98
7. (R.7), X, 483–87
8. (K.1), 706–07 and (H.3), 230
9. (R.7), 622–25
10. (M.9), 90
11. (R.7), X, 570
12. (R.3), 126–27
13. (G.1), 237
14. (W.2), II, 378
15. Book IV, Chap. VI
16. (R.7), X, 514, 523 and 526
17. (R.6), I, 161
18. (R.7), IX, 579
19. (R.7), IX, 467–68
20. (R.7), IX, 563–64
21. (R.7), III, 237, 154, and 308; IX, 521 and X, 102
22. (R.7), III, 149–50
23. (R.7), III, 274
24. (R.7), III, 23–24; (R.11), 80 and (M.12), 37
25. (R.7), VII, 432–37
26. (T.3), II, 108
27. (R.7), IX, 545
28. (R.1), 159 and (H.3), 150
29. (M.9), 75–77; (T.3), II, 99; (H.3), 220
30. (R.7), VI, 167–68

31. (R.7), VII, 739
32. (R.7), VII, 346–76
33. (R.7), VII, 731–33

34. (R.7), VII, 738
35. (R.7), X, 504–10
36. (W.2), II, 338

CHAPTER 15

1. (R.7), VII, 164
2. (T.4), 236–37
3. (R.7), IX, 110–20
4. (R.7), IX, 117
5. (H.3), 186

6. (R.7), IX, 459
7. (R.7), X, 76
8. (R.7), IX, 113
9. (R.7), IX, 110–20

CHAPTER 16

1. (R.7), IX, 607
2. (R.7), X, 10–42

3. (R.7), X, 11–12
4. (R.7), X, 455

CHAPTER 17

1. (R.1), 138
2. (M.12), 33 and 56
3. (R.7), VII, 514–38
4. (R.7), VI, 87
5. (T.3), I, 156
6. (M.12), 282
7. (M.12), 184
8. (R.5), I, 258
9. (R.7), VI, 429–35
10. (R.7), VII, 334–38; (R.6), I, 54
11. (G.1), 120
12. (C.9), 223
13. (R.7), IX, 568; VII, 56–60
14. (R.7), IX, 629–31

15. (W.2), II, 417
16. (C.7), 72; (C.9), 80
17. (R.11), 127
18. (R.11), 101
19. (A.1), 44 and (B.4), 253
20. (R.11), 101
21. (R.1), 173
22. (A.1), 37–38
23. (M.12), 261
24. (R.7), X, 542–82
25. See Goethe's poem *Der Zanberlehrling* (1797) and, of course, Dukas's music *L'Apprenti sorcier*

CHAPTER 18

1. (R.3), 169
2. (R.6), I, 20
3. (R.11), 126
4. (T.1), 3
5. (B.9), 20
6. (R.7), IX, 465–66

7. (M.9), 251–52
8. (M.12), 233
9. (R.11), 10
10. (R.11), 149
11. (C.1) II, 349
12. (M.9), 78

REFERENCES

13. (R.7), X, 446
14. (A.1), 19

15. (W.2), II, 334, 341, 347 and 350

CHAPTER 19

1. (C.9), 103
3. (S.3), 92
3. (S.3), 88
4. (C.7), 154
5. (L.6), 162
6. (G.1), 181
7. (B.6), 222

8. (G.1), 108
9. (R.7), VIII, 315
10. (L.6), 168
11. (G.1), 313
12. (R.11), 123
13. (L.5), 37 and (M.12), 277
14. (M.12), 299

BIBLIOGRAPHY

1. MANUSCRIPT SOURCES

A. GENERAL

The reader should dip into the following *cartons* at the French Archives Nationales, 60 Rue des Francs-Bourgeois, Paris 3:

AA	Section législative et judiciaire
AF	Section administrative (d'Etat)
BB	Justice
C	Procès-verbaux des assemblées nationales
D	Comités des assemblées
F^7	Police Générale
F^{7}*	Registres
F^{12}	Commerce et industrie
F^{13}	Bâtiments civils
F^{15}	Hospices et secours
H	Généralités
KK	Monuments historiques
O^1	Maison du roi
T	Section domaniale et séquestre
W	Section judiciare
Y	Archives du Châtelet de Paris
Z	Juridictions spéciales et ordinaires

B. SPECIFIC MANUSCRIPT SOURCES IN THE ARCHIVES NATIONALES

Admiral and Renault Affairs	W 389
	F^7 4762
	AF^2 275
Agents used by Robespierre	F^7 4436
	W$_{IA}$ 79–80
	F^7 3822
	W 500–01
	F^7 4774–75
	F^7 4432
	AF 47–363

August 10, 1792	F[7] 4622
	F[7] 4774
Barère, Bertrand	F[7] 4432
Champ de Mars Massacre	C[71] 695–700
	F[7] 4622
	D xxix[b] 36
	F[7] 4623
Charlotte Robespierre	F[7] 4436
Committee of Public Safety	AF[II] 180 and 191
	O[2] 449, 453, 469, 543
	AF[II] 33–170
Daily Life of Robespierre	W 79, 500–01
	F[13] 278[2], 281A
	F[7] 4774–75
	AB xix 179
Duplay Family	W[IA] 79–80
	W 500, 534–35
	F[7] 3299[19], 4694, 4775, 6694
	T 1494
	F[4] 2090, 2091
Economics	C 1843
	AF[IV] 1470
	F[12] 1547
Etats-Généraux	O 354
Fête de l'Étre Suprême	C 304, 354–1853
	C[II] 1117–18, 1123–24
	F[14] I, 84
	F[4] 1017, 2090–91
	F[7] 3821
Girondins	AF[IV] 1470
	F[7] 3688
Henriot, François	AF[II] 47
Messe Rouge	F[7] 4774[80]
Militia (*Sans-Culotte*)	BB[3] 80
	F[7*] 2497, 2507, 2520
Spy System	F[7] 4743, 4774, 4775
	AF[II] 46, 358, 289, 111
Théot Affair	C 304
	T 604–05
	F[7] 4685, 4716, 4728, 4774–75
Thermidor 9–10	F[7] 4432, 4433, 4436, 4766
	D xxxv C[2]
	AF[II] 32, 47, 365

	W^{IA} 79, 80
Trials (Germinal)	F^7 1069, 4443–46, 4660, 4687–92
Vadier, Marc-Guillaume Albert	C 304
Villiers, Pierre	F^4 4775^{47}

These works may be consulted with profit:
ROBERTS, J. M.: *French Revolution Documents*, Oxford, 1966.
HARDY, J. D., ed. of *The Maclure Collection of French Revolutionayy Documents*, O.U.P., 1966.

2. PRINTED WORKS

(R. represents Robespierre)

CODE
(A.1)   *Actes du Colloque R.* (Vienna, September 1963). Paris, Société des Etudes R., 1967.

(A.2)   *Annales historiques de la Révolution Française*, ibid.

(A.3)   Anon: *Secret Symbols*. Altona, 1785.

(A.4)   Anouilh, Jean: *Pauvre Bitos* (1956). ed. W. D. Howarth, London, 1958.

(A.5)   Aubry, Octave: 'R. et la Mère de Dieu', *Historia*, mai 1958, pp. 498–99.

(B.1)   Barbier, Pierre and Vernillet, France: *Histoire de France par les chansons* (vol. IV). Paris, 1957.

(B.2)   Barnard, T. C.: *Education and the French Revolution*. C.U.P., 1969.

(B.3)   Barruel, Augustin, Abbé de: *Mémoires pour servir à l'histoire du Jacobinisme*. London, 1797–98.

(B.4)   Beaulieu et Michaud: R. in *Biographie universelle*. vol. XXXVIII (1824), pp. 232–55.

(B.5)   Belloc, Hilaire: *The French Revolution*. 2nd ed., O.U.P., 1966.

(B.6)   Béraud, Henri: *Mon ami R.* Paris, 1927.

(B.7)   Berthe, L.-N.: *Dictionnaire des correspondants de l'Académie d'Arras au temps de R.* Arras, 1969.

(B.8)   Bessand-Massenet, Pierre: *De R. à Bonaparte*. Paris, 1970.

(B.9)   Bienvenue, Richard T. ed.: *The Ninth of Thermidor: the Fall of R.* O.U.P., 1968.

(B.10) Bouloiseau, Marc: *R.* Paris, 1961.

(B.11) Büchner, Georg: *Dantons Tod*, Frankfurt a/M, 1963.

(C.1)   Carlyle, Thomas: *The French Revolution*. 2 vols., London, 1892.
       Carr, John L.: the following articles:

(C.2) — 'Pygmalion and the *Philosophes*'. *Journal of the Warburg and Courtauld Inst.* vol. XXIII (1960), pp. 239–55.

(C.3) — 'Gorgons, Gormagons, Medusists and Masons' *Modern Language Review* vol. LVIII (1963), pp. 73–78.

(C.4) — 'The Expulsion of the Jesuits from France', *History Today*, Nov. 1964, pp. 774–81.

(C.5) — 'The Cultural Background to the French Revolution', *History Today*, July 1965, pp. 457–67.

(C.6) — 'The Secret Chain of the *Lettres persanes*', *Studies on Voltaire and the 18th C.* vol. LV (1967), pp. 333–44.

(C.7) Cattaneo, Mario A.: *Liberta e Virtu nel Pensiero politico di R* Milan 1968.

(C.8) Christophe, Robert: *Danton, a Biography*, tr. P. Green. London, 1967.

(C.9) Clauzel, Raymond: *Maximilien R.* Paris, 1912.

(C.10) Cobb, Richard C.: *The Police and the People, French Popular Protest*. O.U.P., 1970.

(D.1) Dinaux, Arthur: *Les Sociétés badines, bachiques, littéraires et chantantes*. 2 vols., Paris, 1867.

(D.2) Duplay, Maurice: *R., amant de la patrie*. Paris, 1929.

(F.1) Fisher, John: *The Elysian Fields: France in Ferment, 1789–1804*. London, 1966.

(G.1) Gallo, Max: *Maximilien R., Histoire d'une solitude*. Paris, 1968.

(G.2) Garat, Dominique-Joseph: *Mémoires historiques sur le 18e siècle*. 2ème ed., Paris, 1821.

(G.3) Guilaine, J.: *Billaud-Varenne: l'ascète de la Révolution*. Paris, 1969.

(H.1) Hadengue, A.: *Les Gardes rouges de l'An II: l'Armée révolutionnaire et le parti hébertiste*. Paris, 1930.

(H.2) Hamel, E.: *Histoire de R*. 3 vols., Paris, 1865.

(H.3) Hampson, Norman: *A Social History of the French Revolution*. London, 1963.

(H.4) Hampson, Norman: *The Enlightenment*. London, 1968.

(H.5) Henriot, Emile: 'Qui était Saint-Just?', *Historia*, août 1967, pp. 50–53.

(H.6) Herriot, Edouard: 'Fouché et R.', *Révolution Française, 1936*.

(I.1) Iremonger, Lucile: *The Fiery Chariot*. London, 1970.

(J.1) Jennings, T.: *The Rosicrucians, their Rites and Mysteries*. London, 1887.

(J.2) Jones, Mervyn. in (M.2) See MacKenzie, Norman.

(K.1) Kropotkine, Pierre: *La Grande Révolution, 1789–1793*. Paris, 1909.

(L.1)   Lefebvre, Georges: *The Coming of the French Revolution*, tr. R. R. Palmer. Princeton U.P., 1967.

(L.2)   Lefebvre, Georges: *The French Revolution*, tr. E. M. Evanson etc. London and N.Y., 1962–64.

(L.3)   Le Forestier, R.: *Les Illuminés de Bavière et la Franc-Maçonnerie allemande*. Paris, 1914.

(L.4)   Le Forestier, R.: *La Franc-maçonnerie occultiste au XVIIIe S.* Paris, 1928.

(L.5)   Lenôtre, G.: *Paris révolutionnaire*. Paris, 1941.

(L.6)   Lenôtre, G.: *R. et la Mère de Dieu'*. Paris, 1926.

(L.7)   Lenôtre, G.: 'Saint-Just à Blérancourt', *Historia*, août 1967, pp. 44–49.

(L.8)   Léon, A.: *La Révolution française et l'éducation technique*. Paris 1969.

(L.9)   Lévy, Arthur: *Napoléon intime*. Paris, 1895.

(M.1)   McDonald, Joan: *Rousseau and the French Revolution, 1762–91*. U.L.P., 1895.

(M.2)   MacKenzie, Norman: ed. *Secret Societies*. London, 1967.

(M.3)   Madelin, Louis: 'Le deuxième centenaire de R.', *Historia*, mai 1958, pp. 487–97.

(M.4)   Madelin, Louis: *The French Revolution*. London, 1916.

(M.5)   Martin, Gaston: *La Franc-maçonnerie française et la préparation de la Révolution*. Paris, 1926.

(M.6)   Martin, Gaston: *Manuel d'histoire de la Franc-maçonnerie française*. Paris, 1929.

(M.7)   Massin, J.: *R.* Paris, 1956.

(M.8)   Mathiez, Albert: *The Fall of R. and other Essays*. London, 1927.

(M.9)   Mathiez, Albert: *Etudes sur R.* Paris, 1958.

(M.10) May, Gita: *Madame Roland and the Age of Revolution*. Columbia U.P., 1970.

(M.11) Mignet, M.: *Histoire de la Révolution française*. 2 vols., Paris, 1892.

(M.12) Mornand, Pierre: *L'Enigme R.* Paris, 1952.

(N.1)   Naudé, Guillaume: *Instruction à la France sur la vérité de l'histoire des Frères de la Rose-Croix*. Paris, 1623.

(N.2)   Noiset, L.: *R. et les femmes*. Paris, 1932.

(P.1)   Palacios, Alvar G.: *The Age of Louis XVI*, tr. M. H. L. Jones. London, 1969.

(P.2)   Palmer, R. R.: *Twelve who Ruled: The Year of Terror in the French Revolution*. Princeton U.P., 1970.

(P.3)   Palmer, R. R.: 'The World Revolution of the West', in *The Eighteenth-Century Revolution*, ed. P. Amann. Boston, 1963, pp. 1–9

(P.4)   Pizzinelli, L. M.: *The Life and Times of* R. London, 1968.
(P.5)   Préclin and Tapié: *Le XVIIIe Siècle*. Paris, 1952.
(R.1)   Ratinaud, Jean: R. Paris, 1966.
(R.2)   Reinhard, M.: *La Chute de la Royauté, 10 août 1792*. Paris, 1969.
(R.3)   Renier, G. J.: R. London, 1936.
(R.4)   Robespierre, Charlotte: *Mémoires* ed. H. Fleischmann, Paris. n.d.
(R.5)   Robespierre, Maximilien: *Mémoires authentiques, ornés de son portrait*. 2 vols., Bruxelles, 1830.
(R.6)   Robespierre, Maximilien: *Textes choisis*, ed. J. Poperen. 3 vols., Paris, 1956–58.
(R.7)   Robespierre, Maximilien: *Oeuvres complètes* viz:
      I R. à Arras, ed. E. Déprez. Paris, 1910.
      II Les Oeuvres judiciares, ed. E. Lesueur. Paris, 1913.
      III Correspondance avec Augustin, etc., ed. G. Michon. Paris, 1926–41.
      IV *Le Défenseur de la Constitution*, ed. G. Laurent. Nancy, 1939.
      V *Lettres à ses Commettans*, ed. G. Laurent. Paris, 1961.
      VI Discours (1789–90), ed. Bouloiseau, Lefebvre and Soboul. Paris, 1950.
      VII Discours (Jan.–Sept., 1791), same editors. Paris, 1952.
      VIII Discours (Oct. 1791–Sept. 1792), same editors. Paris, 1954.
      IX Discours (Sept. 1792–July 1793), same editors. Paris, 1958.
      X Discours July 27, 1793–July 27, 1794), same editors. Paris, 1967.
(R.8)   Robiquet, J.: *La Vie quotidienne au temps de la Révolution*. Paris, 1938.
(R.9)   Robinson, John: *Proofs of a conspiracy against all religions and governments of Europe*. Edinburgh, 1797.
(R.10) Roland, Madame M. J. P.: *Mémoires*, ed. P. de Roux. Paris, 1966.
(R.11) Rudé, George: ed. R. Englewood Cliffs. N.J., 1967.
(R.12) Rudé, George: *Paris and London in the Eighteenth Century*. London, 1970.
(R.13) Rudé, George: *The Crowd in the French Revolution*. O.U.P., 1959.
(R.14) Rudé, George: *Revolutionary Europe, 1783–1815*. London, 1965.
(S.1)   Schonfield, Hugh: *Those Incredible Christians*. London, 1968.
(S.2)   Schonfield, Hugh: *The Passover Plot*. London, 1965.
(S.3)   Sieburg, Friedrich: R. Paris, 1936.

(S.4)   Soboul, Albert: *The Parisian Sans-Culottes and the French Revolution 1793–94*, tr. G. Lewis. O.U.P., 1964.
(S.5)   Sorel, Albert: *Europe and the French Revolution*, tr. Cobban and Hunt. London, 1969.
(S.6)   Staël, Madame de: *Considérations sur la Révolution française.* C.U.P., 1881.
(S.7)   Stephens, H. M.: ed. *The Principal Speeches of the Statesmen and Orators of the French Revolution (1789–1795).* O.U.P., 1892, II, pp. 287–466.
(T.1)   Thompson, J. M.: R. *and the French Revolution.* London, 1952.
(T.2)   Thompson, J. M.: *Leaders of the French Revolution.* O.U.P., 1929.
(T.3)   Thompson, J. M.: R. 2 vols. O.U.P., 1935.
(T.4)   Thompson, J. M.: *The French Revolution.* O.U.P., 1966.
(T.5)   Tocqueville, A. C. H. C. de: *L'Ancien Régime*, ed. G. W. Headlam. O.U.P., 1904.
(W.1)   Waddicor, M. H.: *Montesquieu and the Philosophy of Natural Law.* The Hague, 1970.
(W.2)   Walter, Gérard: R. 2 vols. Paris, 1961.
(W.3)   Williams, Gwyn A.: *Artisans and Sans-Culottes.* London, 1968.
(Z.1)   Zweig, Stefan: *Joseph Fouché: the Portrait of a Politician,* London, 1948.

SUPPLEMENTARY BIBLIOGRAPHY

Beik, Paul H. ed.: *The French Revolution*, London, 1972
Bertaud, Jean-Paul: *Les origines de la Révolution française*, Paris, 1971
Bloch, Jean: 'Gaspard Guillard de Beaurieu's *L'Elève de la Nature* and Rousseau's *Emile*', *Fr. Stud.*, Jul. 1972, pp. 276–284
Breunig, Charles: *The Age of Revolution and Reaction 1789–1850*, Weidenfeld and Nicolson, 1972
Cobb, Richard: *Reactions to the French Revolution*, O.U.P., 1972
Furet, François and Richet, Benis: *The French Revolution*, tr. Hardman, London, 1970
Furneaux, Robert: *The Bourbon Tragedy*, London, 1972
Gilchrist, J. and Murray, W. J.: *The Press in the French Revolution*, London, 1971
Lewis, Gwynn: *Life in Revolutionary France*, London, 1972
Mariel, P.: *Dictionnaire des sociétés secrètes en Occident*, Paris, 1971
Morris, Governor: *A Diary of the French Revolution*, London, 1972
Palmer, R. R.: *The World of the French Revolution*, London, 1972

APPENDIX I

TWO DEFINITIONS

Parlement. Under the *Ancien Régime*, the *parlements*, numbering thirteen in 1789 but still dominated by that of Paris, were quite unlike democratic British parliaments. In reality, they were bodies of legal experts forming a sovereign court of justice, whose chief initial purpose was the registration of royal edicts. However, because they had become both more refractory and less centralized in the eighteenth century, it was sometimes wrongly assumed that they were the friends of the common people.

Philosophe. The special eighteenth-century sense of this word (nowadays generally italicized to mark the distinction) relates to a person who undertook the free, rational study of nature, untrammelled by reverence for the past and particularly for ecclesiastical authority. The *Encyclopédie*, the first volume of which appeared in 1751, was composed by a group of such men, headed by Diderot, who declared significantly that 'La grâce détermine le chrétien à agir; la raison détermine le philosophe'. Members of the Philosophic Party are usually given the capitalized form, *Philosophe.*

APPENDIX II

THE FRENCH REVOLUTION (1789–95)

DATES	AFFAIRS IN PARIS	AFFAIRS OUTSIDE PARIS
1789 May/June '89 May 5	*A.* ÉTATS GÉNÉRAUX First meeting of États Généraux (since 1614).	
June 1789/ Sept. 1791 June 20	*B.* ASSEMBLÉE NATIONALE Tennis Court Oath.	
July 9 July 14 Aug. 4 Aug. 26 Sept. 11 Oct. 5 Oct. 6 Nov. 2 Dec. 19	*C.* ASSEMBLÉE CONSTITUANTE Fall of Bastille. Suppression of Feudal Rights. Declaration of Rights of Man. King's veto proclaimed. March upon Versailles. King and Assemblée return to Paris. Nationalization of Church property. Use of *assignats*. (Bank-notes)	
1790 (1789–91) June 19 July 12 July 14 Aug. 30	(Internal reorganization of France: 83 *départements*). Abolition of nobility and titles. Civil Constitution of Clergy. Feast of Federation.	 Mutiny of the garrison at Nancy.
1791 April 2 June 20 July 15 July 17 Aug. 27	Death of Mirabeau Flight of King and Royal family to Varennes. Assembly excuses King. Massacre of champ de Mars.	 Declaration of Pillnitz.

DATES	AFFAIRS IN PARIS	AFFAIRS OUTSIDE PARIS
Sept. 14	King accepts the Constitution.	
Sept. 30	End of Assemblée Constituante.	
Nov. 12	Royal Veto re. *émigrés*.	
Dec. 19	Royal Veto re. clergy.	
Sept. 1791/ Sept. 1792.	*D.* ASSEMBLÉE LÉGISLATIVE	
1792 April 20		Declaration of war with Austria and Prussia.
June 19	Royal veto re. *fédérés*.	
June 20	First attempt to invade Tuileries.	
Aug. 1		Brunswick Manifesto.
Aug. 10	Capture of Tuileries.	
Aug. 13	Imprisonment of King.	
Aug. 20	Desertion of La Fayette.	
Sept. 3–5	Prison massacres in Paris.	
Sept. 20	End of Assemblée Législative.	French victory at Valmy.
Sept. 22	Proclamation of Republic.	
Sept. 1792/ July 1794	*E.* CONVENTION NATIONALE	
Sept. 1792/ June 1793	I. 'Gironde' in control.	
Sept. 21	First meeting of Convention. Abolition of royalty decreed.	
Nov. 20	Discovery of *armoire de fer* (in wall of Tuileries.)	
Dec. 1792/ Jan. 1793.	Trial of the King.	
1793 Jan. 16	King condemned to death.	
Jan. 21	Execution of King.	
Feb. 1		Declaration of war with England and Holland
March 10	Formation of Tribunal Révolutionnaire.	
April 5		Defection of Gen. Dumouriez.
April 6	Formation of Committee of Public Safety.	
May 31/June 2	Insurrection in Paris and arrest of 22 Girondin deputies.	

DATES	AFFAIRS IN PARIS	AFFAIRS OUTSIDE PARIS
June 1793/ July 1794.	II. 'Montagne' in control. 'La Terreur'.	
June 24	Constitution of 1793. (An I).	
July 10	Fall of Danton.	
July 13	Death of Marat.	
Sept. 17	Suspects' Law	
Sept. 22	Establishment of Revolutionary Calendar.	
Oct. 16	Execution of Marie Antoinette.	
Oct. 31	Execution of Girondins.	
Nov. 6	Philippe—Égalité guillotined.	
Dec. 4	Revolutionary government decreed.	
Dec. (end)		Revolt in Vendée finally quelled.
1794		
March 15	Arrest of Hébertistes.	
March 23	Execution of Hébertistes.	
March 30	Arrest of Dantonistes.	
April 5	Execution of Dantonistes.	
June 1	Fouché president of Jacobins.	
June 8	Feast of Supreme Being.	
June 10	Prairial Law.	
June 26		French victory at Fleurus. (semaphore and balloons first used.)
July 11	Robespierre attacks Fouché.	
July 26	Robespierre's last speech.	
July 27/28	Arrest and execution of Robespierre, etc. Fall of Montagne.	

APPENDIX III

THE REPUBLICAN CALENDAR (1793–1805)

This calendar was brought into use throughout France in October 1793 by order of the Convention. The republican era was considered to have started on September 22, 1792, the day on which the Convention decreed the abolition of Royalty. Thus September 1792–September 1793 was called 'l'An Iᵉʳ de la République francaise', or simply 'An I', but because the new calendar was not introduced until October 1793, one seldom finds reference to 'An I': for all practical purposes the calendar begins with 'An II'. Napoleon finally abolished it in 1805.

The year was divided into twelve equal months of thirty days, leaving five days at the end of the year which were treated as holidays. Each month was subdivided into three 'weeks' of ten days, called *décades*; the last day of each décade, the *décadi*. was a day of rest.

Months: The twelve months were named to correspond with seasons and weather conditions in France, and were divided into four groups of three:

	VENDEMIAIRE	Month of grape-harvest	Sept.–Oct.
Autumn	BRUMAIRE	Month of fogs	Oct.–Nov.
	FRIMAIRE	Month of frosts	Nov.–Dec.
	NIVÔSE	Month of snows	Dec.–Jan.
Winter	PLUVIÔSE	Month of rains	Jan.–Feb.
	VENTÔSE	Month of winds	Feb.–Mar.
	GERMINAL	Month of buds	Mar.–Apr.
Spring	FLOREAL	Month of flowers	Apr.–May
	PRAIRIAL	Month of meadows	May–June
	MESSIDOR	Month of reaping	June–July
Summer	THERMIDOR	Month of heat	July–Aug.
	FRUCTIDOR	Month of fruit	Aug.–Sept.
	SANSCULOTTIDES	5-day holidays	September

Years:

An II	– 1793–94	An VIII	– 1799–1800
An III	– 1794–95	An IX	– 1800–01
An IV	– 1795–96	An X	– 1801–02
An V	– 1796–97	An XI	– 1802–03
An VI	– 1797–98	An XII	– 1803–04
An VII	– 1798–99	An XIII	– 1804–05

Days: The agronomic and botanical character of the obscure day-names can be demonstrated, for instance, by the first 'week' of the month most interesting to Robespierrists.

Thermidor
Ière Décade

Primedi	Epeautre	(German wheat)
Duodi	Bouillon-Blanc	(mullein)
Tridi	Melon	(melon)
Quartidi	Ivraie	(corn-cockle)
Quintidi	BELIER	(RAM)
Sextidi	Prèle	(mare's tail)
Septidi	Armoise	(mug-wort)
Octidi	Carthame	(safflower)
Nonidi	Mûres	(blackberries)
Décadi	*ARROSOIR*	(*WATERING-CAN*)

The fact that this country calendar was contrived largely by and for urban citizenry shows how influential had been Rousseau and the Physiocrats.

INDEX

(R. represents Robespierre)

6493